Jim Dempsey

40 STORIES BEHIND THE STORY

An Introduction to the Bible

Volume I

40 Stories Behind the Story

Published by:
Intermedia Publishing Group, Inc.
P.O. Box 2825
Peoria, Arizona 85380
www.intermediapub.com

ISBN 978-1-935906-46-9

Copyright © 2011 by Jim Dempsey

Printed in the United States of America

Scripture quotations, unless indicated otherwise, are taken from the New American Standard Bible®, Copyright © 1960, 1962, 1963, 1968, 1971, 1972, 1973, 1975, 1977, 1995 by The Lockman Foundation Used by permission. (www.Lockman.org).

Scripture quotations are taken from the Holy Bible, New Living Translation, copyright 1996, 2004. Used by permission of Tyndale House Publishers, Inc., Wheaton, Illinois 60189. All rights reserved.

Scripture taken from the HOLY BIBLE, NEW INTERNATIONAL VERSION®. Copyright © 1973, 1978, 1984 Biblica. Used by permission of Zondervan. All rights reserved.

Scripture quotations taken from the Amplified® Bible, Copyright © 1954, 1958, 1962, 1964, 1965, 1987 by The Lockman Foundation Used by permission. (www.Lockman.org).

FORTY STORIES BEHIND THE STORY:
An Introduction to the Bible

Book Two:
The Kings, the Poets, and the Prophets

The Kings

Poets and Prophets

Dedications

For the glory of the Lord Jesus, the Master Storyteller,
Who has told us the Story of All Stories,
Who has been the central character in the Story,
and invites us to be part of the Story.

To my lifelong love and best friend, Linda,
who has not only shared the ride,
but who has made it a joy.

To Charles and Nancy Coker,
who have quietly supported and enabled
a life of ministry,
and never hinted that I should look for a
real job.

What Is The Bible?

Our Christian school was an outreach to the community. There were more students from outside our church than from our own membership. One of these, a young woman from a Jehovah's Witness background who could not attend public school because she had gotten married (yes, that was long ago), raised her flag, and I stepped over to her desk to give her assistance. She was preparing for an essay assignment. I have never forgotten her question because it illustrates so much about how the average member of our society views the Bible.

"What page is smoking on in the Bible?"

She was writing an essay on the evils of smoking, and she knew she would have to provide biblical proof for her opinions. As a product of her culture, she had the idea that all the rules about behavior were in the Bible. And, as a product of that culture, she had little actual experience in reading the Bible. (This was thirty years ago, and tragically, knowledge of the Bible is even less in the general population today.)

The Bible is God's Word in written form. This simple declaration is at the heart of all that follows in this book. You can believe that statement entirely, but first, you must know what it means.

The Holy Spirit inspired the human writers to record an accurate history of God's dealings with man. That is what God was intending to give us, a revelation of Who He Is, What He Has Done, and What He Will Do. Satisfying human curiosity and settling human arguments are not His purpose here, and when we try to use the Bible in that way, we do so at our own peril.

The writers each wrote part of the story, as God's Spirit breathed upon them. God inspired them; He did not "high-jack" them. They did not write from a trance, but consciously, with knowledge of their readers, and revelation from God.

I once visited a church building in which the congregation had posted a notice informing the reader that the church believed that it was God who had directly written the Bible as His Own Word and had given it to men of old, who recorded God's message. Therefore, they found it improper to refer to earthly writers as if they were the authors of the books of the Bible. They would not say, "The apostle Paul said . . ." or "John wrote . . ." Taken very literally, this approach can cause problems in the teaching of the Bible.

For one thing, the Bible was not originally written in English so, to follow their logic, having an English Bible would require that we believe in the inspiration of translation, which no legitimate translator would claim. We accept that the translators chose their own words in bringing the Bible into our language. A "dictation" theory of inspiration is not taught in the Scriptures themselves, and is an unnecessary religious belief which can hinder our full and deep understanding of God's Word.

Who the earthly author was is often important to understanding the context of what we are reading, and this should be considered and respected. James was not Paul, and neither of them shared the experiences of Moses or Solomon. Who wrote the book does matter, but it does not remove the fact that God inspired the writing, using the life experiences and even the vocabularies of the writers, who faithfully recorded the revelation.

The date of writing, the writers, and their readers vary significantly. That is why the books themselves vary. Later leaders of the Church compiled the separate books into one collection, our Bible. Those leaders did not *decide* what books they wanted in the Bible, they *recognized* what books belonged there, based on the characteristics of the books themselves.

When we say the Bible is God's written Word that is some of what we mean. Let's add a few examples of what we do *not* mean:

The Bible is not simply a rulebook to keep your behavior in line. Some people's take on the Bible is that it's all about "Thou shalt not," with occasional "Thou shalts." God has given us so much more than rules. He has shown us what he expects, for sure, but He has also given us books of examples of those who lived by His commands, and those who did not. When you read it and understand how the whole thing fits together, you don't just get the "dos" and "don'ts," but a lot of the "what" and "why."

The Bible is not just a fine example of ancient literature, to be studied and respected, but not lived by. Many people's approach to Scripture is that it is respected, but not relevant. Recent generations have no regard for what is not relevant, and scoff at or ignore the Bible completely, believing it to be irrelevant and useless. They are misinformed. Part of my purpose in life is to let people know that without an education in the Bible, we are undereducated, and inadequately prepared to live life.

The Bible is not a mystical, magical text, with special inherent powers to be discovered and used. It has no spells or incantations which may be used for magical purposes. The Bible is about faith, which is way different than magic. You don't get its benefits by just *doing* what it says, but by *becoming* what it teaches us to be.

The Bible is not to be interpreted as a coded document. Is there a "Bible code?" I am not so dogmatic as to say no, but I will tell you that what it says right out in the open, without decoding, is what God intends for you to get. Attempts at discovering a secret code, to get hidden knowledge or to prove the miraculous nature of the Bible can be distracting, causing us to miss the most important message.

The Bible is not a spooky mystery book about the murky future. I have seen folks who seem to have more interest in the antichrist than they have in the Christ. Perhaps there are people who get excited about

Bible prophecy who really shouldn't, since the return of Christ is not good news to those who do not know Him. Biblical prophecy is not given for the purpose of satisfying our curiosity about the future, but as a revelation for the present. In other words, God is not trying to give a few smart people inside knowledge about who "the beast" will be. He wants those who live in that time to receive comfort and direction in how to cope.

The Bible is not an obscure, hard to understand text which only a few experts can explain, usually with disagreement between them. Hear this; you are only responsible for what you can understand in the Bible. Not just what you *do* understand, but what you could if you would apply yourself. There is no excuse for lazy ignorance of God's Word. When you become a disciple of Jesus, you are called to a life-long diligent study of Scripture. God does not intend for the understanding of His Word to be confined to an elite class of scholars. He wrote it for you. Those who make it confusing are mishandling the Word. This is not to say that you don't have to work at understanding the Bible—you do. But have no doubt that if you do the work, you will attain the understanding, in ever deepening levels.

So what is the Bible? Above all, it is the true story of man's redemption. It starts with how we came about, explains how we got separated from God, then tells us what our loving God did to get us back.

THE Story: Redemption

Redemption is a wonderful concept. It is what the Bible is all about. This is how it works: Man was placed on earth as the willing possession of God, then lost control of himself and the creation through disobedience. God, who was aware that all this would happen, put an eternal plan in motion to win man back. What I mean by "eternal" is that the plan was in place before creation, and it extends into our future to infinity. The Bible is the story of that plan and its ultimate, eternal success.

Here is God's "problem." God is both absolute love and absolute holiness. When man sinned, God's love compelled Him to forgive, but His holiness could not allow the presence of sin. This is not something that can be resolved through a wrestling match or coin toss. One cannot win out over the other; rather the two must be reconciled.

The way God did this was to pay the penalty for man's sin Himself. By becoming man (Jesus) and paying the price (death), even though He was sinless, He accomplished the greatest trade in all history. He took on our sin and died with it, so that we could receive His righteousness and live in it. His sacrifice covers us for all time, and our part is to simply accept that through faith.

The Bible's purpose is to tell us how this all happened, so that we can believe and receive it. In addition, we get information about how it will all wrap up. This is the story of redemption from beginning to end.

The little stories are all part of the Big Story. You can state this other ways, if you like, such as calling the individual stories (like the birth of Moses) "micro-narratives," the bigger pieces (like Israel's exodus from Egypt), "macro-narratives," and the story of redemption the "mega-narrative." All the stories are connected, and one moves us toward the next, building our understanding of God and His Plan as we go.

Shall we go?

Book One
A Tribe, A People, A Nation

The Beginnings of Things

1
Creation
Genesis 1, 2

As the Bible opens, all is dark. All is nothing. God's Spirit was hovering over the surface of the waters. I don't know where the waters came from; they are already there when the story starts. Some people teach that there was a great space of time, and a lot of action between verse one and verse two. We are only going to get involved here with what is written in the Bible, not what isn't.

Then God spoke. "Let there be light." This is what happens when God speaks; He gets what He says. And God saw that the light was good. Then he made night and day, and everything else. Day by day He spoke creation into existence:

Day One: Light, day and night

Day Two: The heavens were separated from the waters

Day Three: Dry land, plants

Day Four: Sun, moon, and the rest of the stuff out in space

Day Five: Aquatic life and birds

Day Six: Dry land creatures

There are a couple of things worth noting here. First, light was created before the sun. In the beginning of the Bible, and again at the end, there is light which seems to come from God Himself. He is complete all in Himself, and needs nothing, not even a source of light to see by. Secondly, this creation story follows the generally accepted order of appearance of life on earth. Creationists and non-creationists only argue about the time-span, and about whether it was designed or random.

On day six, God made man. Man's creation is different than everything else. For the rest of the universe, God spoke, and things happened. Everything was formed by the word of His mouth. With man, God formed him from the dust of the earth, then did something really special. He breathed into him. The Bible says that "man became a living soul." This is not the case with the animals, who were spoken into existence, although *Genesis* 2:19 does say that they also were formed out of the ground.

The creation story is told in chapter 1, then again in chapter 2. The accounts don't contradict, but taken together they give the whole story. Chapter 2 gives additional details and perspective.

God made a man, then He put the man into the garden He had created, and gave man instructions to tend the garden. He also told the man not to eat from the tree of the knowledge of good and evil, for that would bring death. All this happened before there was a woman. (NOTE: God gave man a job before He gave him a woman. Women should make sure that this order of things stays intact. Men cannot be relied upon to stay faithful to it.)

After God formed the man, He said that it was not good for the man to be alone. God was not having second thoughts; He was speaking for the benefit of whomever was watching, or listening, or later reading. God declared that he would make man a helper corresponding to him. This was no new idea, since the same had been done for most of the animals.

The man had seen all the animals, which he had been naming, and almost certainly had to be wondering about this. The animals were almost all in twos, matching sets with male and female versions. After a little while of observing this pattern, I think the man would naturally wonder if he was meant to be a single item, a "one-off", or if perhaps there was a match somewhere.

But God did not speak her into being. Neither did He scoop up more dirt, as He did with the man. He apparently wanted them to be made of the same dirt, so He put the man to sleep, and took a piece out of him.

God then expanded that piece to become the woman. This seems to me to be a clone-like procedure, and I suspect that genetically, she had a female version of the man's DNA. When Adam (as the man was called) came out of recovery, God brought the results to him. When he saw her, the male-man, being of considerable intellect, immediately recognized her for what she was, and was very appreciative.

God gives us another principle for life here in the fact that these people had no parents, yet they functioned as a successful unit. Simply put, it is your spouse that you attach and commit yourself to for life, not your parents. Parents became more and more important as experience became more valuable, but they never replaced spouses in priority.

And how does this fit the "big story" of redemption? Well, you have to start somewhere, and the creation is the beginning of it all. The major players are coming on to the stage. God, mankind, and, in the next story, the enemy are introduced, but not really explained totally. That's for later.

This man-couple was bare-beamed, buck nekkid, as the country folk might say, yet they had no shame about it. They were not physically blinded to their nakedness, nor clothed in some holy light, as some have speculated. They were not ashamed of their nakedness because neither shame nor nakedness were concepts they understood at the time. Shame had not been invented yet, so nakedness was an irrelevant concept. Unfortunately, they would soon learn about both.

2
Man Loses It
Genesis 3

They say all was good in the garden for a long time, until the woman messed it up. *They say* she wasn't too bright, a little weak, perhaps. *They say* Adam might have kept his place in the garden if he had controlled his wife better. *They say* it's been man's job to control women ever since they ate the apple. That's what *they say*. "*They say*," are words that have been associated with more baloney than Oscar Meyer.

There is a lot of "they say" out there in regards to the creation and fall of man. Let's see if we can straighten some of it out for you. When we left our original couple, they were in the garden, in control of running everything in a sinless world. It was a sweet gig. No sin, no shame, no sweat, so to speak.

As chapter 3 opens, the third intelligent creature on earth is introduced. He is referred to as "the serpent," although closer examination reveals him as having been influenced or possessed by our enemy, Satan, the devil. (You will have to get all the details in another book; this one is an introduction to the Bible, not a full explanation of it.)

This serpent is not the snake we know today, but an attractive and intelligent creature with the faculty of speech, at least for the time being. I suspect we are not getting all the conversation that had ever passed between the serpent and the woman. In the Genesis 3 account they speak to each other as if they are used to such a thing.

The serpent did what the devil has always done—he questions what God said. "Did God really say that you should not eat of any tree here?" That's how he often starts— exaggerating what God has said. Her honest reply was that they may eat of all the trees but the one in the middle.

She explained to the serpent that they may not eat from it or touch it, or they will die.

Some folk think it is significant that she added the command not to touch the fruit, which was not recorded in God's original instructions in 2:16, 17. This may or may not be important. The orders about this tree were first given to Adam before her arrival, so she may have gotten her information second-hand. Perhaps it was Adam who said, "Don't touch." Maybe they discussed it together and realized that if they didn't touch it, they couldn't eat it.

It is good advice even if not commanded. However, it may be an example of a good idea being mistaken, over time, as a word of God. We just don't know. Religion is full of this, however, and it may have started right here.

The serpent goes about his devilish business in the way he always has. He "explains" what God "really" intends in a way that makes God seem to mean something other than what He said. Satan lies. Then and now. Snakey tells the woman that God actually wants to keep them from receiving the knowledge of good and evil, thus being like Him.

I wish she had thought about this more; maybe talked with her husband about it. They were in a sinless, perfect, God-made garden. God was apparently a frequent "face-to-face" visitor. They knew good. All they didn't know was evil. I know good and evil, and so do you. I don't think gaining the knowledge of evil was an improvement at all, but Satan still tempts us with the promise of "opening our eyes."

Let's talk about the fruit itself. One of the things "they say" is that it was an apple. Recently, I heard a nationally syndicated Christian radio speaker referring to "when Adam ate the apple." Sloppy teaching. The Bible says nothing of the sort; that is just religious folklore. I think the actual fruit is irrelevant. It was the disobedience that brought the knowledge of evil. The disobedience itself was evil, which had never been experienced by the people, although we think the devil knew all about evil.

So she took it, and ate it, and gave it to her husband, *who was with her*, and he ate it. Now, whatever happened, they were in this together. If he was alongside of her as it appears, he had been consenting all along. Another of the things "they say" is that this was all the woman's fault, and this is an example of how women cannot be trusted. That sounds like something the serpent would say.

On the other end of the Bible, in *First Timothy* 2:14, it clearly states that the man was not deceived, but the woman was. Men have used this verse to beat up on women for a long time. They should pay more attention to what they read. Adam was not deceived, therefore his sin was deliberate disobedience. It would be a foolish man who asserted that this makes him in any way better or more trustworthy than the woman. Men and women made different mistakes then, and they still do, but they both make mistakes.

When they ate the fruit, everything changed. Immediately they knew evil, because they had disobeyed. Up to this time they had been more than sufficient in their bare skin, but suddenly they knew the shame of being "unpresentable" as they were. The God-created innocence in which they had lived was gone, so they realized that they were naked, and had to cover up. They made coverings from fig leaves. The figs they used were apparently not the kind we are familiar with where I'm from. Those fig leaves would have itched the first couple to death.

They don't seem to have covered themselves very well, either. As soon as they heard God, they ran and hid in the woods, because they still felt naked. What they felt was nakedness of the soul, the shame of having done a very bad thing for the first time.

But God sought them out. He called to the man, "Where are you?" Now understand this—God knew where Adam was, and He knows where you are. He has never misplaced anyone. Whenever God asks a question it is because He wants us to answer, not because He doesn't know something. In answering Him, we are forced to be honest with ourselves.

Listen to the conversation, keeping in mind that God already knows everything. God peels Adam like an onion. First, it's "Where are you?"

"I hid myself because I was naked."

"Who told you that? Have you eaten of that tree?"

At this point Adam got really pitiful. Remember, God and the woman were his only two friends in the world (I don't think the serpent qualified.) "The woman you gave me did it," he whined. He blamed both the woman and God. Now he had no friends.

God turned to the woman, "What did you do?" The woman blamed the serpent, accusing him of deceiving her, which was true. She believed the serpent when he promised her something she didn't really need or want anyway. Between them, Adam and the Woman literally blamed everyone in the world but themselves.

God did not ask the serpent anything, because He didn't intend to teach the serpent anything. He just started declaring the results of this disaster, first to the snake. The serpent's curses began with the loss of his legs. I suspect that he lost more than that, and perhaps we will see him in his original form again, someday. There would be much bad blood between the snake and the woman. The descendants of each would hate the other.

Then to the devil who got into the snake, God directed the first prophecy of the coming Redeemer. A "seed of the woman" would come and give Satan a mortal (head) wound, while Satan would inflict only a flesh wound on the Woman's Seed. This is our first notice of the victory that Christ will win through the cross. At the very "scene of the crime" of the original sin, God started promising redemption.

To the woman, God delivered the bad news that childbirth was going to hurt. A lot. Ten minutes in a delivery room will make the truth of this really clear. However, the woman would still have the desire for her husband, and he would have a role of dominance over her. Evidence of this is the fact that women often have more than one child. After seeing what they go through in pregnancy and delivery, it is amazing to me that any woman who has had a child would ever have another. Men might get pregnant once if they could, but if they survived it, they would make sure it never happened again. God has put something different in women.

Adam started with a garden to tend that responded easily to his light maintenance. Not satisfied with what God had given him, he listened to his wife, when she mistakenly told him there was more to have. As a result, he traded away the place he had. God removed them from the garden, and locked the door behind them. It wouldn't be easy anymore. The earth would fight him for every meal, until he died.

Oh, yes, he will die. They will both die. They will all die.

3
Wash Away the Wicked
Genesis 4-9

I will tell you nothing but the truth in this book, and the truth is, I have problems with this story. Yet I want to make it clear that I believe everything God says. Faith has to come in somewhere. So, if in telling this story, I raise a few questions that I don't adequately answer, don't freak or attempt to revoke my Believer's Card.

It's a hard story to get your mind around, this flood story, if you think about it at all. I have settled these issues by reminding myself that God gives us the information that He wants, not what we want. We just don't always get all the facts and explanations that our curiosity yearns for.

Some people think we will have no questions in eternity; either we will know everything, or not care. I say we were made to ask questions, and I don't think we'll ever stop. You are not going to become all-knowing like God. The people in these stories are real, and they will still be real when we get to where they are. I want to spend some time with them, to get a better understanding of how things were. There will be plenty of opportunities to get acquainted with Noah over there, and I expect to hear his story, firsthand.

Well, on to the story. A lot of things happened after Adam and his wife, now called Eve, left the Garden. First, they had two sons, Cain and Abel. Then, when those boys grew up, Cain killed Abel out of apparent jealousy.

More people were born, and there is no explanation of where the additional women came from. Some people have shouted, "Aha!" at this as if it is a glitch in the Bible, or proof of evolution, or they have agonized over it as if they themselves were responsible to explain it. It is a question that has been asked for ages: "Where did Cain get his wife?" I'm going to give you an answer for all those who ask. Are you ready? Repeat after me.

"I don't know. It doesn't say."

If that isn't good enough for your inquisitor, then here is a question you can ask: "Why is that a problem?" *Genesis* 4:17 clearly and simply states that Cain had a wife, and they had a son. "But where did she come from?" some people still have to ask. Maybe Cain had a cloning like his dad; maybe God made more pottery; maybe it was his sister. That's not as weird as it sounds; God's commands against such a thing did not come until later. (If you're worried about inbreeding, remember that Adam and Eve were starting with perfect genes.) You just don't get that information here; God doesn't consider it relevant. Cain's wife was there. Get over it.

Genesis 5 proceeds with a list of people who lived a long time, and had lots of sons and daughters. The list mainly pays attention to the firstborn son. This portion of Scripture is intended to move the story along, not to provide a world census. Of note is Enoch, who was lifted heavenward without death. This makes a nice basis for a Bible riddle. Methuselah, Enoch's son, was the oldest man ever on record, yet he died before his father. Finally, that chapter ends with Noah, preparing us for a story we are still trying to deal with.

What about those ages? Did they really live that long? People try to explain this away, by saying that their years were not as long as ours, or something like that, but those explanations usually are harder for me to believe than the story they attempt to justify. There are those who say that these are just errors or exaggerations in the Bible. There's no evidence for that either. It is worth noting that the ages generally get progressively shorter until they reach normal range. I think it has to do with the corruption of creation, due to the effects of sin. Some "puzzles" you just answer by saying, "Hmmn."

Enough preliminaries, let's get on with the story. Man got worse with each generation, until finally God was sorry to have to watch them. This does not mean that God realized a mistake; it just means that he was sorry it happened.

You have to do things sometimes that you are sorry you have to do, but you do them, because you have to. If that confuses you, think of child discipline. No healthy parent wants to make our child so unhappy, but the alternative is an undisciplined child who nobody wants. Without mankind, there is no appropriate object for God's love. God knew man would sin, go bad, and need redemption that He Himself would have to pay to purchase. God knew we would hurt Him, but because of His infinite love, He created us anyway.

Looking over this world, God gave man a limited number of days. Then continuing to look, He recognized Noah's faithfulness. The Bible says nothing about Noah being sinlessly perfect; just that "Noah found grace in the eyes of the Lord." It will become so clear in The Story later, that redemption has nothing to do with "God found perfection," and everything to do with "Noah found grace."

God informed Noah of His plans, then instructed him to make a large "ark," which would hold the first World Zoo. A sufficient number of each species would ride out the coming storm in a boat designed for that purpose. God gave the design and dimensions to Noah, Noah gathered his three sons, and work began.

Work continued for a century, while everyone watched, very likely very amused. Noah was promised that he and his wife, sons, and their wives would be saved from the coming flood by building and entering the ark. Noah complied with all God said, and the job was done (Amazing what you can get done without governmental bureaucracy to tell you that you can't.)

That "two-by-two" thing was only for the "unclean" animals, by the way; the "clean" animals came in sevens. Why the difference? It was going to be a long boat ride, and when they got off, everything was going to be dead and washed away. Apologies to the vegetarian reader, but these people (and the lions, tigers and bears, oh my!) were going to need something to eat for some time, while things repopulated. I don't think they were going to live solely on seaweed and fish, although those were probably on the menu.

It is this part about the animals that stretches my credulity. Imagine every species of animal on earth in one boat. If that's not hard for you to comprehend, then you don't have cable TV. Even the nature shows I see on "free" PBS make me think that this ark would have a hard time holding pictures of all the species, much less the life-sized animals.

So think about the possibilities. Maybe God shrank them as they got on board. Really, really small. OK, maybe the ark was larger on the inside than the outside, due to some space/time warpage thing, like. (I personally like that one, if we're voting for a preference.)

What I really think is that there were fewer species on God's list than there are on our list now. If this is the case, then after the flood, many more species exploded from the originals. God could do that. Perhaps it was already programmed into their DNA. Look what happened with people. Every race and tribe, in all our variety, from white dwarfs to tall, dark, East Africans, came out of Noah's family, genetically.

We just don't know, but one day we will. I hope God's been recording all this, because I've never seen a Hollywood production that did it justice. They don't think enough about the details and logistics; those are too scary to contemplate. Some folks in Kentucky are planning to build a life-sized ark, just to show us all what it looked like. Maybe that will clear some things up for us. *Evan Almighty* was no help; that movie just pretended to be repeating the biblical story. There was a hole or two in the plot, big enough to float this ark through.

God called, "All aboard!" then shut the door. And so, it rained. Not just rain, but the Word says the "fountains of the deep" broke open, so apparently water was coming from all directions. The earth was simply being flushed. After forty days and nights, the water stopped coming. Eventually the water receded. (Cue the "morning music.") The Last Family came out of the ark and released the zoo. God pointed out a nearby rainbow, and told Noah (and the rest of us) to remember His covenant with us—a promise never to destroy the earth again by flood, wrecking the seasons, climate, and growing cycle.

And He won't. Next time He'll use fire.

4
Okay, Break it Up!/Everybody's Favorite Father
Genesis 9-13

After the boat ride, man got a do-over. In our folklore, we often talk about how we descended from Adam and Eve, but we should remember that we all actually descended from this bunch. All our human diversity was latent in them, it looks like.

I'm sure the sediment made the ground very fertile, and Noah started farming. He planted a vineyard, made wine, and got drunk and got naked.

This has been done by many people since then, and the results have been consistently humiliating and tragic. In this case, Noah's son, Ham, ventured into the tent and saw his father in this disgusting condition. He did what too many of us do when we discover someone else's shame. He found people to tell about it, his two brothers ("Patriarchs Gone Wild!").

Those men were more thoughtful than Ham had been. They backed into the tent, and respectfully covered their father up. When Noah came back to his right mind, he angrily cursed, not Ham, but Ham's son Canaan, who was almost certainly a mere baby, probably Noah's first grandchild. Must have been the hangover talking.

Before you harshly judge Noah for his cursing of his grandson, think of the people you have heard (maybe you?) angrily telling their own children, "I hope you grow up and have one just like you!" Those words are a curse on your grandchildren who might not even be born yet, Grandma, and you'd better repent and break those curses. There's still time.

I have heard apologies and excuses made for Noah, but I don't think they are necessary. It is just unacceptable to some folk that a hero of faith like Noah would be so naughty as to get himself drunk, since tee-totaling theology equates alcohol use with absolute unrighteousness. Some have offered speculation that he didn't know about fermentation, and got drunk by accident. It could happen, once. It's even been speculated that fermentation only started after the flood, due to some change in the earth's makeup. If that makes you feel better, alright, but it is not necessary.

We might as well deal with this right here. The Bible is scattered with these examples of alcohol abuse leading to stupidity. What is not in the Bible is a command which says, "If thou tasteth the booze, thou shalt be sinning thy way to hell." God simply records the results, and expects us to learn. In the New Testament, Paul both suggests wine for digestive ailments (no Pepto-Bismol yet), and warns against drunkenness that leads to stupidness. The Bible clearly teaches that alcohol is dangerous, and that fools get tripped up by it.

Myself, I don't even need the Bible to show me this, although I thank God for the warning. My convictions against recreational alcohol use are based on both scriptural and personal observations. I will live by and explain these convictions wherever appropriate, but I will honestly recognize that others in the body of Christ don't agree. They are wrong, but not reprobate, perhaps not even backslidden. However, if you have believed up 'til now that drinking is always absolute sin, do not twist my words as an excuse to get polluted, or even start sipping. You know better, and that makes it sin.

The Bible makes no excuses for what people do, in order to soothe our religious concerns. Bible people are real people, presented "warts and all." What this tells us is that a relationship with God is not reserved for those who deserve Him, but available to all who desire Him.

Now, about all these "real" people. The sons of Noah—Shem, Ham (the cursed one), and Japheth—disembarked and multiplied. Their families are listed in *Genesis* 10. As the next chapter opens, mankind is just one big monolingual family. One of the notable leaders of the time was a mighty hunter named Nimrod. His people, who were expanding eastward, settled on a plain, and decided to make for themselves three things; a city, a tower, and a name.

The folklore version of the Bible says that the people of this city tried to build a tower to Heaven, which disturbed God. Fearing that these people would be able to do anything they wanted, He confused their languages. This version makes God a petty little guy like the Greco-Roman god, Zeus. Our God does not whine like the gods of men. He is not afraid of our towers, but He recognizes rebellion even in its early stages.

In fact, what probably displeased God was that they were disregarding His orders from *Genesis* 1:28, "be fruitful and multiply, and *fill the earth*, and subdue it." They were to fill the earth for God's glory, and be stewards of creation. What they intended instead was to build a fabulous city for their own name, to establish their own glory. God wanted distribution for His purposes; they wanted concentration, to keep themselves mighty in their own eyes.

God fixed 'em. He simply diversified their languages so that they could not all understand each other. God creates diversity, but it terrifies man, then and now. They scattered rather quickly, each one finding the others of his own language, which almost certainly followed family lines. As *Genesis* 11:9 says, ". . . and from there the Lord scattered them abroad over the face of the whole earth."

Now the narrative turns to the descendants of Shem. (By the way, you will see that they are becoming fathers at a younger age, and living shorter lives than the ones listed in Genesis 5.) At the end of the list we come to a man named Abram. This man was one who was faithful to God without the advantages we know. No Bible, no Old Testament Law, no temple or church, no nothing. Just a friend of God who heard from Him directly. God sent Abram out of the land of his people, with only a promise to give him another place later. God also promised a few other things:

- To make Abram a great nation
- To bless him
- To make Abram's name great
- To make Abram a blessing to all nations
- To bless those who blessed Abram
- To curse those who cursed him

So Abram, his wife Sarai, and his nephew Lot, and their people and stuff, set out for the land of Canaan. Abram was seventy-five years old. God continued to speak with him, and Abram built altars and worshipped God along the way.

Funny things happened as they went. Famine drove them down to Egypt, and Abram was nervous. Sarai was one of the Great Babes of All Time it seems, and Abram trusted neither the Egyptians nor God. He ordered her to lie, claiming to be Abram's sister. As expected, she impressed the Pharaoh's wife procurers, and he took her as his wife (Pretty good for a sixty-five-year-old lady, ennit?). Abram got the VIP treatment. God was displeased with this twice-married woman in Pharaoh's house, and plagues followed. When the truth came out, the whole bunch of them got escorted out of town.

After this they went back where they had been earlier. During this time, Abram called on the Lord, but it appears that Lot did not. The land could only support so many flocks and herds, so their hired hands got into it with each other. Abram, not wanting any trouble, gave his nephew the option that should have been his own. Wherever Lot decided to settle, Abram would take his stuff and go the other way. The valley was beautiful and lush, and Lot took it. Abram settled in Canaan, while Lot took Sodom.

Beautiful places often attract, or encourage sinful, pleasure-driven people. The Bible just mentions the wickedness of Sodom here, then records more blessings for Abram, including a promise that all the land he can see will be his and his descendants' forever. Is God joking? At that point, the seventy-five-year-old Abram's descendants totaled exactly zero.

A Nation, and A Covenant

5
You'd Laugh, Too
Genesis 14-18

What we described in the previous section was the beginning of the people. We now have families spreading across the earth. One of these families is going to develop a very special relationship with God. Our storyline is going to concentrate on that family, and follow its progress as it grows into a nation. This begins the story of Israel.

While Lot was living in Sodom there was a war. Lot's side lost. He and his stuff got carried away to another country, but a fugitive escaped to tell Abram. Abram got his posse together and chased the bad guys, who were obviously slowed down by all the plunder. The raiders were caught up with, conquered, and probably forced to apologize. Lot went home with his inventory of people and goods, and the rest of the spoils belonged to Abram and company, but Abram refused to take any home.

He does give a tenth to a fellow named Melchisedek, who was both a king and priest. Guy just walks into the story, blesses Abram, and goes home. He is the first priest named in the Bible, and receives the first recorded tithe. Tithing, or the giving of a tenth to God, is still part of our worship today, and like so many current things, started in Genesis.

God came to Abram in a vision, telling him to not fear, and about how great his reward would be. Abram had a question about this promised reward.

"What kind of reward is it, if I have no heir to pass it on to? Right now, my heir is my executive assistant, Eliezer, and he wasn't even born in my house."

God assured him that it would not be his servant, but his own son who would be his heir. Taking him outside, God said, "Look at the heav-

ens; count the stars. That is how numerous your descendants will be."
Then the Bible says one of the most important things in the story. "Then
he believed in the Lord, and He reckoned it to him as righteousness."

Reckoned? Was God a Texan, like some have claimed? This is in
fact explanation of our relationship with God, and a key to our redemption. We cannot be righteous, but we can believe God. God takes that
belief, and counts it as righteousness. This "reckoning" is an accounting term. The Great Book Keeper accepts our faith and writes us up as
"righteous." The more of His Word we believe, the more of His righteousness we walk in.

To seal the deal, God then made a covenant with Abram. A covenant
is like a contract, but way more. A contract is an agreement between
parties to do something for each other. A covenant is a commitment to
be something to each other. A contract is an arrangement, a covenant is
a *relationship.* A contract is for the stated period. A covenant is *forever.*

In this covenant, God made more promises to Abram and his descendants, none of whom existed at the time. He gave a geographical
promise to Abram and his descendants. The land from the "river of
Egypt" to the Euphrates was theirs forever; promised to Abram and his
descendants—whenever they got there.

I'd love to tell you how faithful Abram received his long awaited
miracle boy, at the end of a trial period marked by uninterrupted obedience. Didn't happen like that. Sarai, in an apparent fit of really good-
hearted helpfulness, suggested that maybe her servant Hagar could be a
surrogate to raise up seed for Abram. (No, really, it was *her* suggestion.
Her exact words were honestly, "Please go in to my maid. . .") So Hagar
was promoted from wife's maid to second wife.

Another biblical issue that stresses newcomers arises here. God did
not create Adam and Eve and Eva. Multiple spouses are not His plan.
But marriage is marriage, no matter how many concurrent (or consecu-
tive) unions are going on. The relationship with Hagar was not a case of

adultery; no "action on the side." The words of Sarai show that culturally, as senior wife, she considered the potential child to be hers. I'm not advocating this; it's messed up. I'm just explaining it to you.

Later in the Old Testament record (*1 Chron.* 1:32, 33) we read that Abraham, as he is called there, had sons by a concubine, Keturah. Concubinage is even less ethically and morally honorable than polygamy. Concubines do not have the rights or privileges of wives, and their children can be ignored in the inheritance. This is why they aren't mentioned in the story until the *1 Chronicles* inventory.

No, this isn't right. A concubine is a partner in adultery, and God will speak much more clearly about this in times to come. Remember, we're just in the first book of the Bible. Morals and ethics have developed through the centuries, and we know better than to do some of the things they did then. Abraham's imperfections are no excuse for you to be a polygamist, or a "swinger."

However, *Genesis 25*:1 tells us that Abraham married Keturah. Why the apparent discrepancy? I'm not sure, but I can speculate. Keturah could have been, at separate times, both a concubine and a wife. We can easily see how Abraham could have been hesitant to "make an honest woman" of Keturah until after Sarah died. Again, you have the rest of your life to dig deeper into this, if it bothers you.

The "potential" child was a reality before long. Hagar got pregnant, and as soon as she did, bad blood started between her and Sarai. Hagar got an attitude, and Sarai blamed Abram, and Abram now knew why polygamy was such a bad idea. Abram weaseled a bit and allowed Hagar to be treated harshly by Sarai, and the girl fled.

The angel of the Lord found Hagar in the wilderness by a spring. He didn't call her "Hagar, Abram's pregnant wife." He said, "Hagar, Sarai's maid . . ." He corrected her attitude, instructing her to submit to the boss-lady's authority. He also pronounced a blessing upon her son, who would be called Ishmael ("God hears"). "The angel of the Lord" is a title used in the Old Testament occasionally, to indicate an appearance of the Lord before His birth into our world. This was one of those, and the message was from God Himself, whom Hagar referred to as "The Lord *El Roi*," "the Lord Who Sees."

Remember, she had already named the boy, "God hears." God both saw and heard Ishmael. He knew where he was, and He still does. Redemption extends to the sons of Ishmael, both then and now.

God's word was good, and Ishmael was born, when Abram was eighty-six. At ninety-nine, God appeared again, and changed Abram's name to Abraham. Abram means, "exalted father," which up to now had been an ironic joke; even the birth of Ishmael had not exalted him much. Abraham means, "father of a multitude," a really big laugh at ninety-nine. God restated the earlier covenant, then added a provision for Abraham to keep. Up to now, it had been all God's contribution. Abraham would now have to come across with a personal sign of the covenant—circumcision.

Circumcision is difficult for some people to talk about, and hard to understand for an even greater number. It involves the removal by cutting of the foreskin of the penis. This would be done in infancy in the future generations. If that seems hard on baby boys, remember that it was no party for a ninety-nine year old man.

Let's have a "grown-up" discussion about this. I used to just "give God the benefit of the doubt" about this idea. However, the more I have studied God's Word, and come to understand His grace, the more I have come to understand this sign. It's about the Covenant. The covenant between Abraham and God is sealed with blood. Circumcision is Abraham's contribution—a token; God's contribution will be infinitely more before He is done. If you require more explanation about the motives and significance of this ritual, there are many sources that study it in more depth. In this book we just tell the stories.

But here are some things you should be thinking about. God does nothing for no reason. The result of circumcision is that God's covenant partners will be marked, for all generations to come, in the most intimate of ways. The sons of the Covenant will be reminded daily of their special relationship with God, and whenever they are exposed to each other, they will be reminded that they are not alone. This sign was passed from fathers to sons, through many generations. Perhaps more significantly, all the "seed of Abraham" that descended from this generation on would literally pass through the center of this sign of the Covenant. There would be one Exception.

By now Abraham was living as a friend of God. Think of it, entering into a covenant with God Himself, who has chosen that relationship with you. The sign of that covenant was a simple symbolic act, cut into the flesh of all generations to come. There was no hesitance to comply.

Sarai's name was changed, too, to Sarah (princess). Abraham was promised that she would be blessed, and would bear his son. At this, Abraham fell on his face and wondered at the idea of he and Sarah becoming parents together, he at one hundred and she at ninety. He declared his wish that Ishmael would serve God, but God said, "No, Sarah will have a son, and he will be named Isaac (he laughs)." It is through Isaac that God would fulfill this covenant, He promised.

What about Ishmael? God has given promises of Ishmael's blessing to both Hagar and Abraham. The Arabs of today trace their lineage to Ishmael, and Christian sources have generally, although not unanimously, agreed. There is a book to be written about the "Blessings of Ishmael," but Christian writers have loudly ignored the subject. This attitude hinders evangelism of the Arab world today. Nobody admits hatred of the children of Ishmael, but we like to dismiss them as "Abram's mistake," which is "causing trouble" to this day. Our opinions often don't match what God actually said.

After everyone was circumcised, God came to visit Abraham at home. Sitting out in front of his tent Abraham saw the Lord approaching. Three men actually appeared to talk with Abraham. He immediately got busy providing appropriate acts of hospitality. After lunch, they asked where Sarah was, and were informed that she was in the tent. Knowing where she was (they were the Lord, after all), they delivered the Big News Flash; this time next year, Sarah would have a son.

This had to be too much for Sarah, and she laughed to herself. The Lord asked, "Why did Sarah laugh, saying, 'Shall I indeed bear a child, when I am so old?'" The Lord was being nice; that's not exactly what Sarah had said.

I don't intend to be shocking or off-color, for entertainment's sake. I say what I say to bring home the concept that this is fact. Sometimes we zip through this part of the story, and make it to be more of a fairy tale than a reality. This stuff happened, and it was wondrous. What Sarah is recorded to have actually said to herself was, "After I have become old, *shall I have pleasure, my lord (husband) being old also?*"

Sarah knew about "the birds and the bees." If she was going to have the "miracle of birth," that meant there would have to first be the "miracle of conception." The only way she knew for that to happen was through the "miracle of sex." Some of us think it's pretty spectacular in our twenties; at ages ninety and one hundred, "miracle" hardly covers it.

Sarah laughed and the Lord took notice, then she denied it out of fear. She needn't have been afraid. God had already named the boy, "Laughter." He surely wasn't going to be offended if Sarah giggled a little. The Lord understood why she laughed. If we think about it, we all understand why. It was funny, I don't care who ya' are.

6
You Can Get Out of Sodom, but Can You Get Sodom Out of You?
Genesis 18-19

After the birth-to-be announcement, there was an abrupt change of subject. You can almost hear the tires screech. God had something important on His mind, so to speak, and He "decided" that it was best to share it with His friend, Abraham. God wanted a man of such strategic importance to understand what was about to happen in Sodom. The men/Lord were headed down to Sodom to "see if it was as bad as they had heard." Now we know that God already knows everything. He knew exactly how bad Sodom was, along with its twin city, Gomorrah. Sometimes God does things so everyone else can see what He already knows.

The Lord simply told Abraham that the outcry of S&G was "indeed great," and that their sin was "exceedingly grave." No details are given here about judgment, but Abraham knew God and got the picture in some manner. I can see him standing there as the men walk away. He was thinking. Then he had a bold idea, and moved on it.

"What if there are some good folk there?" Abraham appeals. The Lord replied that for fifty righteous there He would spare the city. Abraham apparently didn't think much of Sodom, so he negotiated further. Forty-five, forty, thirty, down went this backward auctioneering until it got to twenty, and then ten. There it stopped, and the Lord departed, and Abraham went home.

Angels can be bad. Not necessarily evil, just baaaad. A couple of these "special ops" type angels went to Sodom in the evening. They are never referred to as anything other than "angels" or "men" here, so they are apparently not the Lord, like the men in the chapter before.

When Lot saw these angels he naturally invited them in. First, for hospitality's sake, and also for their security, since Lot only knew them to be regular men. They were going to sleep in the square, but Lot urged them in, and gave them a big supper. After supper, the neighbors showed up, and it became obvious why Lot had compelled the angels to come into the house.

This story is not good bed-time reading for the grandkids. The men of Sodom surrounded the house and demanded that Lot bring his guests out for some after-dinner rape. Lot stepped out on the porch and tried to persuade his neighbors otherwise. He even offered his two virgin daughters to the mob.

No, I don't know what he was thinking with that. I have told you, I'm just telling the stories, not explaining everything. Buy a good *Genesis* commentary. I will say that it is obvious that Lot was not quite the hero of faith, or friend of God that Abraham was.

For whatever motivation, Lot offered his daughters for abuse. However, the Sodomites were having none of that, to the great relief (perhaps) of Lot's daughters. I don't think the men of Sodom liked girls, at least not these. The gang accused Lot of being judgmental, and worse, he was from out of town. As they pushed forward, they were about to smash Lot, and break down the door. From within, the angels grabbed Lot, pulled him in and struck the mob men with blindness, so that they couldn't find the door.

The SWAT-angels then instructed Lot to get his family and sons-in-law together and evacuate. When Lot went to Sodom, the Bible says it was already full of wicked people. Now it was boiling over. Let's come back to this down the page; for now I want to get on with the story.

The angels revealed their orders to Lot. They were there to destroy the place. Lot went to the boys who were engaged to his daughters to warn them to leave town with him. They thought it was a joke.

As day broke, the angels were more demanding, but Lot was hesitating. So the angels grabbed Lot, his wife, and the girls, and began to remove them forcibly. Having gotten them out of town, an angel ordered them to run to the mountains. Lot apparently could not run uphill, and asked for indulgence to just go to the next little town. He received this concession, and went to Zoar.

By this time the sun is up, and the brimstone is coming down. Folks have kicked around theories of what this really was, maybe a small asteroid or meteor. As if it makes some difference. Read the book as it is written and get the picture. Fire from above came down below and Sodom was toast, along with its twin, Gomorrah. Call it what you want, God sent it because this festering sore had to be removed.

Let's get back to the subject of the Sodomite wickedness. Because the men of Sodom wanted to rape the apparently male angels, and refused Lot's daughters, some have emphasized their homosexuality as the great sin causing their destruction. This single-minded focus on a particular form of sin is not required by the text. If we are not careful, the focus on just one type of sin (with which *we* have no struggle), can have the effect of distracting us from all of our own sins.

Yes, they were homosexual, obviously. Yes, the Bible is clear that homosexual behavior is sin. But these freaks were just what we Ethnic Texans call, "rurnt to the gristle." They weren't wicked because they were homosexuals; they were homosexuals because they were wicked, first. Make them heterosexuals, and they'll still be wicked. I believe their wickedness came out in lots of ways.

How do I know this? Because this is how evil works, from the inside out. Sexual perversion doesn't start out so obviously. It begins with being a little too fleshly, then moves on to sinful thinking. Next comes a moral failure through weakness, then deliberate "sneaky sex." The conscience is destroyed, and desires get nastier and bolder. Next thing you know, you're trying to gang-rape angels. Sin makes you stupid.

There is a strange little verse here. Verse 19:26 says that Lot's wife, following him, looked back, and became "a pillar of salt." No explanation or commentary, just the casualty report. Maybe after all their hesitating and second-guessing the angels, God had just had enough. Maybe she dilly-dallied too long, and got scorched-in-place by the blast. Whatever. The lesson is that sometimes you got to get your rear in gear and flee evil like you mean it.

Lot did make it into the mountains eventually, and that is where an R-rated episode takes place. The family is now reduced to Lot and his two daughters, whose fiancés were blasted away in Sodom, those slow-witted boys. They all live in a cave; life seems to be rolling downhill like a snowball headed for Havana.

Some writers have offered somewhat mitigating rationales for what happened next. However, this is not necessary or useful. The girls could not have actually thought that the whole earth had been destroyed, since they had fled to Zoar after leaving Sodom. Their subsequent behavior can not be made out to be honorable in any misguided way.

The oldest suggests to her sister that "since their old father is the only available man left on the earth," they should get him drunk and have sex with him, thus preserving the family line. If it was such high-minded practical wisdom, why didn't they discuss it with him while he was sober? Not their style. Both the girls bore sons from this trashy behavior. The sons became the fathers of nations which will give their people trouble later on.

So, Lot saved his family? Well, his wife didn't get away, and the two daughters he saved acted like raunchy chicks. As I said in the chapter title, sometimes you can get the girls out of Sodom, but you can't get the Sodom out of the girls.

When God's judgment comes, there are three places you can be. First, you can be in it, like the Sodomites. That's the worst place, avoid that. Or, you can be pulled out of it by the grace of God, like Lot. He got out, but lost all he had, including his wife. Now he's holed up in a cave with his two sleazy and pregnant daughters. (This is a *Jerry Springer Show* just waiting for taping.)

But there is a third place you can be when judgment comes. You can be where Abraham was, watching it from a distance. As a favor to His friend Abraham, God spared Lot from the judgment of Sodom, just barely. Some of us were spared from God's judgment by the prayers of others, just barely. Be thankful.

7
The God of Abraham, Isaac, . . .
Genesis 20-26

This is going to be a long story, two chapters worth. There is much ground to cover. I am forcing myself to put this all together for the sake of staying on track with our overall plan.

I told you what a friend of God Abraham was. I never said he was perfect. He had a problem on road trips. Apparently, he had a fear that his good-looking wife would be taken from him and that he would be killed off. Remember when they traveled to Egypt and God sent plagues because Sarai was taken as a wife by Pharaoh? Abraham had instructed her to lie about their marriage, and they got kicked out of the country when God exposed them.

That should have been an adequate lesson, but no. They are traveling again, and Abraham is telling the same lie again. As he expected, Sarah has impressed the King of Gerar, Abimelech, and has been taken as a wife. In those places, in those days, when the king saw a woman he liked, he just drafted her. She didn't get a say in the matter, and besides, in Sarah's case, she was going along with it, to keep her husband healthy.

By the way, has anyone noticed that *Sarah is at least ninety years old*! This is some kind of woman here. At sixty-five, and again at ninety, kings are grabbing her for their harems. The Bible says nothing about "a famine of women on the earth," so the kings were not desperate. She must have been pretty amazing, if not downright hot. (I saw Raquel Welch recently, and she's holding up pretty good, but she's not ninety.)

Well, God couldn't allow this, since He had already reset Sarah's biological clock. He threatened the king with death and Abimelech pleaded his innocence, since he didn't know, and never touched Sarah, anyway. God said, "Yes, I know, "and let him live. Everyone was still frightened of God's judgment, however, and Abraham was summoned to explain his actions.

Abraham gave his lame excuse. First, he had assumed that the pagans in that place would have no fear of God, and would have just killed him for his wife. Anyway, she was his sister for real, sort of. They had the same father. (Boy is their kid going to have a lot of questions!) Abraham said they carried on this scam wherever they went; it was an ongoing thing.

Unlike in Egypt, this king gave Abraham a lot of money and stuff, and threw out the welcome mat throughout the whole country. In return, and because it was his fault anyway, Abraham prayed all the curses off the people and king of Gerar.

Right after that, when everyone was back where they belonged, and Abraham and Sarah had a decent place to live, the Lord made good on his long-awaited promise, and Sarah conceived. A son was born to Abraham. This made everyone laugh (I told you it was funny!), so they named the boy Isaac, which means "laughter," or "he laughs," depending on your grammar.

When the boy was weaned, Abraham threw a big party. Sarah saw the son of Hagar at the party, and all the old resentment came back. Now Sarah had a son of her own to look out for, and she wanted everything for him. Abraham was disturbed by this, because Ishmael was his son, after all. God spoke to Abraham, to ease his mind about the situation. God was going to make Ishmael a great nation, for he too had come from Abraham.

God directed Abraham to send Hagar and her son away, which he did the next morning. However, it has been noted that God did not tell him to send them away in poverty, with nothing but some bread and water. Abraham's action seems to be indicative of an attitude some people still have about the descendants of Ishmael, "Yes, I know God said He would bless them. Let God bless them, but I'll have nothing to do with them."

Hagar and son went into the desert and were about to die, when God spoke from heaven and repeated His promise to make a great nation of the boy. He showed Hagar where to get water, and they survived. Ishmael grew up and married an Egyptian girl.

Abraham lived on in that land for some time and God came to talk with him again. God called him to go and give Isaac as a burnt offering. Next morning a small party sets out into the wilderness, for about a three day trip. When they arrive at the sacrifice spot, Abraham leaves the servants behind and heads up the mountain with Isaac.

You know Abraham was in some intense thought along the way. We don't know exactly how old Isaac was, but he was old enough to do some thinking of his own. He asks where the lamb is, since everything else is with them for the sacrifice. Abraham's answer is a sermon title we have been preaching ever since, "God will provide for Himself the lamb . . ." Indeed He has, as Jesus was identified by John the Baptist in the New Testament, "Behold the Lamb of God, who takes away the sin of the world!"

As I said, we don't know the age of Isaac at this time. I'm betting however, that the boy could have refused to participate in this offering, had he not agreed to it. For the 100+ year old Abraham to bind Isaac and place him on the altar required a certain amount of passivity on the part of Isaac, if not actual cooperation. Isaac was trusting Abraham, and Abraham was trusting God, and it seems that not a word of this had been breathed to Sarah, for obvious reasons.

Just as Abraham was preparing to take the knife to his son/sacrifice, the angel of the Lord spoke from above, stopping Abraham from proceeding. The covenant had been tested, and Abraham had been found faithful. Looking away, Abraham saw a ram caught in the brush, so the wood and fire and knife were still put to good use.

God repeated and expanded his covenant blessings to Abraham, adding the promise that in Abraham's seed, all nations will be blessed. This has been fulfilled in multiple ways, the greatest being the birth of Christ as a descendant of Abraham.

Our story moves on. Isaac grew up, and Sarah died. Abraham gained years and blessings, and as an old man required his servant to swear that he would not allow Isaac to take a local Canaanite wife. He had to promise to go back to the country and people of Abraham, to find a suitable Mrs. Isaac.

The servant loaded the camels, ten of them, and headed off to the old country. Abraham was very plain in his instructions that the wife must come from Abraham's people, and Isaac must not go back there. The young couple would share her background, but his future.

Arriving in town, the servant sought the help of the Lord. He asked for a specific combination of events to show him which girl was The One. As he finished his request, a lovely young virgin with the right pedigree, Rebekah, came to the well where he was waiting. What the servant had asked for was that a girl would give him a drink, then offer to draw water for his camels as well. This babe did exactly that, offering to draw water for the camels *until they finished drinking*, which was no small thing. Remember, he had at least ten camels in his convoy, and camels drink prodigiously after a long trip. This kind offer could have taken up her whole day. What a sweetheart!

When the servant asked about her family, he was overjoyed, and worshipped the Lord for making his journey immediately successful. He also gave her bracelets, and a ring for her nose. The passage that follows is an interesting insight into the courtship practices of that people and time.

Rebekah's family invited the man to dinner, receiving him and his camels hospitably. But before he would eat, he had to tell them his business there. He explained who he was, why he was there, and caught them up on the results so far.

It was Rebekah's father and uncle who were making the decisions here, you may have noticed. They agreed that Rebekah would go to be married to Isaac, and no one asked her anything until they were discussing the actual day she would leave. Fortunately she was agreeable to all this, and they set out for her new home right away. She took her nurse, a person who appears to have functioned in that culture as a personal assistant, and off they went.

I confess to being the romantic type, and I think verses 61 through 67 of *Genesis* 24 are rather sweet. Humpity-bumpity, a long camel ride, then Rebekah looked up to see Isaac walking in the field, meditating. She had no reason to know who this fellow was, but something arrested her attention, and she slid right off her camel. She asked her servant escort who this man was, and I think I detect some hopefulness in her inquiry. Lo and behold, it was the very man for whom she had left her home.

She saw him, but he could just make out the camels. Being the modest girl she was, she covered up before he got to where they were. We may think it bizarre, but you would marry a girl in those days without ever having seen her face. If you think that's a weird deal, think about this girl agreeing to go to another country to marry a guy she only just now heard of. Isaac moved into his departed mother's tent with his new bride, and started a new phase of his life.

Rebekah was apparently unable to conceive for almost twenty years after they married, but Isaac prayed for her and the Lord answered the prayer. Did He ever; she was carrying twins! Seems like Rebekah was having a tough pregnancy; fighting in the womb or something. When she asked God about this, He explained that two nations were represented in her womb, and that their struggle was starting early. Twin boys were soon born; Esau and Jacob.

Even from the womb, Jacob was a grabber, getting what he could. His name meant "grasper" or "supplanter," and his life followed his name. Esau was an outdoorsman, and his father favored him, since Isaac had a real taste for wild game. Jacob was more of a city guy, and was favored by Mom. Esau was the firstborn, which carried big weight, even if you were only ahead by a few minutes.

Jacob spent his life trying to grab what was meant to be Esau's. Esau cared little for the birthright he had coming as firstborn. He traded it off one day for a bowl of red bean soup. Since he was a reddish color when born, and the soup was red, Esau got the nickname, "Edom," which meant "Red." (BAD PUN ALERT: We English speakers might say that whenever "'esaw" beans, he'd "Eat'em.")

Back to Isaac. God directed him, and repeated His promises of blessing which had been given to Abraham. Like his father, Abraham, Isaac settled in Gerar, where Abimelech was king. And—here we go again—like Father Abraham, he lied about his wife, because he was scared. When the king spotted Isaac and Rebekah acting in an unsibling-like manner from his window, he remembered the family history and uncovered the falsehood. Fortunately, he chewed them out, but didn't throw them out. They stayed in the land and got wealthy.

God's blessing often incites jealousy. As Isaac retraced his father's steps, the locals, now referred to as Philistines, quarreled over water rights, as desert people are prone to do. Isaac kept moving on, until he came to a place where he could live, and drink, in peace. He named the place Rehoboth, or "broad places," and there the Lord appeared to him, repeating the promised blessing.

When God is blessing you, some people get jealous, but others want in on it. Abimelech came to Isaac to make a covenant, even though he apparently hadn't cared much for the fellow and his deception. They agreed to keep each other in peace, and went on their separate ways.

8
. . . and Jacob
Genesis 27-35

As Jacob sought after God's blessing, Esau continued to despise it. He married ungodly wives and caused grief to his parents. This brotherly contrast is important to the story of redemption. Jacob represents those who, although they are not born to the blessing, have an attraction to the things of God. They want it, even if they go about getting it in wrong ways. Esau shows us those who are born into the covenant, but despise it. They disrespect it, and thus lose the benefit of it.

Jacob is not perfect, but he desires God's blessings, even if he has to steal them. Esau is completely worldly, living for the now, not spiritually oriented at all. Jacob will literally fight God for His blessing, and it is this desire that God responds to with that blessing.

Since this book is all about redemption, we can't just slide over these two boys. I don't want to start anything controversial, but the difference between Jacob and Esau is like the difference we will see later between the People of God in the Old Testament, and the People of God as described in the New Testament.

The New Testament explains these brothers' relevance to redemption. In Romans, starting in the ninth chapter, continuing through the eleventh, Paul makes reference to Jacob and Esau, relating them to both the Jews and Gentiles who have had faith in Christ. Under the Old Covenant, you got credit just for being a Jew, a member of the nation of Israel. Membership in Israel plus faith in God (obedience) made you one of the People of God. This is like Esau, who was given the birthright simply by virtue of escaping the womb first.

But under the New Covenant, membership in the People of God is by faith alone and is much less exclusive. This is like Jacob, who was blessed because he wanted to be, and sought the blessing on purpose. God corrected his shady methods, but honored his desire. God saw this before they were born, and said, "The elder shall serve the younger."

This analogy only works as far as the Bible takes it. If you overdo it, you can get into error. The New Covenant people do not replace the Old Covenant people. It takes both groups together to make up the People of God throughout history. At the same time, we must be clear that both will be redeemed only by God's sacrifice in Christ.

One more thing happened that belongs in this part of the story. Isaac got old and blind. He was hungry for some wild game, and called for Esau. He promised his official fatherly blessing to Esau, if he would go get him a wild game supper. Rebekah was listening, and desired this blessing for her favorite son, Jacob. She quickly went to Jacob, and they schemed up a scam. Rebekah had learned a recipe to make *cabrito* which tasted like venison. I'll bet she had been fooling the blind old man for years.

Jacob, who was no dim bulb, knew that his brother was hairy and rougher than himself, so he was afraid that Dad would feel his arms and blow the plot. Abraham might curse him instead of bless him. Rebekah then says a powerful thing, accepting the potential curse for herself, telling Jacob to get the little goats and follow her orders. She'll cook the meat; Jacob will put their skins on his arms to fool Isaac.

So Jacob, dressed in Esau's clothes, with kidskin sleeves and turtle-neck, took the savory dish in to his father, who was immediately suspicious. "How did you get it so quickly?" he asked. As liars sometimes do, he claimed God's help.

"Come closer, and let me feel." Jacob and his scheming mother had anticipated this, and the goatskin trick worked. Isaac recognized Jacob's voice, but this son continued (I counted six times) to deceive him, and finally, Isaac embraced the younger son and gave him the blessing intended for his brother.

When Esau came in with his honestly hunted food, there was great uproar. Esau pleaded for a second blessing, but there was not much left to give. I would think that, if you gave a blessing in error you could just say, "Never mind." Guess it doesn't work that way. "No do-overs, no slipsies!"

Esau held a grudge, and planned to kill his brother as soon as Dad's funeral was over. Rebekah heard of his intentions, and warned her boy Jacob. She counseled Jacob to flee to his Uncle Laban's house for "a few days" until things blew over. With Isaac's agreement, a cover story was told to explain his departure—he needed a wife, and they couldn't stand the local girls, like the two Esau had married.

In favoring one son over the other, they lost both. Esau cared nothing for his birthright, married ungodly women, and was planning to murder his hated brother. Jacob had tried to receive good things in bad ways, had lied to his father, stolen from his brother, and would never see his precious mother again. She advised him to leave for a "few days," but he would not return for many years. Rebekah would die waiting for his return.

Off went Jacob to his mother's relatives. Strangely, Isaac blessed him some more, but gave him strict orders to pass over the local Canaanite girls, and find a wife over there. The Bible says that Jacob came to "a certain place" to spend the night on his way to Haran. At that place God spoke to him in a vivid dream, and promised that his people would spread out from there in every direction. God also promised to bring Jacob back to that place, which Jacob called Bethel, "the House of God." Jacob vowed that, if God would take care of him and bring him safely back, Jacob would serve God, and give a tenth of all he had to God. God didn't need the stuff, but this was important for Jacob to do.

Jacob asked the first guys he came to in Haran about his uncle, Laban, and heard that he was well. As a matter of fact, Laban's daughter Rachel was just coming to the well with the sheep. Jacob helped her get the flock watered, then, in a weepy revelation, he told her who he was. She ran home to tell Daddy, and Jacob was warmly received. Remember that they sent Jacob's mother away with Isaac's servant, and there is no mention of her ever coming back. It would be a big deal for her son to appear there. Jacob stayed as a helpful guest for a month, then Laban offered to put him on the payroll.

Laban had these two daughters. Leah was the eldest, and seems to have been a plain-looking girl, perhaps. Rachel, the youngest, was more of a hottie, at least in Jacob's heart. He was in love with the girl, and offered to work seven years for her hand in marriage. As is the case with intense romantic love, the seven years just flew by and the wedding date arrived.

If Jacob had been a young crook, then Uncle Laban was an old pro. After the big feast he slipped Leah into the tent with Jacob for the wedding night. I don't know if it was really, really dark, or if Jacob had just drained a couple too many wineskins, but he didn't notice until the morning after. Girl must have just kept her mouth shut. Jacob would not have thought it so unusual for his bride to be shy and quiet on her wedding night. Laban claimed that it was not the custom there to marry off the youngest ahead of the oldest, and nobody had spoken for Leah, so here you go. Seems like someone would have mentioned this to Jacob, over the last seven years. Perhaps Laban just conveniently "remembered" this custom in time for the wedding.

So Jacob agrees to a deal. He would fulfill his duty as a new husband to Leah, completing the "honeymoon" week with her. For that, he would receive Rachel as his wife also, and then work another seven years for her. Seven years service, two weddings, then another seven years service. Of course Rachel was his choice, and he loved her more than her sister.

God took note of the awkward and somewhat sad position of Leah, the despised. He gave her a fertile womb, while Rachel the favored remained barren. This precipitated an episode which I like to call, "The Baby Bowl." The two sisters began to use childbirth as a means to compete for Jacob's attention, if not affection.

Leah takes the early lead. She may not be much loved by Jacob, but she gets loved enough to get frequently pregnant. Four sons come before she takes a break. First quarter score: Leah 4, Rachel zip.

Rachel was jealous of this, and begged Jacob to "Give me children or I die!" Jacob reacts angrily, and reminds Rachel that conception is in God's hands, not his. It's obviously not Jacob's fault; he has little trouble getting children with Leah. Does Rachel really think that Jacob is holding out on her, delivering seed only to her sister?

Now if you read the Scripture here, you notice that the girl's maids went with them when they got married. We know how Sarah used this, and now Rachel follows the same pattern. She sends Jacob in to her maid, Bilhah so she can bear children in Rachel's name. This she does, twice. Score at halftime: Leah 4, Bilhah (for Rachel) 2.

"Oh, so that's how it's going to be!" says Leah, and as soon as her own heir-force slows down she drafts her maid, Zilpah, into service. Zilpah is quite up to the job, and provides two more sons. Heading into the final quarter: Leah 4, Bilhah/Rachel 2, Zilpah (for Leah) 2.

At this time, the first son Reuben has grown enough to go out and pick mandrakes. Rachel has a taste for mandrakes, and strikes a deal with Leah to give her a turn with their husband for some mandrakes. When Jacob comes in that evening, he is informed by Leah that he is to stay with her for that night. He has been traded for a mess of mandrakes. I'm thinking that he feels less like a father of faith right now, and more like a pinball, or—can we even say it—a stud service? And guess what?

Leah's back in business, producing sons five and six, and as a topping on the sundae, a daughter. (For novelty, perhaps?)

After all this, God gets back to Rachel, and she bears a son, Joseph. She will repeat the accomplishment once more later, but we'll talk about that then. For now, when the dust settles, the final tally looks like this:

Team Leah		**Team Rachel**	
Leah:6/1	*Zilpah:2*	*Rachel:2*	*Bilhah:2*
Reuben	Gad	Joseph	Dan
Simeon	Asher	Benjamin	Naphtali
Levi			
Judah			
Issachar			
Zebulun			
Dinah			

Leah, the sentimental favorite as the underdog, produces more children than the other three combined. This is even more impressive since she probably had far fewer opportunities for conception than did Rachel. We don't know what Jacob thought about the maids, but at least they came out even in the end. Let me also remind you that all these women were taken as wives, not concubines or adulteresses. And don't forget the names of these kids, especially the boys; they will become important as the Story moves along.

The relationship between Laban and Jacob went bad. This may have been inevitable, since they were both somewhat ethically challenged. Jacob wanted to leave, but Laban offered him a new contract. Problem was, Jacob was under God's blessing, so any contract they agreed to would work out to favor Jacob. The other problem was that Laban was a cheat, so he continued to try to rookie-do whomever he dealt with, nephew/son-in-law included. The more he tried to cheat, the more he lost to Jacob.

After more of this than Jacob could stand, he decided to make a break for it. He had noticed that Laban's sons were unhappy that the whole estate was being swallowed up by their cousin. Also, Laban was getting increasingly surly. Time to go. Jacob rehearsed the whole history to Laban's daughters, who were his senior wives, and all agreed to depart.

Depart they did, and on the way out, Rachel stole her father's household idols. Three days later, when Laban found out the whole bunch of them were on their way to Canaan, he gave chase. On the way, God warned Laban in a dream to be careful how he dealt with Jacob. When he caught up with Jacob's party, he blew a lot of smoke about how he was wronged by Jacob's departure, but did not take his desired retribution, because of the dream. He claimed to understand everything except one, "Why did you steal my gods?"

Jacob spoke as if righteously offended. He declared that he had snuck out because he was afraid Laban would not let his daughters go, but whoever took the idols would die. He challenged Laban to publicly show what was taken. The tents were searched, Leah's and the two maids', then Rachel's. Rachel had hidden the idols in her camel's saddle, which was apparently kept in the tent. As her father began to search through her tent, she apologized for not rising in respect—as she sat upon the saddle where the idols were hidden. She blamed her immobility on her menstrual period, tricky girl. Surely the daughter of her father, wasn't she?

Jacob, knowing nothing of Rachel's theft and deception, had endured enough. He went off on Uncle Laban, letting loose twenty years of resentment and frustration at Laban's shabby treatment. Laban still would not concede and confess. He claimed everything as rightfully his.

Yet he pretended to be the big man, and suggested a covenant between them.

The *Mizpah,* as Jacob called it, has been misunderstood in the present day. Lovers and friends wear those broken-in-half medallions with romantic sentiment, asking God to watch over them while they are apart. It was not in fact a covenant of friendship, but a settlement based on mutual distrust. It was a contract calling upon God to watch their backs, while they promised to leave each other alone.

Now, there was only one issue left. To go home, Jacob had to face Esau. He developed a plan, this time not to deceive his brother, but to appease him. Jacob knew that Esau was coming to greet him with 400 men, but he didn't know their intent. First, he divided all that was with him into two groups, thinking that if Esau attacked one, the other would escape. Then he prayed sincerely that God would be good and faithful to the promise to bring him home safely.

Next day, he selected lots of good livestock as a gift for Esau. He divided them into droves, and instructed his servants to keep a distance between droves. Imagine what is going to confront Esau. While anticipating the arrival of Jacob, he will meet a nice little herd of livestock, which he will then be told are a gift from his soon-to-arrive brother. This happened once, twice, three times, then some more. All of this was sure to wear on any murderous resentment that may have been remaining in Esau's heart. At least, that was Jacob's hope. For all he knew, Esau might have killed them all, and Jacob, too, when he got there.

The servants were telling Esau that Jacob was behind them, on his way. However, Jacob was not moving yet. When the presents were all on their way Jacob stayed in the camp. For the night, he stayed behind. In the dead of that night, he sent his stuff, his people, his wives and his children on ahead. They crossed the brook into "Esau County," and Jacob was the only one left behind. Alone—but not quite.

Jacob wrestled with a man until daybreak. This was one of those theophanies I told you about, an Old Testament appearance of the Lord in physical form. At daybreak, the man knew that Jacob would not let go, so he touched and dislocated Jacob's hip. Yet Jacob was a desperate man, at the crisis point of his life. He would not let go until the man blessed him. Jacob knew Who he was holding on to.

The man asked, "What is your name?" Remember, I told you God asks questions for our knowledge, not His. Jacob spoke his name, a name fitting to his life as a cheater, a grasper, and a deceiver,

"Jacob."

It was a confession, *"I'm a cheat. I bought my brother's birthright for beans, when he was at a weak moment. Then I outright stole his blessing from our father through deception. That's what I do. That's who I am."*

"Not any more," said the Man, "from now on you will be known as *Israel,* 'He who strives with God,' for that is what you have done." Then Jacob asked the man's name, but it was not given to him. Instead, he just received His blessing.

The sun came up, and Jacob limped on over with the rest of the party. Soon they came face-to-face with Esau and his 400. Surely there was trembling as Jacob readied the company. The children went to their separate mothers, and everybody stared as Jacob went forward to face the music, and meet his brother. Seven times he bowed, and at last they were drawing near.

Then Esau ran.

It was not a run to warfare. It was not a run to vengeance. It was not the same run that had chased Jacob away twenty years ago.

It was a run to embrace. It was a run to forgive. It was a run that recognized that, when you total it all up, your brother *is* your birthright, and twenty years is too long to be deprived.

They hugged. They kissed, as people over there do. They wept, in sorrow for what they had lost, and in joy for what had been restored. They met their in-laws and nephews, and the niece, and their uncle. Esau went on back to the ranch house, and Jacob's company came along more slowly, because they had all the baby livestock to bring with them.

And Jacob made good on his vow. When he bought some land of his own, he put up an altar and called the place, "God, the God of Israel."

I wanted to make that the end of this chapter, but there's more, and it's relevant to the Big Story. One more episode, and it's an ugly one. Back to the "R-rated" Bible.

The kids grew up. You remember Dinah, the daughter. She was the one girl produced in the "Baby Bowl." By now, she was beyond her little girl days; apparently one of those attractive young women who have the power to reach in through a man's heart, grab his brains, rip them out, and throw them in the creek. Unintentionally, of course.

While Jacob was settled in the land of Shechem, Dinah was out for a stroll, and came upon a young man, also named Shechem, the prince of the land. He was not your virtuous Disney-style prince, it appears, and could not restrain himself, as a decent young man should do. Overcome with "love" and hormones, he forced himself sexually on Dinah. However, having raped her, he still had feelings for her, and attempted to woo her, which I would think would be a real challenge after you have raped a girl.

Looking at it from Dinah's perspective might be helpful, though. As a now deflowered woman, she was considered "damaged goods" in her culture, defiled. She no longer was among the young virgins attractive to the eligible bachelors of her people. She would be asking, "Who would want me now?" There was one obvious answer.

Practically speaking, she has to settle. If Shechem was not too ugly, and didn't smell bad, perhaps he could be tolerable. After all, even having had her, he still loved her. He was rude and selfish, but he was sincere. He had started out all wrong, but with the help of his father, he was now trying to make things right.

Shechem's dad, Hamor, went to see Jacob. Dinah's brothers were out in the field when the elders conferred. When they returned, they were incensed, as you would be. Hamor spoke with them all in good faith, saying, "Let's make the best of an unfortunate situation. We have daughters for you to marry, and land for us all to share. After all, my son really does love your sister." Hamor made an open offer, a blank check, to pay whatever Jacob's people required as dowry. This sparked a wicked idea in the boys.

Deceitfully they replied. "We cannot let our daughters get hooked-up with uncircumcised men. You will all have to be trimmed." Hamor's eyes must have widened a bit at this, but they had promised, and this seemed tolerable, if bizarre. Prince Shechem did not hesitate, for he desired Dinah greatly, and after all, given the nature of their first encounter, he did owe her and her family. Turns out he was not the creep we originally thought. Maybe this could work. (Shades of "Luke and Laura!")

So for the benefit of the merger, everyone in Shechem-town followed the prince in circumcision. (I told you this wasn't a Disney-type prince story.) On the third day after, you can imagine (although you probably don't want to) how they were painfully sore. On that day, two of Dinah's brothers armed themselves, snuck into town, and killed the whole bunch of them, and took Dinah home. They looted and pillaged and plundered, right down to the herds and wives and children. Their father was upset, since he had made the deal with Shechem and Hamor in good faith, and now the hot-headed boys had brought the wrath of the countryside on Jacob and his people by deceiving and massacring those Hivites.

The boys' response? They didn't care. Hot-heads often don't. They were stupidly simple minded: "Should he treat our sister as a harlot?" You can almost hear them grunt as they walk away, dragging their knuckles in the dirt.

Yeah, those brothers really did a good service for their baby sister— she lost her virginity, and got nothing at all for it. Had to move back home with the charming boys who slaughtered her husband and in-laws. If you are starting to think that women in those days often got swapped around like cattle, then I must be doing a good job of communicating, in spite of my subtlety. Now Jacob had to leave the country, where he was unpopular again, and return to the place where he met with God before—Bethel.

Why am I telling you this nasty story? Well, have you noticed a strange inconsistency in the narrative? Look at the end of *Genesis* 33. Jacob has had his name changed to Israel, made up with his brother, and settled in Shechem for his happily ever after. Then chapter 34 happens, and the new name, "Israel," is not mentioned. The man is called Jacob, and his sons act like "sons of Jacob," and he's in trouble again. As much as we would like to ignore this chapter, it is there, and it's important to the Big Story.

You see, God renamed Jacob as Israel in 32:28 as a promise, but it would take a while for "Jacob" to actually become "Israel." Those nasty boys of his were just being sons of Jacob, their father. Your life is a "big ship," and takes a while to turn around sometimes. When God redeems you, the change in your spirit and soul is instantaneous, but the results can take a while to work their way to the outside, especially if you've taught your old habits to your children.

When you become a believer in Christ, you are changed by God from "Jacob" to "Israel." That happens right then; that's how God sees you. That's your vertical relationship. But you have an earthly, horizontal relationship with everything and everyone around you, and that change may not appear so instantaneously.

God wanted Jacob to be Israel, move back to Bethel, and faithfully worship his one God. When Jacob obeyed, God returned to again call him Israel, although his original name continues to be used as well. It's not that we ever stop calling him Jacob; we just see him taking on more and more of the characteristics of Israel.

The family moved on, and Rachel was pregnant again. She died in childbirth, and named the baby, "Ben-oni" (The son of my sorrow), but his father called him "Benjamin" (the son of my right hand). The two sons of Rachel would be very important to the story of the people as it would unfold.

To Egypt, and Back

9
Dream Your Way to the Top
Genesis 37-50

I love this story. If you get it, you will love it too. It is one we may see elsewhere in literature: the brat who gets what he deserves, and learns from it, becoming a greater man than anyone but he himself ever dreamed he could. The "Beauty and the Beast" fairy tale is built around this theme. But this is not just literature. This is a true story from the "Redemption Files." The story of Joseph will teach you how to be faithful to God. It will teach you how to become a man or woman of God.

You remember that the "Baby Bowl" produced all those sons of Jacob. Toward the end, almost as an "Oh, by the way." The Lord remembered Rachel, and she conceived. This boy Joseph (we'll talk about Benjamin later) was destined from birth to be his father's favorite. Let us count the ways.

First, Rachel was still the wife of choice for Jacob. She was the object of his love in a way her sister could never be. Any child of hers would be at an advantage to start with. Then, there was the long barrenness before Joseph came. Years of deep sorrow intensified the joy when the announcement came, "Rachel is with child!" Can you imagine the anticipation of that long pregnancy? Finally he was born.

Born to be spoiled! He was the son of his father's late life. Ben Cartwright had only two sons before his "Little Joe." I think this "Little Joe" was number eleven. Jacob had nothing to prove with this boy; everyone knew what kind of man and father he was by now. This kid would not be expected to be disciplined and provide labor like his older brothers. He would just stay close to Dad at the house, getting loved in a way more fitting for a grandson.

Away from the house, he wasn't greatly loved. You would think that Jacob would have learned a lesson about parental favoritism in his own tragic family history, but no. Imagine the self-image little Joseph must have had, openly acknowledged as his daddy's favorite, even though he was the most unproductive of Jacob's sons. The more Jacob favored him, the more jealous resentment grew in the other brothers.

Jacob whipped out a beautiful gift for Joseph, a coat of many colors. Colors were harder to come by in those days, so this was an extravagant gift. As if he were afraid Joseph would not be hated enough, his father gave him assignments that ensured the resentment of the others. Joseph reported to his father that the brothers were goofing off on the job, and they disliked him intensely.

Joseph was not helping the relationship. He was just a kid, so you really can't expect greater wisdom at the start. His brothers already would not speak to him on friendly terms, and then Joseph got a dream from God. The point of the dream was that he would rule over his brothers. When Joseph shared the dream with his elder brothers, it went over like a pork chop at a bar-mitzvah. They hated him more, and then he got another dream. This one included his parents, and it was too much even for his doting father. Israel had a talk with the boy. The brothers' hatred got worse, but his father kept the dream in mind.

The brothers went to the pasture, and Joseph was sent to check on them. They saw him coming from a distance, and their hatred began to boil. Upon the very sight of him, they began to plot his murder. They would kill him, then say that a beast got him. As hateful plotters do, they said to each other, "Then we'll see what becomes of his dreams!"

You need to understand that if you have a dream from God, there will be those, in hell and on earth, who will say the same about you. They will hate you for your dream, and even plot against you. They will say in their hearts, "We'll see what becomes of his dreams!"

But brother Reuben was of a slightly different mind. He counseled the others to not kill the little snot, but rather throw him in a pit. After all, he was their brother, and why should they become murderers for such a useless cause as Joseph? Actually, it was Reuben's intention to come back later and rescue Joseph, for which he knew Dad would be very grateful.

The boys pulled off Joseph's fancy coat and threw him in a dry hole, then they broke for lunch. Reuben had somewhere to go. While the rest of the boys were polishing off their lamb tacos, a caravan of traveling Ishmaelites appeared. As these gypsies approached, the enterprising siblings decided that this squirt of a brother of theirs should not go to waste. Selling him to the gypsies would 1) get him out of their hair once and for all, 2) keep them from having to kill him and, 3) put some money in their pockets, being the first actually useful thing Joseph had ever done for them, they figured.

When Reuben got back, the pit was empty, and Joseph was off to Egypt. Although unhappy with this result, Reuben joined his brothers in the deception of their father. You see, they knew that if Dad found out what had really happened, he would send them all to Egypt to get Joe back, and no one wanted that. They took the cheap way out; they bloodied Joseph's coat, then played dumb when they showed it to Jacob. They let their father surmise the story from the evidence they provided. It was low and cruel.

While Israel went into mourning, Joseph went into Egypt, and into slavery. Here he was sold to Potiphar, an officer of Pharaoh. At this point, Joseph begins to show the pattern of his life. Somewhere, he had developed true character and integrity, although the narrative doesn't say how. At first reading, this may look like a flaw in the story, literary-wise. How does the spoiled Joseph suddenly become an honorable young man of faithfulness and integrity?

It's not as abrupt a change as it appears. Under the pressure of having his life come apart, the real Joseph came out. We know Joseph had something going on with God, because of the dreams God had given him as a plan for his life. Someone at home had been doing a remarkable job of preparing Joseph for life. (Could it have been the changed Israel?) Additionally, the Bible says that the Lord was with him, so he was successful.

Potiphar recognized Joseph for what he was, and put him in charge of all he had. Potiphar's wife recognized Joseph for what he could do for her, and tried to give him all she had. Joseph refused her attempts at seduction, due to his loyalty to Potiphar and the Lord.

The frustrated floozy got angry at being turned down, and falsely charged Joseph with attempting to do what she had been attempting to do. Potiphar does not seem to have been exceptionally bright, at least not a good judge of character. Perhaps he just wanted to keep peace in his home. He had Joseph put into the king's prison, which was unfortunate for not only Joseph, but Potiphar as well. Now Potiphar's ho-wife could just have her way with Joseph's replacement, if he was hunky enough, and not the kind of man Joseph was.

Too bad Potiphar could not see what he had in both his wife and his household servant. The chief jailer did, however, and soon Joseph was in charge of the jail. Watch this; this is what Joseph did, more than once. One verse he arrived at his next difficult situation, the next verse he was running the place. This was the story of his young life.

So Joseph sat and served time in jail, but it was the king's jail. This meant he was surrounded by important prisoners. Among his cellmates were the king's chief cupbearer and his baker. These guys both had dreams one night, the kind you know are important, but you don't know why. Joseph, being the sensitive type, perceived their concern the next day and listened to their dreams. He was continuing to hold true to his faith in God, even though he was now thrown into a hole for the second time. "Do not interpretations belong to God?" Joseph asked his buddies. He had some experience with this sort of thing, and gave them both interpretations. One was very positive, the other tragic.

The events happened just as Joseph said they would, but it didn't help him any. The baker was killed by the king, end of story. The cupbearer was restored to his place, but forgot all about Joseph. Joseph still sat in jail, for two more years.

Then the king had a dream. Skinny cows and fat cows, skinny corn and fat corn. Weird stuff. No one in the house could explain the dream, and Pharaoh was upset. This jogged the memory of his cupbearer, who got helpful all of the sudden. When he told the king about meeting Joseph two years earlier, Pharaoh sent for him. One good thing about jail; if someone forgets you there, at least they will know where to find you when they remember you later.

Joseph no doubt "cleaned up good." He came to the palace, and was his usual faithful self. Now, this boy had endured enough trauma and dirty dealing from his family, employer, and colleagues to fill up a week of *Oprah* shows, yet he showed no bitterness. Joseph was smart; he had to know that he was finally in the position to start making his dream happen. Joseph was also wise; he knew that if it was truly God's dream, he didn't have to make it happen.

Not a word to the forgetful cupbearer who just left him behind. He didn't mention how Pharaoh should deal with the knucklehead Potiphar and his trashy old lady. He didn't even ask for his freedom and an escort home for vengeance on his brothers in return for his services. He didn't bargain at all, he just did what he was there to do, put himself in the service of the king. Joseph was class.

The boy was now the thirty-year-old man, and he continued his life-long pattern of exceeding expectations. He heard the dream, and immediately explained not only what it meant, but what Pharaoh should do about it. Famine was coming, and God had given Egypt a plan to get through it.

Pharaoh saw what everyone else had seen. He recognized the hand of God's favor when he saw it, and he wanted the benefit of it. He put Joseph in charge, just as everyone else had, and the land of Egypt was spared starvation in the coming famine.

At this point, in *Genesis* 41, something else important happens. Joseph becomes a father. He was married to Potiphera, an Egyptian priest's daughter, who bore him two sons in the time before the famine. As wonderful as this is on its own, there is a really cool but subtle point here, not to be missed. The boys are named Manasseh and Ephraim.

Manasseh means "forgetfulness." Joseph said, "God has made me forget all my trouble and all my father's household." Forgotten. The hatred and abuse of his brothers, forgotten. His own early mistakes, behind him. The loss of his home at an early age, forgotten. That evil, lying woman and her doofus husband, forgotten. Thirteen years of slavery and prison, while trying to learn to become a man in a foreign dungeon, forgotten. Neglected in prison by those he had helped, forgotten. Losing his family, forgotten, as he started over with a family of his own.

Joseph had gotten over it all. This was not amnesia or Alzheimer's. This was the forgetfulness of God's grace, in which *we still know the facts, but forget the offense*. Joseph named his firstborn, "Forgetfulness," and gave testimony to God's ability to bring us out of grief, and heal the grief out of us.

When we accept this forgetfulness of God's grace, we can move on with our life, and become fruitful. Joseph named his second son "fruitfulness," and said, "God has made me fruitful in the land of my affliction." In his blessed forgetfulness and fruitfulness, Joseph looked like the owner of a happy ending. But this is God's story, and just when you think it's time to roll the credits, it gets ridiculously better.

By my figuring, Joseph was just past thirty-seven years old. He is the Palace Wonderkid, the HHIC (Head Hebrew In Charge), himself. The plan God gave him has saved Egypt from starvation. People from "all the earth" are coming to buy food from his nation.

Meanwhile, back in the "old country" Jacob has heard that there is food to be had in Egypt. Apparently, there were no flocks or herds left to be tended in their dried-up pasture. So, the patriarch walked into the room one day and said to the boys, "Why are you all staring at each other? There is grain in Egypt—go buy some!"

So ten of the brothers headed to Egypt to get groceries. Count them up; sons #1 through #10, all sent on this mission. However, unbeknownst to them, brother # 11, Joseph, was already there. See also that the youngest son of the beloved Rachel, #12 Benjamin, was not about to be let out of his father's sight. Not after the incident with Joseph.

This story gets fun in a hurry. Joseph was the one with whom all the foreign customers were required to deal. Imagine this. Eight or nine years have passed since the day Joseph came out of jail, and into the palace. All the things we have discussed above have happened, and just when life could not get any sweeter for Joseph, one day at work, he looked up and there were all ten of his older brothers. Surely Joseph was smart enough to have anticipated this possibility, but now here they were for reals. What would you do? This looks to us like the "AHA!" moment.

Joseph was a wise and patient young man, however. I can see him just sitting back and taking a deep breath, "OK, now what?" Perhaps he had it all planned before they arrived. I think of Bible people as real people, and I look forward to spending time in eternity with some of these guys. I want to hear this story from Joseph himself, as well as from Reuben, and Simeon, and Benjamin. I want to ask of these, and other folk from the Book, "What was that like? What were you thinking?"

"And Joseph remembered the dreams," says *Genesis* 42:9. That's a sermon title begging to be preached. It's one of those phrases the Holy Spirit will use to teach us deep things, if we will take the time to meditate on it. Those dreams had been set aside, perhaps even forgotten, as Joseph re-built his life in Egypt. If he ever wondered about their meaning, he had to just leave that all in the hands of God. Now, those brothers have just crossed the desert and walked right back into Joseph's destiny. "Oh yeah, I remember. I had dreams about this." Not only did he remember the dreams, he had a plan.

Joseph's first step was to accuse them as spies, up to no good. His strategy seems to have been to test their character first. "Let's see what these guys are made of now." They vehemently denied being spies, using their claim of being "sons of one man," to appear more benign, since they represented just one family, not a whole foreign kingdom.

Joseph countered with a test. "If you guys are on the up-and-up, bring that other brother down here. I will keep all but one of you, and the one will go home and get the youngest." For three days they cooled their heels in prison, then Joseph gave them their first encouraging word since their arrival. "Do this and live," he said, "for I fear God." This had to be good news to the brothers, that they were in the hands of a God-fearer, rather than a crazy pagan. Nonetheless, they were still distressed.

It is here that we see how deeply they were still affected by their sin against Joseph and their father. Their guilt is chewing on their souls. "We didn't listen to the boy when he pleaded with us in his distress, and now that distress has come upon us." For twenty years, the cries of Joseph had echoed in the minds and souls of his brothers. All they could do was regret, and dread God's judgment. Now it was coming. Reuben even exercised a right he had been reserving the whole twenty years, the prerogative to say, "I told you guys not to mess with the boy!"

As they discussed this in agony, they had no clue that Joseph heard and understood every word, because he had been using an interpreter.

It is a wise lesson I have observed that you don't have to tell people everything you know. Joseph had to feel a little vindicated at watching his brothers "twist on the spit" in regret for their meanness. However, any joy he had at this was short-lived. The emotions of the moment began to work on Joseph, and what he was hearing and seeing made him weep.

Why? Well, put yourself in his place. The shock of finally seeing the others, realizing that God is bringing your dream to reality, hearing that those mean boys actually have regret for what they did, the adrenaline rush of knowing a powerful secret that they don't, the anticipation of a full family reunion. All of this overwhelmed Joseph, but he gathered himself and went on with his plan.

Sort of. Instead of keeping them all and sending one back, Joseph did the opposite. He kept Simeon, and loaded everyone else down for the return trip. I'm thinking that by this time, Joseph could see that the brothers were loyal enough to each other and their father not to leave Simeon behind to rot in prison. But he still wanted to see if they would face their father, and bring Benjamin to Egypt. Before they left, he put their money back into their bags. After they left town, they found it, and were greatly troubled, believing, "God has set us up!"

Back home, the conversation was not pleasant. Jacob chewed his boys out royally. "Joseph is gone, Simeon is gone, and now you want to take Benjamin!" Reuben offered his own son's lives in payment if Benjamin was not returned, a powerful, but probably symbolic move, since Jacob was not likely to kill his grandsons in his grief. Jacob was not hearing of it. The risk was too great.

But the food dwindled, and Jacob was eventually resigned to meet Joseph's demand. With little hope, but lots of gifts and money, he sent all his remaining sons to Egypt, into the mercy of this foreign big shot.

At this point, Joseph began to get creative with the situation. His patience was remarkable, but it seems he really did want to observe his brothers' reactions under unpredictable and stressful situations. So began a series of surprises for the boys. When they arrived, Joseph invited them all to dinner, but they came thinking they were in trouble. Imagine the relief and surprise when Joseph's house manager told them, "No, your God blessed you! I had your money, and here is your brother."

Reunited with Simeon, they went to dinner. When Joseph arrived, the drama intensified. They presented the present they had brought, but Joseph was really not interested in their stuff. His eyes were focused on Benjamin, his only full brother, whom he had not seen in twenty odd years. This was too much again for Joseph, and he had to run out and have a good cry.   Speaker of the House Boehner has nothing to apologize for.

When he pulled himself together, (those Egyptians and their mascara, you know) Joseph had more surprises for the brothers, who must have been growing more and more confused. The diners were segregated three ways; first, the Hebrew brothers, then Joseph, then the Egyptians. The brothers did not know they were being hosted by a Hebrew, but the Egyptians did, and for all their gratitude and respect for Joseph, they still wouldn't eat with him.

And then another weird thing. They were assigned seats by age, eldest to youngest, which astonished them, since no one had given that information to the Egyptians. Who knew? When the food was served, their portions came from the table of the boss, whom they only knew as Zaphenath-paneah, and whom up to now they believed to be an Egyptian.   Benjamin was loaded up with food, and they all enjoyed it, but what was this fascination that the "Egyptian" had with their little brother? Curiouser and curiouser.

When it was time for them to go home, Joseph had them loaded down, and was sneaky again with Benjamin's pack. In addition to putting the money back, he also had his best silver cup stashed with baby brother. Then as they got out of town, Joseph sent his steward to accuse them of rudely stealing his master's special cup, out of which he drank and did hocus-pocus stuff (according to the steward). The boys had not learned to be careful yet, and rashly denied the charge with an oath. The guilty one would die, and the rest would become slaves, if the charge was proven.

Well, of course the fix was in, and Benjamin had been framed. His brothers tore their clothes in despair, and they all went back to the city. It must have been a long ride. They fell before Joseph, who twisted the knife a little more, "Don't you know a guy like me can practice divination?" Judah pled "no contest." They had not a clue as to how this terrible thing had come about. They were feeling truly at the mercy of God and Joseph. The worst of it was that they could not claim innocence because, although they may not have been guilty of this theft, each of them knew they had an awful family secret, which was that they were in fact guilty of something far worse than lifting a fancy cup.

Joseph had one more test, for he wanted to know if the brothers had deeply changed from the cruel and jealous jerks who threw him in a hole and sold him to the gypsies. He offered to let them all go, but keep Benjamin. Twenty years ago, the "sons of Jacob" hated their younger brother, and listened coldly to his screams as he was taken into slavery. Were these men different? Had they yet become "sons of Israel?" When they had to save themselves, would they sell out Benjamin, and once again put their poor father through that pain of bereavement?

What if they did? The worst outcome would be that Joseph would have his own true brother back. After the other ten went home, Joseph could console his younger brother with the revelation of the whole story. He would explain how their older "brothers" had not proven worthy of the name, and say, "It's you and me, kid." Together, they would decide what to do next. It could be fun to run Egypt with your little brother.

I don't think that was where Joseph's head was, however. You see, he was not just testing them for his own interest, but doing the greatest favor he could for them. He was giving them a "do-over." It was a chance at . . . wait for it . . . *redemption.*

The mistake they had made with Joseph could have been repeated with Benjamin, but Joseph was betting that twenty years of regret had made a difference. He had been watching them for months, if not years. You know there had probably been long conversations with Simeon after he had been held back, questions and discussions that Simeon did not understand. (Someday, I want to ask Simeon if he ever even suspected what the truth might be, who his powerful host actually was.) The Vice-Pharaoh had seen how all the brothers had come back to him, when it might have been easier just to let Benjamin return to face him alone. Joseph was extending an opportunity for his brothers to make the right choice this time, to make everything right.

Judah was the one who spoke up. He explained the situation between the brothers and Benjamin, and that he had become surety for the boy. He rehearsed the facts of which Joseph was already aware, and pleaded with Joseph to accept him as a substitute slave for Benjamin.

It had been Judah who had suggested to his brothers that they sell Joseph into slavery. Now Judah was offering himself as a substitute for little brother Benjamin, in order to spare Jacob the grief that would surely kill him. This irony, and the obvious change in the hearts of his brothers over the past twenty years, came flooding over the heart of Joseph, and it was once and for all too much. No longer able to control himself, he sent everyone from the room while he revealed himself to his brothers. His weeping was heard in the next room, and was even reported to Pharaoh.

He bluntly admitted, "I am Joseph! Is my father still alive?" His brothers did not respond. They were stunned and dismayed. They thought they understood it all now. It all finally made sense. They'd betrayed their brother into slavery, but somehow he'd made it to the top of the kingdom of Egypt. Now they had been manipulated into "payback-time," and were at his mercy, and rightfully so. Of course they would be his slaves, or worse, and they would never see their homes or families again! This all seemed crushingly obvious to them now.

But Joseph was so over that, and he begged his brothers to get over it too. Joseph's ultimate purpose in life was revealed. He explained that God was in it all, to save the lives of their family and all Egypt. He informed them of the five years of famine left, and instructed them to go get Dad, for there was a place for them all in Egypt with him. Everybody wept with joy, and there was happiness even in Pharaoh's household.

Now let's have some fun thinking about Jacob/Israel. Back home, he sat in anxiety. Twelve sons, and one was no more. The death of his favorite son over twenty years ago was still the greatest heartbreak of his long life, but now every one of his sons were gone, most tragically his youngest, Benjamin. The two precious sons of his beloved Rachel were gone, as were all the boys God had given him. They may never be seen again. Could this foreign official in Egypt even understand his grief? How cruel he must be to toy with the soul of an old man like this! "If I have lost them all, so I have lost them. I have lived too long!"

Weeks, maybe months, of anxiety and grief had torn at Jacob when word came that a party was returning. As it drew near, things appeared more and more strange. They had left as a caravan of donkeys, but were returning as a wagon train. And it was obviously a well-loaded train, at that. You know that Jacob was counting his sons in the distance— "There's Reuben and Judah, Simeon (He made it back!) and the others . . . where's little Ben? There— there he is! My God, they are all back! Praise be to God, He has given me back my remaining sons! What mercy he has shown this old man!"

What mercy, indeed! Little did he know. Perhaps as the wagons rolled up, the more nimble brothers leapt off and headed for Dad with the incredible news. There was certainly a long embrace from Simeon, and maybe everyone talking at once. Or, perhaps the brothers had their pecking order firmly enough established that one of the eldest came to Jacob as spokesman, with the formal notice that . . .

. . . incredibly, we all made it back.

. . . more incredibly, Joseph is there.

. . . still more incredibly, we are all going back to Egypt, with you, Dad.

. . . because, most incredibly of all, Joseph is in charge there!

Can you hear old Israel just saying, "Wow!" with each further unbelievable piece of news. He's beyond cartwheel age, but after hearing it all, he makes a flat but satisfied statement in reply. "It is enough: my son Joseph is still alive. I will go to see him before I die."

As they set out, God spoke words of assurance to Israel, and the whole nation of Israel with all their possessions went to Egypt. Upon arrival, Joseph had a long weep on his father's neck, as you would expect. As to practical matters, the land of Goshen was set aside for the Israelites, since they were shepherds by occupation, which was detestable to the Egyptians.

The meeting between Israel and Pharaoh reminds me of a meeting between birth parents and adoptive parents. Pharaoh had probably been very paternal toward Joseph in personal relationships, even though he had put Joseph over his whole kingdom. Now Joseph's 130-year-old natural father had arrived, and Pharaoh showed him due respect and kindness. In a move more important than either probably realized, Jacob blessed Pharaoh.

The last days of Israel were days of blessings and prophecies pronounced on his sons. He claimed Joseph's first two boys as his own, so that when you see lists of the twelve tribes of Israel, you will see Ephraim and Manasseh listed there. Israel had a dignified homegoing at age 147, and Joseph fulfilled a promise to take his father's body back to Canaan for burial.

One last poignant episode occurred after Jacob's death. His brothers feared that Joseph would take his vengeance, now that Dad had died. They sent word to him that Jacob had requested mercy for all their wrongdoing. A guilty conscience is a horrible burden to carry. When they were together, Joseph tearfully assured them that there was no need to worry. Joseph said words that we still forgive with today, "You meant it for evil, but God meant it for good. . ." God had sent Joseph ahead to Egypt to preserve His people through the famine. They would be there a long time. The story of how they will return to their own land will be one of the most important stories in the Big Story.

Through the famine, Joseph had collected all the money in the land, then the people's livestock, then their land and themselves. Egypt apparently became a socialist monarchy (no, I never heard of one either, except here), with all property owned by the king, on behalf of the people. By heeding Joseph's foresight from God, Pharaoh now owned everything in the land. And the land. And the people on it.

10
The Prince of Egypt: The Real Story
Exodus 1-15

The book of *Genesis* held our first nine stories. One book, nine stories. By contrast, the next three stories take in four books of the Bible. It is a narrative huge in scope, involving many years and multitudes of people. You have to get this story, and the next, to understand the rest of the Bible.

Perhaps you think you know the story. It's one of the better-known narratives of the Bible. Hollywood has taken a few stabs at it, but they usually get it wrong. I have never understood why people think they need to improve on God's material. Let me tell you how this Moses and Egypt thing really went down. I am retelling it here, but not changing it.

We are finally out of *Genesis*, the book of beginnings. Of our forty stories, almost a quarter are in the first book. It's that important to our understanding of the Story of Redemption. This story begins well after the time of Joseph. All from his generation were gone, but the people of Israel were increasing still. They were not just a family anymore; they were a nation. *Exodus* 1 opens with a little historical material, then shifts to an ominous tone in verse 8, "Now a new king arose over Egypt, who did not know Joseph."

This king was short-sighted and ill-informed. His nation had become forgetful. The study of history is important for any society. Because the story of Joseph had not been passed through the generations, this Pharaoh did not know what a blessing these people had been, nor did the people of Egypt. So, when they continued to increase, the Egyptians got nervous.

The Egyptians claimed to "deal wisely" with the Hebrews, as we see them called, but it doesn't look very wise in hindsight. First, they afflicted them with oppressive labor, as if hard work would lower fertility rates. Check out oppressed people anywhere; I don't think that works. Next, the wicked king commanded the midwives union to practice infanticide of newborn males. Killing babies is a really ugly practice, which ungodly societies continue to this day. It is a symptom of a nation on its way to destruction.

The midwives were better people than the Pharaoh, as were most of the Egyptians. They feared God and would not kill the babies. God blessed them for this, but the Hebrews kept increasing. This brought about a bizarre order. Verse 1:22 says that "Pharaoh commanded all his people" to throw their newborn sons into the Nile.

One of these babies was born to a couple of descendants of Levi. He was a beautiful little boy, and they could not stand to see him become croc meat. They kept him under wraps for three months; but realized they would have to let him go. The Bible doesn't say directly, but we can recognize the direction of God in all this. The baby's mom must have spent sleepless nights in prayer before her mind and heart were at peace with this plan. If God did not tell you to do this, you would be nuts.

She waterproofed a wicker basket with tar, and put the baby in it. Then she set God's little tar baby into the reeds along the bank of the Nile. The baby's sister stood by to see what would happen, perhaps with a bagful of rocks to keep the crocodiles away.

The daughter of Pharaoh was an elegant woman, but she needed a bath from time to time, just like anyone. When she went to the river for a dip, she took her entourage of maidens, because lots of bad things can happen when you are bathing in the Nile alone, and besides, the girls all needed washing too. On this day, as they approached their bath-beach, she saw the little girl on the roadway, awed by the impressive presence of the Princess of Egypt. Cute little Hebrew girl. Lucky to be a girl, not one of those poor little Hebrew boys. "How could my father be so insanely cruel?"

"What is that in the reeds? Go get it!" The maid she sent dutifully retrieved the package, but did not open it. It was gooey with tar and pitch, and she handled it as little as she could. When the princess opened the basket, the history of the world changed. The woman saw the boy, and the boy cried, and her heart dissolved, as yours would have. She immediately understood everything, almost, "This is one of the Hebrew's children!"

She got it. Someone had birthed a baby boy whom they couldn't stand to murder at her father's command. They couldn't kill him, but they couldn't keep him. What agony that poor family must have gone through! He was a precious child, and she understood. She wouldn't kill him either. Being the daughter of Pharaoh has to count for something. She would take this boy home, and dare Daddy to try to take him. He was afraid of the masses of Hebrews; well, this one baby was no mass, and he would be raised as a member of Pharaoh's household, anyway.

Suddenly at her hip was that cute little Hebrew girl from the road.

"Shall I go get a Hebrew nurse for you?"

"Sharp kid; she knows how life works," the princess thought. The princess or any of her maids could wipe a bottom and change a diaper, but this boy was hungry. That would require an ability they all lacked.

This was centuries before infant formula, and to provide for a baby required a nurse, which in those days meant a milk-producing lady, not someone with a B.S.N. It was not unusual for someone who was lactating to have a surplus to give to a baby without a mother, and without storage or refrigeration this meant that the nurse would have to have the child at hand, so to speak.

So Pharaoh's daughter sent the girl, who of course went straight to her mother, who was the boy's mother. By the end of the day, the baby was back home in his own bed, none the worse for his adventure in the river, and now under the protection of Pharaoh's government. Pharaoh's daughter was going to pay the woman to nurse her own baby? Sweet.

Did the princess know what had actually happened? If she had any capacity for thought, she should have had at least a suspicion. If the parents had this much love for the child, how could they abandon him? For the mother to hang around would be too obvious, but a little girl arouses no suspicion. A little girl, who just happened to know right where to go to find a wet-nurse with a vacancy in her home. Hmmm, wonder what happened to the baby she was nursing? The princess does not appear to have been overly curious. Sometimes you don't ask questions unless you really want the answers.

It takes one verse for the boy to grow up, and the princess gives him the name, Moses. This seems to be an Egyptianization of a Hebrew word related to being "drawn out" of the water. His growing up has been a popular subject of movie speculation, but the Book doesn't actually say much. Somehow he had the idea that he was Hebrew; perhaps his birth family had just raised him with the truth. With these sympathies, he got in trouble by intervening when one of the Hebrews was being mistreated. He killed and buried the abuser. The cover-up lasted one day, and when it was blown, Moses fled to the wilderness.

In Midian, he met and married into a fine local family, who made him part of the family herding enterprise. Life was good. Meanwhile, Israel suffered. They cried out to God, and God heard.

Speaking of "heard," Moses was out with the herd—the flock, actually—when he beheld a strange thing. A bush was burning, which was not that unusual. But the bush was not consumed, which was weird. It just burned on, and Moses decided to get over there for a better look. As he approached, God called his name from the middle of the flame, and the amazed Moses said, "Here I am."

The Voice warned him to not come closer, but to remove his shoes on this "holy ground." He identified Himself as the God of Moses' fathers. This scared Moses, and he hid his face. Introductions out of the way, God states His business in *Exodus* 3:7, 8.

"I *have seen* the affliction of My people . . ."

God sees.

" . . . and *have given heed* to their cry . . ."

God listens.

" . . . for *I am aware* of their sufferings."

God understands.

"So *I have come down* . . ."

God will do something about it.

God further explains that He has come down to 1) deliver them *from* the Egyptians, and to 2) bring them up *to* a better land. Redemption is like that. We are redeemed out of our bondage, and we are redeemed into a world of God's promises. Next, He gets to the bottom line with Moses. "Therefore come now, and I will send you to Pharaoh, so that you may bring My people, the sons of Israel, out of Egypt."

There followed a period of Q & A with God, during which Moses gave numerous objections to the plan, and God patiently answered, for a while. God eventually got angry and made allowance for Moses' brother, Aaron to be Mo's spokesman. Moses agreed to return to Egypt with his family.

God gave Moses a couple of signs to perform, in order to convince everybody that he was legit as a deliverer. I've been thinking about these signs, and I think they were mainly to help Moses feel better. Try to identify with this: You're coming against the greatest superpower in the earth in its time. Although you were raised there, you've been gone for forty years. You've been gone because you killed an official, and had to get out of the state. You're eighty years old. You are going to demand, in the name of a God they despise, that they release their labor force, destroying their own economy. And what can you do? Turn a stick into a snake, and make yourself a leper! Oh, they'll cower at that power!

God was always honest with Moses. He told him that these signs wouldn't change Pharaoh's mind. Pharaoh was evil, and God was looking to whack him for what he already was and had done. When God is ready to judge evil, He sometimes makes the condemned stupid.

After requiring the circumcision of his sons at God's command (which very much irritated his wife, since she did the actual cutting), Moses and Aaron arrived in town to set the Hebrews free. Those Hebrews were happy to hear that God had heard of their suffering, and had sent help. They anxiously anticipated their immediate deliverance. They were overly optimistic. They didn't really know what the Lord actually had in mind. Now would be a good time for us to discuss that.

You remember that the whole Bible is about redemption, buying man back from the Fall. God is going to use this story of Israel's deliverance to draw a picture of His Eternal Plan. He often uses earthly things to help us understand heavenly principles. We call these earthly pictures "types."

You have to understand this, or you will get confused. We say, "A pig is a *type* of animal." This means that a pig is a "kind" or "sort" of animal, an actual literal beast. This is *not* what we mean here. Down the page, I will say, "Egypt was a *type* of sin." This *does not mean* that the nation of Egypt was a kind of sin, but that in this story, Egypt *represents the concept* of our bondage to sin.

There are many types in the story of the Exodus, and understanding them helps us understand God and His Plan. In literature you may encounter foreshadowing, which is similar, and allegory. C.S. Lewis' *Chronicles of Narnia* have been enjoyed by generations, some simply reading a children's fantasy, others recognizing the story of the gospel woven throughout. Stories like this work on two levels, which is why, for now, you can still find the *Narnia* books in a public school library.

Our story is on two levels, and we will try to keep in touch with both. The two levels explain each other. First off, Israel just wanted deliverance. They probably cared not a fig (still thinking about Lewis) that they were a type of redemption. They just wanted out, but God was doing something bigger. You see, Egypt was a type of sin. As such, Israel's deliverance had to mirror our deliverance from sin. It had to be total, not just "good enough."

Here's the biblical context: in *Genesis* 3:15 the first promise of the Redeemer is given, and Satan is promised a fatal head wound—complete destruction. In the New Testament, we will read that Christ has destroyed the works of the devil, indeed the devil himself. Christ has triumphed completely, and the language used to describe this is that of military conquest. The keys to everything will end up in the hands of our Deliverer. This complete vanquishment has to be foreshadowed in the *Exodus* story. Israel can't just sneak out; their God must be shown to be greatly superior to the "god" of the Egyptians. Pharaoh, a type (picture) of Satan, can't just decide to let them go. It must be clear that he is overpowered by Israel's God, and has no choice in the matter. This may be the proto-typical "power encounter."

Secondly, they were not just delivered from somewhere, but to somewhere. God had promised (*Exodus* 3:8) to bring them out of Egypt, into a good place. The story of how they got from one place to the other was given to us as an example of the Christian Life, the Walk by Faith. It is a crucial model of how we are to live. Way before John Bunyan wrote *Pilgrim's Progress* to show us how we travel the road of salvation to Heaven, God gave us the story of Israel's journey from Egypt to Canaan, to serve as a model for us. The difference between these two stories is their destinations. Bunyan's Pilgrim arrives in the Celestial City,

Heaven. Israel arrives at their promised land, not Heaven, but rather the land of their destiny. More about this later.

Their story is our story. We who trust in Christ were delivered from sin and its oppression, just like Israel was delivered from Egypt. That is the point of the whole story, and that is how I will tell it and explain it.

Now back to the story. Because they had no way of knowing all that God was doing, Israel expected now that a deliverer had come in the Name of the Lord, they'd get out of town quickly. They were disappointed. When Mo' and 'Ron showed up before Pharaoh, he was so not impressed. He began with the obvious and expected "Who are you?" Pharaoh said "I don't know the Lord, and I won't let you go anyway, and besides, why are you stopping work now?" So the nasty king made labor much more difficult for the Hebrews, who reacted with rejection toward Moses and Aaron. They didn't see the mission of Moses as having any positive results.

Being booed by his people was one thing Moses had not expected. Confused, he asked God why this had happened. He came to help, but had only made things worse. It seems that God's answer was that He had to give Pharaoh a fair chance to do right, but the boy got ugly. Now God would take the gloves off. He had a covenant with these people, and He was going to come through on His part of it. Moses tried to tell this to Israel, but they were too tired and depressed to hear him.

So God explained the plan to Moses: God would make Moses as God to Pharaoh, and Aaron would be his prophet. However, even though the king saw Moses as God, he still wouldn't listen to him, because God would harden Pharaoh's heart. Then God would put his hand on Egypt, and all Egypt would know who God is.

Off to the palace went the octogenarian deliverance team. They delivered God's ultimatum, to little avail. The snake trick cut no ice with Pharaoh; his magic boys could do that, but then Moses' snake ate theirs. That should have clued him in right there, but it didn't. So let the plagues commence. First, Moses and Aaron turned the water of Egypt into blood. Not red water, real blood. It killed the fish, and the waters were all foul. But, the Egyptian magicians could also do that, so Pharaoh felt pretty good about himself.

The next week God predicted and produced a plague of frogs. Frogs everywhere, in everything. Sounds like it would be funny, but it's not *your* refrigerator full of green hopping madness, is it? And you know what? The magicians did the same, just to show they could. More frogs, how bright was that? So Pharaoh called for Moses, and promised to let the people go if the frogs were taken away. (Apparently his magicians could only call frogs, not control them.) I have this on my list of "Funny Stories in the Bible."

Pharaoh said, "I give up! Take the frogs away."

Moses said, "The honor is yours to say when."

Thoughtfully, Pharaoh said, "Tomorrow."

My friend Jerry Morgan preaches a message entitled, "One More Night With the Frogs," and I have probably preached some version of it, too. Given the opportunity for immediate relief, Pharaoh the Brain chose another froggy night, due to his unrelenting pride. Do you think the old boy bragged to Mrs. Pharaoh about this over dinner that night, across their elegant dinner table covered with the croaking stampede?

Mrs. Pharaoh: "These FROGS, they're everywhere!"

Frogs: "Ribbit…"

Pharaoh: "Don't you worry your pretty little head about these frogs—your man is the king, and I got Moses straightened out about this."

Frogs: "Croak!"

Mrs. P: "Wonderful! I knew you would handle it."

Frogs: "Ribbit, Ribbit!"

Pharaoh: "Yup! When I got through with Moses, he even gave ME the honor of telling HIM when to take the frogs away!"

Frogs: "Croak! Croak!"

Mrs. P: "And YOU told HIM, RIGHT NOW, huh? How long will it take them to go?

Frogs: "Ribbit, Ribbit, RIIBBIITT!"

Pharaoh: "They'll be gone by tomorrow."

Mrs. P: "Tomorrow? That's the best Moses can do? Didn't you tell him who the King is? Didn't he understand what you ordered?"

Frogs: "Croak, Croak, CRROOAAK!"

Pharaoh: (Mumbling) "Oh, I think Moses understood what I said."

Frogs:"RIIBBBIITT!"

Mrs. P: "Okay, just what did you say? Moses said 'Say when,' and you said—?"

Frogs: "CROAKERIBBBIIIT!!"

Pharoah: "Well, er um—I said, uh, well, tomorrow…"

Mrs. P: You said WHEN?"

Frogs: "CROAKITYRIBBIIIT!

Wanna bet Pharaoh slept on a frog-covered couch that night? Nah, probably not—he was the king, after all, but I'm sure it was a cold, lonely place over there on his side of the bed, with just frogs for company. God was faithful, even though the king was not, and there was a big frog kill. When he saw that there was relief, Pharaoh hardened his heart, and went back on his word. So God said, "Let's kick it up a notch."

This time, the dust of the earth was turned to gnats. Ever been in a bug swarm? White flies, black flies, mosquitoes, no-see-ums; all parts of the world have their bugs, and these were worse than yours. The magicians tried to duplicate this, but failed this time, fortunately for everyone.

Perhaps they failed because this may have been the first wonder in which life was actually created. The frogs "came up" from the rivers, but the dust "became" gnats. Their demonic arts may not have been capable of this magnitude of wonder, or maybe God was just tired of them, and said, "Enough of that." There were plenty of gnats on man and beast, regardless. The magicians were more easily impressed than Pharaoh. When they couldn't do it, they declared it, "the finger of God."

The next morning, Moses was right there when Pharaoh got up, like that creepy freaky king on the Burger King ads. He informed the king that there were plenty more bugs to be swarmed at Egypt, but in the Goshen trailer park, where the Hebrews stay, no bugs. God wanted everyone to know the difference, and God wanted the Egyptian people to know who was truly responsible for their misery.

This story is full of lessons, and here is one. With the insects swarming, Pharaoh told Moses, "Go! Sacrifice within the land!" But that is not what God had commanded. When Moses first came back to Egypt, he gave the word from God. "We will go out to sacrifice to our God." The king said, "Get back to work, you idlers!" After a few plagues, the king says, "OK, you can take some time off to sacrifice here." This is the offer of compromise. That is how Satan works, and the lesson here is not to fall for it. Compromise is not a characteristic of the fruit of the Spirit.

Moses wouldn't have it. "We have to leave town, you know our sacrifices will offend the Egyptian people, and they will stone us." Pharaoh made a counter-offer, as if he could negotiate with God. "Just don't go far, and by the way, pray for me while you are at it." In his defense, we should recognize that as the most powerful monarch in his world, he was used to doing business this way. He was doing what he knew to do, but he had never dealt with anyone like Moses or God before.

Moses said, "I will go speak to God now, to get rid of your bugs, but you had better not be lying again!" Moses did as he said, and God did what He was asked, and Pharaoh was lying, as he had been all along. Neither Moses nor God was being deceived. Pharaoh thought he was all slick, jerking Moses' chain. But God and Moses were in complete control. This back and forth, "yes-I-won't" treatment that Pharaoh was giving was not fooling God; God knew it was coming all along. It was

His patience that was allowing it. Pharaoh kept being a wicked jerk, and God kept building a case against him.

So God gave Pharaoh a day's notice that all the livestock were going to die, except those belonging to Israel. Sure enough, next day—dead animals in every yard and pasture. And sure enough, lots of healthy, happy cows and sheep in Goshen, where Israel lived. But Pharaoh's heart just got harder, and he continued to refuse God's orders. I don't want to be too judgmental, but it seems that Pharaoh may have been a stupid, stubborn man.

As I said earlier, Hollywood usually fails to tell this story right, but one of the things that does seem correct is the portrayal by Yul Brynner of Pharaoh in *The Ten Commandments.* I think Yul captured the essence of what this guy was about, at least from what the Scriptures show us. He seems to be a simple, straightforward hardhead; your garden variety, basic pagan ruler sort of dude. Maybe there was more to him than that, but it doesn't show in the Bible narrative.

God sent Moses to a kiln, to get some soot, which he was to throw into the sky, while Pharaoh watched. The ashes became a fine dust, and where the dust landed, boils broke out on man and beast. (There were still beasts alive, since Israel had flocks and herds, and probably sold cattle to the Egyptians after all theirs had died.) Remember the magicians of Egypt? When they were summoned this time, they couldn't come, because of the boils on them. God was asserting His complete power and authority by increments, and misery was increasing exponentially in Egypt. But God was hardening Pharaoh's heart still, because He planned to destroy his nation completely.

Next morning, Moses was there to deliver the daily report. He had become the Al Roker of plagues. Today's forecast: killer hail. There was a difference in this plague, however, a turning point, I think. Now the announcement was given to all of Egypt, so that those Egyptian citizens who chose to hear God could bring their livestock and servants to shelter. The Egyptians who sheltered-in-place were spared; those who did not were hailed, and not in a good way. But in Goshen, no hail.

Now Pharaoh made a contrite sounding speech, but remember, he'd had practice. He thought he still had Moses on a string. Moses showed a little impatience; after all, Moses was not God. Mo said, "OK, I'm going out now, and when I get out of town, I'll stop the hail. But nobody thinks you are going to let us go."

At this point, I am thinking of Sam and Ralph, a couple of my favorite Warner Brothers cartoon characters. I hope you know them, the sheepdog and the wolf. All their cartoons are the same. In the opening they are at the breakfast table together, with paper and coffee. They get in the truck and carpool to the pasture together. They wait by the time clock and punch in right on time together. Then they go to their jobs, one protecting the sheep, the other trying all day unsuccessfully to steal sheep.

They wreak havoc on each other, and the wolf repeatedly gets the worst of it, smashed, punched, exploded, and otherwise maimed in typical WB fashion, occasionally with a break for lunch. Usually, in the middle of one of these disasters, the 5 o'clock whistle blows, and they knock off in mid-thrashing to punch the clock and go home together, two buddies coming home from work, as amicably as Fred and Barney ever did. "G'night Sam." "G'night Ralph." I don't care what this says about me, I sit and laugh out loud every time. This is why God made cable.

I see Moses and Pharaoh almost this way, although much more bitter than Sam and Ralph. Moses comes before Pharaoh with the latest plague report, and leaves. Although he is pronouncing vast destruction on the land, nobody bothers him as he goes. (You wonder why nobody suggests that Pharaoh just kill Moses. Maybe they are all afraid of God, even though they don't realize just how big He is.) Next morning they all watch as the disaster unfolds, and they suffer all day. In the afternoon, Pharaoh sends for Moses and pretends repentance. Moses pretends to believe him and goes out to stop today's pestilence. "G'night, Mo." "G'night Phay." Next morning, Moses comes back in to restart the cycle. I think this scene in *Prince of Egypt* catches the spirit of what was happening fairly well, and is one of that movie's high points.

After the hail, however, God let Moses preach a little. "How long will you do this?" Moses asked. "If you don't let us go, tomorrow there will be locusts." Great, more bugs. But these insects were different. Locusts are grasshoppers on steroids. Whatever crops survived the hail would be munched up by the locusts. This plague couldn't be undone in a day. The people would starve. The damage was getting more and more permanent. Pharaoh's entourage began to crack. Some counseled letting the troublemakers go.

Pharaoh called our heroes back in to negotiate. "Moses, who do you plan to take with you?"

"Everyone and everything."

"I don't think so!" retorted Pharaoh. He used religious language to make a personal accusation and rebuke towards Moses, then kicked the men out of the palace.

Let me preach a little here. God is here again giving us an example of how the devil works. He tells you "It's one thing for you to serve God, but who do you think you are to expect your children to be forced to believe, just because you do?" This tactic is especially effective in the American culture, with our democratic and individualistic values. I have actually heard parents excuse letting their children grow up ungodly and hell bound by this "logic."

"My parents made me go to church every time the doors opened!" they whine. "I hated it, and I told myself I would never do that to my kids. I believe little Junior should be allowed to make up his own mind about those things."

Have you informed Child Protective Services about this parental philosophy? Do they know that Junior will be making his own decisions about nutrition, education and personal hygiene and security? After all, your parents made you take a bath, brush your teeth, eat things you didn't want to, and be nice to people you wanted to be mean to. Surely you want to spare your own children that abuse!

When the police bring your enlightened-parent-raised child home from his drunken, shoplifting, granny-bashing excursion, will you explain to them that you would not abuse him by forcing your personal ideas about ethics onto his free mind? No? So it's only his eternal soul that you don't have the backbone to deal with? Ok, back to the story, for now.

The locusts were scrambled, and delivered by the east wind right on time. They ate every green thing in the land, except in Goshen County, we assume. Pharaoh whined, Moses made supplication, and God sent a west wind to blow the locusts out to the Red Sea as quickly as they had blown in.

Then it got spooky. The next plague was darkness. Not just night, but a darkness they could feel. By nature, light drives away darkness, but it seems that this darkness smothered the light. Egypt couldn't even light their lamps, but in Goshen, the light bill had been paid. Egypt was immobilized for three days, feeling around until Pharaoh called for Moses, to give him another compromise offer. "Go, take your little ones even. But not your flocks and herds."

Another trick of the devil unmasked. First, it was "Let's negotiate the terms of your deliverance." Then it was, "You can be delivered, but you have no right to take your children." Now it's, "You can go, but you'll have to leave all your wealth behind, in order to serve God." Many of us would never let the world have our kids, but we buy into the lie that Satan controls all the material wealth. Perhaps we don't say it deliberately, but we accept it.

Have you ever said, maybe in the presence of your family or friends, "Yep, I could move up a notch or two in the company I guess, if I'd go along with the stuff the bosses do, but I can't live like that. I have morals and ethics that won't let me." You think you're really standing up for God, and perhaps you are, but you're also repeating a satanic lie, and I'm sure he appreciates it.

Here's what you need to understand: whether you are successful in your occupation is up to you and God, not the enemy or others. If God's purpose for your life is fulfilled by your wealth, then you are obligated to be wealthy. If He needs for you to be poor, He will let you know. Don't let man (even yourself) or the devil decide for you.

Moses wouldn't buy the con. R.W. Shambach and I preach from this text. "We must serve God with our livestock, and we don't know yet what God will require. Therefore, *not one hoof will be left behind!*" (*Exodus* 10:26) I have that underlined in red in my Bible. You see my "stuff" is dedicated to the service of God. If I surrender it to the enemy, I will not have it to put it into God's service. What God has promised, do not let the devil talk you out of.

Some might have counseled Moses to be glad for what Pharaoh was allowing, take the best deal he could get, and go. But Moses wasn't negotiating for a deal. He was patiently waiting for Pharaoh to agree with what God had already said: they were all coming out, with their children and their stuff, and all that God wanted them to have for the trip. Not one hoof left behind.

Moses had heard God say that with a mighty hand and outstretched arm He would deliver Israel. He didn't need to deal with this puny king, and he knew it. I think I'll stop and shout. Put down the book and praise God a while. Above all, remember that redemption is total. Don't let the devil or anyone else convince you to let him have a part of your life—not your body, your soul, your spirit, or your stuff! It is all redeemed for the glory of God.

Pharaoh, unfortunately, never got it. He drove Moses out of the room, saying, "Get out! If I see you again, you will die!"

Moses replied in great finality, probably shocking those who had gotten used to this ongoing "Sam and Ralph" thing, "You got that right! I shall never see your face again!" Chapter 11, verses 1 through 8 back up just a little, then bring us to the same dramatic point of Moses' departure. These verses describe what will be the last plague.

God tipped Moses off. "One more plague, and then he will let you go. Actually he will drive you out, so do this. Borrow lots of loot from your Egyptian neighbors. Get lots of silver and gold. God gave the people favor with the Egyptians and Moses carried a lot of weight with everyone except Pharaoh, so they all made out like bandits.

I think what Moses started saying in *Exodus* 10:29, he finishes up in 11:4-8. The firstborn of everything in Egypt will die. Man or cattle, high-up to humble, all will be touched. But among Israel, none of this, so Pharaoh will know the difference between God's and his.

God instituted a commemorative meal that night in Israel. The dinner was full of symbols and types, and God called it the Passover, for the Lord would "pass over" the houses of Israel. Nights like this one are what this book is all about. God's instructions were simple: Israel was to take the blood of the lamb that was slain for the Passover meal, and paint their doorposts with it. Then they were to stay in the house, "under the blood" until morning. When death moved through the land, God would see the blood, and would "pass over" those houses.

I used to think that this meant that God was going through Egypt, killing off the firstborn, and that he was "skipping over" the houses with the blood. Now I believe that the image we are supposed to get is one of death moving through all of Egypt, with God "passing over" each bloody doorway in protection, keeping death out. He sent the death, then He put Himself between death and those who pled His mercy in obedience. This fits with the way God is, His holiness demanding judgment while his mercy provides a way of deliverance. That's redemption. If you have not accepted it yet, now would be the best time to do so. Ask God to forgive you and let Jesus be your "Passover Lamb."

Death came to Egypt at midnight, and the firstborn throughout the land died, wherever the blood was not. We can only imagine the horror, although I'd rather not, please. They had lost their crops, their livelihood, their peace and security, and their land was a stinking mess, but they still had each other. In one night a death-blow was stricken to the kingdom of Egypt. Their culture placed extreme value on their firstborn. In addition to the tragedy it brought to each family, the death of every firstborn turned the economy and society inside out. It was a trauma to Egypt in ways we cannot even imagine. Step out of your door, and hear the screams and wails from every direction.

Just not in Goshen, where the people are commemorating the night with a set of ordinances God has instructed them to follow, to ensure that they never forget what has happened here. God claims His right to their firstborn, which they are to redeem from Him through all generations to come.

Before the night was over, Pharaoh called for Moses and Aaron, but we are not sure he actually saw them both, based on 10:29. We do know that he ordered them and their people out of the country immediately. The people had obeyed Moses' direction to borrow from their neighbors, and these same neighbors were now urging them out before their bread could even rise, lest all of Egypt be dead before morning.

It is an interesting premise for a movie. It's on my list of things to rent, when I get around to it. *A Day Without Mexicans.* In this film, a strange occurrence causes California to wake up one morning and find that all those of Mexican descent have disappeared. The obvious point is made about how much we can both despise and depend upon the same people. This is what was happening in Egypt, and just like in the movie, it was suddenly "A Day Without Hebrews."

It had been 430 years to the day since the sons of Israel, with their father, had moved into Egypt. God was leading Israel out, but He didn't put them right on the interstate to Canaan. That led through hostile territory, and they weren't ready for battle yet, even though they were marching in battle formation. There was a pillar of cloud to lead them in the day, and a fire by night. They marched out with the bones of Joseph, for Joseph had made his brothers promise not to leave him there, and that promise had been passed on to their children for almost four centuries.

Let's review typology again. Slavery in Egypt teaches us about our bondage to sin. Our forefathers took us there, we were born into it, and could not get ourselves out. We were delivered from that bondage through the blood of the Lamb. Now we are leaving sin, and headed for the life of promise that God has for us. But there is a decisive act of God yet to come, and He maneuvered Israel into place to do it.

They were all going to get baptized.

God instructed Moses carefully, "You put Israel here, and you camp there, by the sea. I am going to harden Pharaoh's heart again, then I am going to slam the door on his head (my paraphrase)." They did as they were told.

Sure enough, Pharaoh and Co. changed their minds. "Why did we let the Hebrews go? If they won't be our slaves, we should at least have the fun of killing them all. Let's get 'em!" Off they went, 600 select chariots, then all the rest of the other chariots, and their officers. They caught up with Israel at their oceanside encampment. There they had the Hebrews, between the devil (Pharaoh) and the deep Red Sea, you might say.

People of those days reacted to this kind of trouble in much the same ways we react today: they cried out to God, and blamed their leaders. Moses was unperturbed, because God was keeping him informed ahead of time. His speech to the people went like this; "Yes, the Egyptians are coming at us, but do not fear. Hold still and see the salvation that God

will give you today. The Egyptians you see coming today you will see
no more!" His next, last statement to them may have had a little personal spin included, "The Lord will fight for you, . . . while you keep
silent." Then follows another of those scenes I want to see someday on
God's Home Movies. If Tom Clancy had been there . . .

The air space over the Red Sea, 1800 hours

The angel assigned to the Sons of Israel was drifting out over the
Red Sea, enjoying the night breezes. He had been briefed on the expected action of the Egyptians and their motivating agents, so he was watch-
ful, although relaxed. Unlike earthly special ops, these angelic guys had
no need of radio communications; they sent word directly spirit to spirit,
and this angel's spirit came alive with orders from On High, "Move to
the rear, they're here." He blew away in a rush, taking the pillar of fire
in a spectacular glowing streak from the front to the rear of the camp.

As he moved across the scene he took note of the near-panic below.
"Oh yeah," he thought, "they were all about 'marching out in victory'
this morning, when they thought they were putting distance between
them and the bad guys. Now that the 'boogey-man' is coming down
on their heads, they're ready to eat Moses and Aaron." He was a little
amused, but not angry, or even disappointed. They all knew that these
were just men, and untested ones at that.

He chuckled a little at the thought of the deliverance that was coming, then sobered immediately, as he thought of what it would cost in
human souls. Mothers, wives, and children who had thought they had
been spared grief in the operation against the firstborn, and some who
had not, would have their worlds further shattered tonight. He was coming into position now, and picking his spot.

It wasn't so important to make a dramatic arrival, since these poor
losers were likely never going to return to tell anyone about this. But he

did need to be effective. He saw the strategic location from above and dropped in.

On the Red Sea highway

It had been a difficult time in the City of the Sun, but tonight should take care of it, the charioteer consoled himself. Weirdo Moses, coming back after forty years they say. Crazy old man, they'd thought, then the threats he made started to happen. They'd thought he'd just learned some magic tricks, and their guys could do that. But it got deeper, and scarier. The heavens and earth seemed to be fighting against them. The whole kingdom had been destroyed, and then . . . that last night of death, throughout Egypt.

He thought about his father, and his brother, and of countless other fathers and brothers across the land. And sisters and mothers. And children. Children who had no part in this, who didn't ask for this fight, and didn't understand why their life had become day after day of ever changing horrors. He remembered the look on the kids' faces when they came back into the house the day the animals died. They had all thought it was as bad as it could get, until . . .

And we just let them walk away! His stomach turned again as he thought of it. The Hebrews! If they had only recognized their place! After hundreds of years of being loyal servants, what had caused them to go bad? Well, surely having your baby boys thrown to the crocs would provoke even the best slaves. But what those "sheep people" were already doing to their week-old baby boys shouldn't even be allowed! That infanticide thing was a long time ago, however, and it seemed they had gotten over it. Until Moses showed up again and got the "mud men" all stirred up. Should have killed the agitator on day one.

As they topped the ridge, the glow in the sky gave way to a view of the Hebrew camp. The glow had been a source of discussion as the sky darkened. No one could really figure out what the brickboys had been doing to generate such a light. Now they would get a good look at it. "Yeah," the charioteer thought, "We'll get a look at it—as we ride by it on the way to slaughter the Hebrews like dogs!" They would make those locusts the Hebrew god sent look like a flock of butterflies. Now they were drawing into position for their charge, a rolling wall of death. Their attention was drawn upwards by what seemed at first to be a flash, then an extra moon.

Over the Egyptian Cavalry, 1815 hours

The angel was descending. Time to put the brakes on the chariots. He streaked downward and dropped a curtain onto the plain, just in front of the cascading war wagons. The angel had not been ordered to touch the Egyptians, although he expected that would happen before long. For now he just dropped the cloud/fire on the target, and watched the cavalry back off. "There, that'll do ya, dudes." The men in their chariots could not see beyond the wall of black, but they knew the object of their attack was just there. So they waited. And everyone held, and the night passed. A stormy one over on the beach, judging from what they could hear of the wind blowing on the water. It blew all night.

Hebrew encampment, Red Sea

In the camp by the sea, the Hebrews stood and stared. Almost as soon as the chariots rumbled into view, the pillar had roared around to their rear guard. Since it remained light on their side, they had no way of knowing what the Egyptians were seeing (or, not seeing) but at least the chariots had stopped. That had shut up the whiners who were boohooing about "dying in the desert."

A man of Israel stood at the edge of the camp and faced the flames. Was there no end to the wonders they would see? What would God do next? He had stopped the chariots, but there was nowhere for the Israelites to go. The Hebrew thought that he had better get back to his family. Whatever was going to happen, he had a duty there.

Above the Hebrew encampment, Red Sea

The angel was stationed far above the whole scene and was watching with curiosity. He did have power to get into this fight, but had not been authorized to do so. His orders were to hold things steady. He sensed that this would be one of those "covenant things" in which the Lord would get hands-on involved with His people.

As the pillar had been dropped, the angel had noticed Moses moving toward the sea with purposeful steps, as if there was coordination. Was he getting communication from above also? Could be. As he got to water's edge, he had everyone's attention in both heaven and earth. This was going to be good.

Moses reached out toward the sea, and the Lord backed up his motion with power. The water was swept away by a terrific east wind, a blast more powerful than the locust-lifter they had used earlier, and more focused on one point—the point where Moses pointed. It stood the waters up in heaps, and was drying the sea bottom—or what had been the bottom.

In the tents, Hebrew encampment

The Hebrew was back with his family by the time things started shaking down at the beach, and word came up from the water that something was up, big-time. He jumped on a rocky hill and strained his eyes seaward. His eyes widened, and his jaw dropped. He made funny grunts for a few seconds, then broke out laughing. From where she was with the kids, his wife could see him above, but nothing beyond. Even so, she could tell that what he was seeing was something spectacular. He looked out at the water, then laughed into the air, then looked back at her, and did that silly giggle again, then repeated it all.

From the crowd ahead she could hear the babble of general excitement, and now occasionally someone ran by saying something goofy, like, "Into the sea . . . blowing away the water . . . dry bottom . . ." Her husband was coming down from the rock and then in their direction at a dead run. When he arrived, he began striking the tent they had only just put up. As he worked in a mad hurry, he tried to muster the breath to speak coherently, but didn't quite succeed.

"Sea is moving . . . Moses is making a gap through the middle . . . a definite miracle if ever you saw one . . . the people are going in . . . I think we're all going through . . . it has to be now, tonight!"

She gathered the kids and their kit, and they headed into their close encounter of the God kind.

Airspace above the Red Sea, 0000 hours

The angel couldn't help but smile. This was sweet. When had God ever gotten into the middle of His people's business in such a positive way? After all the horrors they had visited upon the poor Egyptians, this was such a precious break.

Sometimes people like to watch ants, and on occasion, angels like to watch the little people from up above. The throbbing mass of humanity on the shore funneled into the narrow split across the sea. Just uphill, the dark curtain held the incensed Egyptians at a frustratingly harmless distance. Eventually, the camp of Israel drained into the "walkway of the waters." By dawn, they would be coming up out of the other side. Back to business, the angel reminded himself, heading back to check on his fire pillar.

Sea floor, Red Sea

Generations later, they would still talk about the "night of the crossing." The Hebrew kept his family close as they descended into the sea bottom, the brisk wind whipping around them. Everyone was quiet as they began to walk steadily across, but you can only keep little boys under control for so long at a time. It started with a toddler, who broke ranks and sprinted, giggling, for the wall of water on the right. Before any sober, responsible adult could get to the rugrat, he was at the water, which towered over them all. Some of the women screamed as the baby slapped the water innocently, and everyone held their breaths, in spite of themselves. The water stood firm and they all exhaled, which was just a little more east wind added to the environment.

At this development, the tight edges of the marching column began to dissolve, and the lines spread out to fill the whole pathway. They didn't waste time, but they began to enjoy the trip a little more. The children found wonderful treasures on the sea floor, and everybody got a souvenir. By night's end, the adventure was coming to an end, but the memory would be with them for eternity.

Operations Center, Red Sea

The angel wondered what would come next, and just before daybreak he got the word. He picked up his fiery pillar, and headed across the Red Sea, to where the Israelites were ascending on the other side. Time to move on; someone else would deal with the army behind them.

Egyptian Cavalry Battalion, Red Sea Highway, 0600 hours

The charioteer held his reigns and fumed. Yet another bad night at the hands of the Hebrew god. But they were right at the backs of these slaves, and there was an ocean on the other side, so vindication was just ahead. The commanders would decide on a route around this darkness, and then their swords would drink their fill of Hebrew blood. Then quickly and quietly, the wall went away. Just like that, the way a tornado retracts into a cloud when it is spent. The captains of the chariots reacted immediately, and the whole army rolled forward with a shudder. Now it would be finished, this Hebrew slave rebellion. But what's up with this? No Hebrews!

They first focused on where they believed the slaves would be camped. Nothing but haze and litter. Lifting their eyes, they became amazed once again. Where there had always been a smooth uninterrupted seascape, there now appeared to be two separate seas—and a valley full of runaway Hebrews in the middle. As they saw more clearly their astonishment grew. These were not two seas, but the one sea split in half, and heaped up on either side. They cursed their gods for their impotence, and marveled at the power of the Hebrew deity. Is there no end to what the Hebrew Lord can do?

The commanders realized that their hope of vindication was marching away from them at a rapid pace. Strategically, they sensed that if the Hebrews got away to the other side of this sea, it would all be over. In desperation and anger, they ordered the chariots to follow the Hebrews into the seabed.

Red Sea, far shore

The angel was watching from the front, but he could see all the way to the rear. Angels are more in tune with God than with what crazy, unstable, angry pagan men are going to do, so it raised his eyebrows a little when the chariots headed into the path through the sea. Angels don't make many jokes, but he thought to himself, "Well, they *are* in over their heads this time."

Any mirth he felt at his witticism, as well as any hilarity at the hapless Egyptians, was dissolved as he was overshadowed and overwhelmed, by The Presence. Angels operate always in the presence of God, but there are some points in time and space that can only be described as a manifestation of The Presence. The angel acknowledged The Presence from his spirit, and stood by to watch quietly. This was it. This was going to be special.

Egyptian Cavalry operations, Red Sea floor, daybreak

It began simply enough. A chariot hit a mudhole, another one's wheels wobbled. Here and there they locked up, or veered off course. Within seconds, however, it was evident to all that they were in trouble. That was when they began to crack. You can only fight against God for so long. There's a reason He is called the Almighty, and the Egyptians fully comprehended this now.

The Commander of the Chariot Forces made a cogent, but tardy decision, and made a futile order—his last.

"Call for retreat!"

Red Sea shore, near Hebrew HQ

At that specific point in time, God was speaking to Moses. The Hebrew was not far away, and he could tell that Moses was hearing from elsewhere. The children were anxiously chattering, and even his wife was asking questions, but he motioned to them to hush, and pointed toward Moses on the ledge above them. The man of God extended first his view, then his hand, out over the sea, and the eyes of all Israel followed. As the day broke, the sea returned to its normal state. There was a thunderous rush of water, and they felt it. They heard it and saw it. And then as the tide settled, and a few scattered Egyptian things began to bob to the surface, they started to fully appreciate what it meant, once and for all.

Egypt was gone.

Slavery was over.

The promises of God through Moses, and the promises of Moses, in God's Name, had proven 100 percent true. They had been totally delivered.

Some wept gently. Some fell to their knees and sobbed violently. Some broke into song. Some shouted in victory. Miriam, Moses and Aaron's sister, took up a tambourine and led the women of Israel in a dance. And others just stood there and held their babies, and smiled the smile of the redeemed.

It was not profanity to say, "Oh my God, what a morning!"

11
"Into The Promised Land: Take One"
Exodus 15-40
Leviticus 1-27
Numbers 1-14

Israel had been delivered through God's power and the blood of the lamb. Our salvation is accomplished by grace through faith in the blood of the Lamb of God, Jesus. After we are delivered from sin into salvation God instructs us to be baptized—buried in water as a symbol of our death with Christ, and raised out of that water as a symbol of our new life in Him. God began teaching this at the Red Sea. If you think this is just me trying to make the Bible prove something it really doesn't say, review the first eleven verses of *First Corinthians* 10. Paul teaches this very truth there.

Deliverance was behind them, destiny was ahead of them. This is where the new believer in Christ stands. Don't forget this as you read their story, which now continues.

Soon the Red Sea disappeared behind them, and they kept walking. In three days, they had found no supply of water. They came to a place, Marah, that would be called Bitter Springs, if they had been walking across the American West. The water was unfit to drink, and the people could stand it no more.

The multitude grumbled to Moses for water, and he cried out to God. God directed Moses to a tree, which Moses threw into the bitter waters of Marah. This act miraculously sweetened the waters, and the people got a drink. God said, "OK, if you will listen to me, and do what I say, I will keep you healthy. I am the Lord, your Healer."

I can almost hear the "Rawhide" theme song at this point (*Rollin'* *rollin' rollin'—keep them Hebrews goin'*). This is a long drive, and people can be harder to move than cattle. Soon they had moved on to a pleasant oasis at Elim, where there were springs and date palms. Now everyone is watered, well-fed, and happy, right?

Well, they couldn't stay in the oasis, so they headed to Sinai, as God had directed. Halfway between Elim and Sinai, in the wilderness, they got hungry and started to snack on their leadership. The whiners went on about how they wished they had died in Egypt with a full stomach. They had pots of meat and all the bread they wanted. Now they accused Moses of bringing the whole nation out into the wilderness to kill them with hunger.

This is a constant theme during the exodus, and yes, it is as stupid as it looks. In misery in Egypt, God had heard their cries for deliverance, and came to deliver them. They were living as slaves, being forced to kill their own infant sons, when God came to set them free with a mighty hand. They had seen His miraculous workings against Egypt, and His protection of His people in Goshen. They had been preserved from all the plagues, even from the Passover night which was a horrible tragedy in Egypt. When Egypt gave chase, God had dunked their chariots, and promised Israel that they were free from Egypt forever. This had all been accomplished through their trust in God and through Moses' faithfulness. Now, after a walk in the desert, how do they respond to their Deliverer? "What have you done for us, lately?"

Moses tried to refocus the attention of the people to where the responsibility was actually centered, "The Lord hears your complaining against Him, for what are we, that you grumble against us?" God promised that tonight there would be meat, and tomorrow morning, it would rain bread.

Phase One: At evening the camp was covered with quail. Apparently it was a similar operation to the plagues that God had brought upon

Egypt. Quail would be infinitely better, however, than flies or frogs or locusts, to most peoples' tastes. I'd be fine with either frog legs or quail, I like them both, but you're not going to get a mess of frogs in the desert. Quail are more practical, and I think they are kosher as well.

Phase Two: In the morning a dew settled on the camp, and when it lifted, a fine flaky substance was left coating everything. When the Israelites came out and saw it, they said, "What's this?" The notes in my Bible say that in the Hebrew tongue, this is "*Man hu?*" The name stuck, and we still call it manna. It seems to have been a versatile carbohydrate, from the ongoing context, and very nutritious for people on the road. Imagine the land, as far as you can see, covered with vitamin-fortified grits every morning. Well, that's a pleasant image for me, anyway.

Moses had to give instructions for proper manna management. God intended for there to be enough for each day's needs, but He wanted His people to keep trusting in Him. Therefore, they were told to gather just a day's worth each morning, and not enough for leftovers. Nothing wrong with leftovers, but God was teaching them, and us, some important lessons.

There are always the hard-heads and can't-believers in the crowd, and they gathered extra. Next day, their leftover manna was rotten and wormy, and Moses was angry. The anger of Moses is a much too common occurrence in this story, and it will eventually cause more unhappiness. Watch and learn.

The exception to the leftover rule was on the day before the Sabbath. Then everyone got two days worth, and it kept. Also, God told Moses to put a pot of it up for historical value, as a witness through the generations. For the next forty years, manna will be the staple of the Israelite diet; it must have been amazing stuff. When Jesus later instructs His disciples to pray ". . . give us this day our daily bread." He must have at least had a thought of manna in mind. We use manna as an object lesson and example of God's faithful provision to this day.

On we roll. Next thing you know, we are in another dry space. No water, and no patience. No water, but plenty of "whine." The thirsty people were confronting Moses, and accusing him again of a conspiracy to kill everybody with thirst. Perhaps some were picking up rocks, maybe Moses heard a voice down in the crowd growl, "Git a rope!" Moses reported to God that the tourists were getting restless, and God sent Moses out before the people with a delegation of elders and his stick. This was the stick with which Moses had been doing the stuff all along. It had become a symbol of the authority of God.

Moses was to go out to a large rock and strike it with the stick. God would be there, and He would bring the water out of the rock. Paul tells us in his writing to the Corinthians mentioned above that this is another type. The rock is Christ, who was smitten to provide living water for our souls. Remember this; it will be important later in the story.

They all got a drink, but Moses called the place *Massah* (test) and *Meribah* (quarrel), because of all the attitude shown by the people toward God. Moses' resentment over this seems to have lingered with him too long, and took root a little too deeply.

As if that were not enough, Israel now met their first opposition since getting on the road. The people of Amalek came out to fight. As the battle ensued, Moses sent Joshua out to lead the fight, then went up on the mountain to overlook the head-knocking. When Moses held up God's staff in his hands, Israel prevailed. But we all get tired with our hands in the air, more so for octogenarians. When Moses drooped, Amalek began to take the advantage.

A couple members of his entourage, Aaron and Hur, noticed this pattern. They sat Moses down on a rock and supported his arms until the sun had set and Joshua & Co. had sufficiently whipped the Amalekites. God told Moses, "Write this in a memorial book, for I am going to blot out Amalek from the face of the earth." Come to think of it, we don't ever hear anything about Amalek on the evening news these days, do we?

That's the way life went in the wilderness crossing. Moses got some good advice about delegation from his father-in-law, which helped. They lived on the manna, and traveled from one watering hole to another, even if God had to drill a well. Soon they came to Sinai, the place at which God had called them to meet Him. Moses climbed that mountain, and had a very long talk with God. Actually, Moses mainly listened.

God had delivered Israel *from* something, and now he was calling them *to* something. To accomplish this destiny, they had to *become* something. That is their story, and yours and mine. Their becoming was about to get started for real. At Sinai God would remind the people of the covenant He had with them through Abraham, and the people would commit themselves again to that covenant.

God was awesome and terrible, with thunder and smoke kind of like the Wizard of Oz. But God was for real. The people kept their distance, and Moses moved back and forth between God and the people, who thought they would die if God Himself spoke directly to them. This was where God would establish the Law for the nation He was bringing forth. You may know about the Ten Commandments, but there is much more to the Law.

God gave commandments and ordinances, and dates for the calendar, and instructions about how to take possession of the land He had promised. He told them what offerings to bring for the Sanctuary they would build, and how to design and construct the Ark of the Covenant, sort of a chest wherein the glory of God could be found. God gave Moses the entire design of the Tabernacle, where the people would offer worship and atonement, and where God would meet with their representatives. The designs for the furnishings of the Tabernacle and the garments of the priests were given. Instructions came on how to consecrate and provide for the priests, and how to make and use the anointing oil. This went on for some time, with Moses literally getting the Word, and the people below trembling at the fire, and thunder, and clouds, and smoke visible from below.

As I said, this went on for some time. If you had been there, you would probably have been in such awe of God's Presence that you would have been at the bottom of the mountain gathered in worship the whole time. At the very least, you would have behaved yourself. Not these desert wanderers. In one of the strangest episodes of this story, the people gave up on Moses and leaned on Aaron to make a golden calf. They then called the calf their god. Next day, they partied before their new god.

Up on the mountain, God told Moses to head down and tend to these people. He even suggested that He might kill them all, and raise up another nation out of Moses. Remember when we said that God does not ask questions for His knowledge, but for ours? This incident is like that. God is not intending to wipe out Israel and start over, but is putting the proposition before Moses for his response.

And what was Moses' response? It was the right one. First he suggests that killing Israel now would be a reproach in the sight of the Egyptians, an opportunity to say "Aha! Their god took them out of Egypt just to kill them!" Then he pleads the covenant relationship with Abraham, Isaac, and Jacob. One does not vaporize one's covenant partners. God, of course, knew all this, but wanted Moses to confirm it and put it on the record.

It is important that you understand this well, or you may fall prey to one of those bozos who try to show you "contradictions" and flaws in the Bible and the story of redemption. When *Exodus* 32:14 says that God "changed His mind," that is written to put the event in terms that we human people will comprehend. That is exactly how it was seen from Moses' perspective, but God simply does not change.

So Moses took two stone tablets that God had engraved, and went down the mountain to see what God was so angry about. When he saw the scene, Moses got really ticked, himself. Moses got so mad he threw the tablets to the ground, shattering the words God had just given. Then he burned the calf, ground it to powder, put it in the water supply, and made them all drink it. I wonder if anyone had gold kidney stones later?

Aaron gave the lamest sort of excuses for his behavior and absence of leadership, but Moses saw it was time to cull the herd. You may remember this scene from *The Ten Commandments*. This is where Charlton Heston gets rid of that pesky and annoying evil Edward G. Robinson once and for all, Chuck throws down, literally, pitching the stone tablets at E.G's bunch. The earth opens, and they are swallowed up—down, actually. Pretty cool in the movie. I was disappointed when I found out that it didn't happen. Not at this point, anyway.

What did happen was that Moses called a squad of Levites into action, and they moved across the crowd, whacking about 3,000 of the backslidden and rebellious sons of Jacob. I'm thinking they knew what was what, and knew who to slay. Moses went up to God the next day to atone for the people. He gave an eloquent and poignant plea to God for forgiveness, and God let them live, albeit on a sort of deferred sentence basis.

The tablets were replaced, the Covenant renewed, and the people moved on. They keep walking, right out of the book of *Exodus* into *Leviticus*. The Tabernacle was built according to the plan God gave Moses. The Tabernacle was a big tent, in case you're wondering why they would build something while they were on the move. It was beautiful, and rich in furnishings and decoration. Remember all that stuff they borrowed from their Egyptian neighbors? Here's where a lot of it went—what didn't go into the calf. They had instructions on taking it down and putting it up, and it served them well for a long time.

As *Leviticus* opens, Moses receives laws from God regarding when and how to make sacrifices and offerings, and how to prepare the priests and other Tabernacle issues. They instituted sacrifices in the Tabernacle, placing them on the altar and sprinkling the blood, just as God commanded. Remember, God was teaching them, and us, about redemption purchased by blood. This is important and powerful stuff. The fire of the Lord came down and consumed the sacrifices, and the glory of the Lord appeared to all the people. It was a good day. Then there was a bad day.

It is too often the case that when God is doing great things, man is tempted in his silly flesh to take glory for himself. This was one of those times. Nadab and Abihu, the sons of Aaron, offered "strange fire before the Lord, which He had not commanded them." God responded by sending His own fire, and they were toasted to death. Aaron couldn't complain after God explained through Moses how unacceptable their behavior was. It was important that they all learn about the holiness of God, that any old religious-looking act was not what He expected.

Our ideas about what is pleasing to God are inadequate, like "strange fire." God was not going to put up with another Cain (*Gen.* 4), and He got this point across forcefully. We had to be shown that we were not going to redeem ourselves.

Immediately thereafter, God teaches that His people will live separated lives from this world. He does this by giving laws about which animals to eat, and which not to. Then followed laws about maternity, leprosy, health, atonement, and who you can have sex with. This is the first we hear of incest being a problem. The nation of Israel was growing up, and the people of God were instructed that they could not live like the Egyptians behind them, or the Canaanites ahead of them. They were to remain a pure and holy people. They were also warned about spiritual adultery, or idolatry, as we know it.

God warned them about the evil things the Canaanites were into, and when you see what those guys were doing, you understand why they were about to get wiped out and displaced. Earlier, in *Genesis,* we saw the beginning of these nations, and a little about how they got where they were at this point. Now they come back into the story as tribes who went into Canaan and got horribly corrupted. They were into child sacrifice, and all manner of hellish immorality and idolatry. The promise of a home in Canaan to Israel was the pronouncement of judgment on the Canaanites, Perrizites, Jebusites, Amorites, Samsonites, Termites—the whole bunch! But that's still to come in the next story.

There is a whole lot of redemption in all these laws, and preachers and teachers have been mining them for centuries. Once I understood about the Big Story, this part of the Bible got more interesting.

Leviticus closes, and *Numbers* opens with a census. More instructions and laws are given, and the habit of "following the cloud" established. You remember the cloud? They followed it out of Egypt, and it had been leading them since. It was the Presence of God, which settled on the Tabernacle. As long as it stayed, they stayed. When it lifted, they took up stakes, and when it moved, they moved. A good rule for life— follow the presence of the Lord.

But before long, the people were complaining again, and God's fire came out and torched a bunch of them. Apparently, not everyone in the camp was of the sons of Israel. The NASB says that there was a "rabble among them" (Num. 11:4). I think these were people from Egypt who "jumped ship" when things went bad for the home team. Now, having left Egypt with what looked like a winner, they were stuck in the wilderness with nothing to do but whine.

Their whining infected some of the Israelites, too, and soon there was a chorus of discontent, "We remember Egypt! We had fish, and cucumbers, and melons, and leeks and onions. Now there is nothing to eat but this manna! Who will give us meat?" Anyone who has spent much time in a feeding ministry will tell you, there are indeed people who complain about a free lunch.

Neither Moses nor God was happy about this, but Moses was really burned-out. Look at his complaint to the Lord about his ministry (Num. 11:11-15). My NASB shows some form of first person reference fourteen times. Moses' prayer was full of "I," "me," "my." So God gave him some help. Seventy elders were appointed to help with the administrative load. Then God dealt with the people.

"Moses, tell the people that this will be a month of meat. They will eat meat until it is coming out their noses. They will be sick of meat in thirty days!" Never dare God. He doesn't take dares to perform tricks for you, but if you are disrespectful, he may give you your stupid demand, as a judgment on you. Look and learn.

Moses raised a logical point. "Where are we going to find meat for 600,000 people for thirty days?" God's reply can be paraphrased as, "Duh, Moses! I'm like, GOD, remember? This is what I do." The seventy elders were gathered and anointed by God for their service, and everyone got ready for the big meatfest.

Critters of all kinds do what God says. The quail didn't know why they were over the sea, and I don't either, except that God had them there for Meat Month. God sent a wind, which blew the birds into the camp, and dropped them there. For as far as you could walk in either direction, to a depth of ninety-six inches, the quail piled up. In a straight line to the horizon, I think you can walk farther than you can see. This means there were eight feet of quail, as far as you could see, which was probably not too far, unless you were over eight feet tall, or climbed a tree. The people went a little nuts over this. You would think they would have recognized God's sarcasm in the overkill. You would think, they would have gratefully trusted His provision, since there were so many blooming birds. They did neither.

They were crazy-greedy. Not my judgment, the Bible says it. They went out and gathered quail for two days. If they had any bird dogs, I'm thinking the poor puppies just exploded from stress on the first day. The people gathered piles of quail, and all around the camp, they stacked them, as a safeguard against future meat shortage. They did this because they were greedy and unthankful for God's provision.

God was offended, as He rightfully should have been. While the meat was still in their teeth, He struck the greedy with a plague, before they could even bite down on their bird. They buried the dead there, and called the place, "The Graves of Greediness." As if that were not enough, there was grumbling among the top leadership, and God had to straighten that out with a face-to-face rebuke, and a well-placed case of leprosy. Days can get tough in the desert, even if you are following God's cloud.

By this time the folks were close enough to Canaan to send an advance team. At least a dozen men, one from each tribe, set out with Moses' instructions to spy out the land and its people. They checked out the place, and brought back samples of its produce.

They returned after forty days to give their report. It was a mixed bag of information. As it turns out, the land was as wonderful as they had been led to believe, flowing with milk and honey, but the people of the land were terrifying. The Canaanites were strong, their cities were fortified. They also found there were the Anakites, apparently a particularly nasty people to deal with. The rest of the land was infested with other peoples who would be tough to confront.

I don't know what these guys thought would be there—maybe a big sign at the Jordan, "Welcome Israelites!" Caleb stepped forward to calm down the meeting, which was getting fearful. "Let's go now!" he exhorted, "we can take these guys!" It wasn't that Caleb didn't know how bad all these "-ites" were, but he knew something more. He knew that God was bigger, and God had promised the land to His people.

The mass of the sons of Israel, however, were still being influenced by the "bandwagon whiners." Ten of the spies put out the word that the land could not be taken, "We're just grasshoppers to them! The land will eat us up!" Upon hearing this report, the people cried all night. You might, too. Deliverance from Egypt, everything they had gone through crossing the wilderness, now at the verge of entering into the anticipated land of blessing—then denied!

Wailed all night, they did, and God was really upset with them when the next day came. The people wanted to elect new leaders, to take them back to Egypt. Caleb and Joshua went among the people, pleading with them to believe God and enter the land. Moses and Aaron fell on their faces before God in the Tabernacle. All of Israel was in an uproar, and people were about to stone Mo' and 'Ron, when the glory of the Lord appeared at the Tent.

God repeated His offer to kill them all, and start over with Moses. Moses responded again that such an outcome would not bring glory to God, and of course he was right, and of course, God knew that already. But God was way angry, and the people deserved whatever they got.

Or didn't get, as it turned out. God read the judgment to the people. They had rebelled ten times, and not trusted God's words to them. This was beyond enough. All of them would be turned away from the Promised Land to die in the wilderness. The exceptions were two. First, Caleb and Joshua, who had been faithful in believing God's promise, and strove with the people to obey Him, would return to enter.

Secondly, all those below twenty would enter. In their rebellion, the unbelieving people had accused God of bringing their little ones out of Egypt to "become plunder" in Canaan. Now God said, "Your little ones will go in, but you will not." The spies went in for forty days, and Israel would now wander the wilderness for forty years. But the ten men whose fear and rebellion had turned Israel against God (again) did not wander any more. They died on the spot.

12
Into the Promised Land: Try Again

Numbers 14-36
Deuteronomy 1-34
Joshua 1-24

Yes, God was going to take His people into the land of promise, but not these knuckleheads. After they heard how badly they had offended God, they changed their wishy-washy minds. They decided they would take the land, after all. Moses was unimpressed with their newfound courage. Admitting your sin is not the same as repenting of it. They thought they could just ask for a "do-over" and God would forget that just one day before, they had insulted Him and had been close to murdering His chosen leaders in an ungodly coup.

Moses warned the people not to try to move without God's blessing, but they still weren't listening. Now they thought they had God figured out. They'd get back on His good side, and that "forty-year" thing would just be forgotten. Moses waited in the camp until they returned, as many of them as survived the beating.

Now God was still giving them laws, and talking to them about how to behave when they entered Canaan, because they were still going. Eventually. At least, the younger generation. In this part of the Bible, it's not always easy to tell what happened when, but you can get a better grasp of that by closer study later. There are good sources for that, but in this work, we're just following the narrative.

Some people never get it. There was a committee of men who should have known better (we'll call them the "MSKB"), who rose up against Moses, even after all this. These rebels, along with about 250 other community leaders, assembled against Moses and Aaron, to call for a change. What they wanted was democracy. In our American culture's view of things, their request would be perfectly reasonable, even noble. "God can speak to any of us; He is here with us all. Why should Moses and Aaron be the bosses?"

Here's why. God was visiting the Tabernacle personally. He was talking to Moses face-to-face, and everybody knew it. When that is happening, you don't need democracy. You follow the cloud, and do what God says. This uprising was in fact an attempt to stop that. Rather than follow God, as Moses was leading them to do, they wanted to take control and figure things out for themselves.

When Moses heard their complaint, he was humble as usual, and a bit fearful, I suspect. Not for himself, but for the MSKB. He kept control of the agenda, because God was still directing him. Tomorrow they would meet. Since the MSKB were claiming that they were as much chosen as any one, particularly Moses and Aaron, each of them would bring his incense holder to the meeting, and God would make clear His choice for leadership. There would be an election, but only God would have a vote. Two members of the committee, Dathan and Abiram, were so presumptuous in their rebellion, that they refused Moses' summons to the meeting. Now Moses was truly angry, and God was very unhappy also, as it turned out.

Next morning, everyone got together to settle this thing. The glory of the Lord appeared, and God separated out the MSKB. Then Moses called the action, "If these men die a natural death, then the Lord has not sent me. But if the earth opens up and swallows them, then you will understand that they have spurned the Lord." Then that is exactly what happened. Just like in *The Ten Commandments*, except the movie puts it in the wrong place. Earth opens. Bad guys and all they have fall in. Earth closes. Fire came out and fried the 250 used-to-be leaders. Eleazar, son of Aaron, picked up their incense holders, and made a pretty plating for the altar.

So all Israel sought the Lord and supported their leaders, right? No. Next day all Israel was again gathered against Mo' and 'Ron, blaming them for all the earth-swallowing and fire-consuming and rebel-killing that God had done the day before. After all, reasoned the people, all those guys wanted to do was help lead worship. Obviously, this crowd did not have all the information about the events of the day before. No CNN to give them the hour's headlines, or Fox News Channel to argue about them. And what you don't know, *can* hurt you, as we will see.

As he heard their grumbling, Moses had to be thinking, "Not again!" And he and Aaron fell on their faces in the Tabernacle (again) as the glory of the Lord descended (again). God said to His boys, "Get away from these people as I consume them." God didn't even ask Moses this time, as He had twice before. Moses recognized what was happening, since God had indeed suggested it twice before. Now he was going to do it, and Moses knew that if God had wanted his opinion about this, He would have asked.

While Moses was on his face interceding in prayer, he saw a possible remedy. He ordered Aaron, the priest of the two, to get up and take fire from the altar in his incense holder, and run to where the plague was dropping the people. According to Moses' directions Aaron ran out with the censer and placed himself between the living and the dead.

Incense throughout the Scripture speaks of worship, and that is its function here. The rebellion of all the people caused the plague. The obedience of one man, representing all of them as priest, lifting worship to God, stopped death in its tracks. Once again, God has arranged things so that a picture of our redemption is played out on the earth. But the rebellion still caused 14,700 to die.

God further demonstrated his choice of leadership by causing Aaron's dead rod to bud, as a sign of His favor. This issue of leadership was going to have to be settled, since they were about to leave on a forty-year wander in the wilderness. They took care of some more housekeeping, Miriam died, and soon they were back to their regular habit of grumbling against Moses. This time they were thirsty again.

God instructed Moses to go to the rock as before, and speak to it, that it would bring forth water. Remember that anger issue I told you Moses had? It came back to bite him here. Losing his temper a bit with this bunch of whiners, he not only spoke angrily to the rock, but struck it twice. The water came, but God was unhappy. This loss of control cost Moses entry to the Promised Land. He would not get to go in because of this.

Wow, that's a heavy price to pay for hitting a rock. You think? Let's talk typology again for a while. Run ahead again to *1 Corinthians* 10:4. Paul tells us that this rock represented Christ. The first time it was struck, in *Exodus* 17, it represented Christ being smitten for our salvation. That happened once—Jesus suffered and died once for all. When Moses came back to the rock he was told to speak to it—to claim by faith what had already been accomplished. In hitting it he seems to have destroyed the type. Christ was not to be smitten again. We are to receive our blessings through Him by "speaking to the rock," claiming His promises, which are already paid for.

Moses rebuked the people before he struck the rock on the second trip, saying, "Must we fetch you water out of this rock?" This shows his attitude to be one of anger with having to "do it all himself." He took action against the rock which God did not command. The water was there for the asking, but, here comes Moses, swinging his stick—which no one told him to do.

Remember that Paul said that all these things were written for us? That means *all*. Moses did not destroy the type; we still get that point. Moses actually became a type. He is a type of man-made religion, which claims to be providing the spiritual water by its own actions, when the Once-smitten Rock has the water already in Him for the asking. Did you see what God told Moses in rebuking him? It was for not treating the rock as a holy thing that Moses was disciplined. This happened not only to Moses, but Aaron was included; he would die before they entered in.

Altogether they spent forty years in this wilderness, long enough for all those who refused to go in the first time to die off, except Joshua and Caleb. There were more lessons about grumbling to learn, and more ordinances, and more funerals. There was more conquering to do, since some of the kings along the way were very inhospitable.

You may find this next part amusing. I do, and I have never seen it portrayed in one of those "bathrobe Bible operas" Hollywood used to produce in the old days. Israel was camped in Moab/Midian country and the local king, Balak, was worried. He sent word to a free-lance prophet named Balaam that he needed a curse placed on Israel. Balaam was a prophet-for-hire, but he was the real thing. He apparently knew God, but not Israel. Lots of people like that; saved, but clueless as to what God is doing in the world with His people.

When this guy spoke with God about Israel, God gave Balaam orders to turn down Balak's offer and leave Israel alone, so Balak's people went home empty-handed. Balak sent another, more high powered delegation, with an even better offer.

Put yourself in Balaam's place. He would not disobey God, but there just wasn't much good-paying work for true prophets, and he undoubtedly needed the money. He took the second offer to God, asking permission again to do what God had already told him not to do. He must have been happy that night when God said, "OK, go with these guys, but don't say or do anything other than what I tell you." Next morning, he saddled up his own faithful donkey, and headed out. Balaam wasn't green, but *Shrek* kind of reminds me of Balaam, for reasons we shall soon see.

God had allowed Balaam to go, but He wasn't happy about it. I think Balaam had some attitudes that needed adjusting. Remember, Balaam didn't know Israel, or much, if anything, about God's promises and plans for them. If he had asked, God would have filled him in. It seems, however, that he was just a little too enthusiastic about this high-paying contract with Balak. Perhaps he was riding along on his donkey, thinking of just which whammy he would lay on this rabble out of Egypt. God could see what he was thinking— "Just show me the money, and tell me who to curse!"

God was angry. He hadn't gifted Balaam as a prophet so that he could prostitute the gift to pagan kings. The angel of the Lord dropped in front of the prophet, sword drawn. Balaam's improper attitude blocked his spiritual perception, so he didn't see the danger. The donkey saw it, and turned away. Donkeys aren't usually so spiritually perceptive, but neither did she have an impure attitude like the prophet. For God's purposes, He made sure the donkey was aware of the angel. Balaam whacked his mount to straighten her out, and headed into a narrow place between two walls. When the donkey saw the angel again, she turned aside, smashing Balaam's foot against the wall. More beating.

The angel went ahead, to a narrow place where there was no room to either side. This donkey wasn't stupid, so this time she just lay down in the road. Balaam was fairly ballistic by now, and proceeded to beat the donkey with sincerity, but then the donkey spoke up.

"What have I done to you, that you beat me three times now?" Honestly, I'm not sure if this was ventriloquism on the part of the angel, or if the donkey was given a temporary upgrade in her intellect and faculties. I prefer to think the latter, and this is my book so I'm going with that.

What makes me giggle here is the reaction of Balaam. What would have been your reaction? What would you have said? Pick one from this list:

1. "Whoa, dude—a talking donkey? No more wild mushrooms for me!"
2. "Forget the prophet business—we're joining the circus!"

3. "Have you been listening all this time, just pretending to not understand?"

4. "What is this, a magic stick I'm beating you with?"

5. "Oy vey! You can't walk straight, you smash me into walls, you lay down in the road, now you want to argue! You're no good as a donkey, so you want to be a lawyer?"

What I find goofy is that Balaam reacted none at all to this astounding phenomenon. He went on to argue with his ride like this was something they did every day! "I'm beating you because you're making a fool of me! If I had a sword, I'd kill you!" Yeah Balaam, and then you'd walk the rest of the way to Moab, or come in on the back end of someone else's donkey. That'd impress everybody.

And as for being made a fool, who's standing in the road arguing with an ass? You're having a bad day when that happens—and the ass wins the argument! She very rationally pleaded her case, asking, "Am I not your own donkey, who has been carrying you your whole life? Do I *ever* act this way?" To which Balaam had to thoughtfully answer, "No."

Well, my wife points out that Balaam was a prophet who dealt in the supernatural as his normal life. She thinks that he had likely seen things as strange as a talking donkey before, so this was nothing that would freak him out. I think she is probably right, and this story gives us insight into the life of the prophet in those days.

The Lord allowed Balaam to now see the angel, and was the prophet's face red! With Balaam bowed to the ground the angel asked, "Why you beatin' that donkey? I came to kill you, and if she hadn't seen me and turned away, I would have chopped you down, and let her live!" Balaam apologized to the angel, and we hope, to his donkey. He offered to go back, but now that his head and heart were corrected, the angel said, "Go on, but only do exactly as you are told."

When he got there, Balaam was up front with Balak, "I only can do what God says." Sacrifices were offered to the Lord, and God met Balaam. He said, "Go back to Balak, and say this . . ." When Balaam got back down the hill, he made the king very unhappy. He pronounced a blessing on Israel, since that was what God told him to say.

Balak did not get it. He took Balaam to another place, thinking he'd get another result. This time the result was a rebuke to Balak, and a greater blessing on Israel. "Balak" may be a Moabite word meaning "stupider than average," because he took Balaam to a third location to see if he could get Israel cursed from there. More sacrifices; same result. Balaam blessed Israel the third time and Balak went off. "What's up with you? I brought you here to curse these people, and you have blessed them three times! Just go home. I promised you great honor (a big honorarium, we suppose), but the Lord has messed that up for you."

Balaam has spoken with a talking donkey, an angel, and God on this trip, so the ranting king didn't impress him much. "Didn't I tell you before I left home that even if you gave me your house full of silver and gold, I would say only what God said? Now let me tell you what God says these people are going to do to you!" He read the riot act to Balak and his buddies, then they all went to the house.

This story shows us that when God has chosen blessing for His people, no enemy can change God's result. But the damage that Balak couldn't do by hiring a curse, the Israelites did to themselves by their own sinful behavior. Balak wanted to hire Balaam for a lot of money, and Balaam wanted the money, so he counseled where he couldn't curse. He let Balak know that all he really needed was to send over the Moabite women.

The home town ho's invited the Israelite boys over to the Baal festival, and the Israelites enjoyed it way too much. They whored around with the Moabite wenches, and bowed before the Moabite gods. The

Lord said to Moses, "This time, you do the killing. Let every judge take out his own people who have been partying with Moab."

This had to have been a terrible tragedy throughout the camp, being forced to kill your own people to purge the nation. While they were still weeping, one of the old boys brought one of the Midianite (Moabite) floozies home to his tent in broad daylight, with all his relatives, and the leaders, and God, and everybody watching. Apparently, this was too much for one Phinehas, Aaron's grandson, to stomach. Taking up a spear, he went right into the tent where they were clinching each other, and skewered them through together, giving them a somewhat more intense "hook-up" than they had imagined. God was pleased with Phinehas' jealousy for Him. A plague of judgment had broken out, and his actions stopped it. However, 24,000 people were dead from all this.

They next counted everybody, established more laws, and installed Joshua as successor to Moses. They were getting closer to going in to their promised land, and God was getting them ready for it. We think of receiving a promise as a process of us patiently waiting for God to make good on what He said. God intends for it to be a process of Him getting us ready to receive that which He has planned for us. If we sit around idly waiting for Him to come through, like we're expecting a package to be delivered, we're not participating in His plan for us, and we may not receive the promise.

Now, God had not forgotten that it was the Midianites who had caused the last round of killings and plagues. So for Moses' last assignment, God instructs him to whack the Midianites. They mustered an army of 12,000, including Phinehas, who had previously shown a talent for dealing with seductive Midianites. This army was sent to Midian, and they killed every male.

They even killed Balaam. The Scripture tells us that he was the one who advised Midian to seduce Israel with women when the curse thing didn't work out, so he had it coming. They took a lot of plunder. The army still had a soft spot for the Midianite women, so they spared them, along with the children, but they took all of these back to camp with them.

This did not sit well with Moses, who was being led by God, rather than by his pants. He reminded the boys that these women were the whole reason for all this killing in the first place. He ordered the killing of every male child that had been spared, and every female that was not a virgin.

No, I don't know what test they used to determine virginity. I could perhaps find out, and explain that here, but it would be a diversion from the story. When you study *Numbers* in Bible college, ask your professor. I didn't think to. However, surmising from the known behavior of the Midianite women, the only ones left with virginity may have been very young little girls. It may seem harsh of God to have had all the little boys killed, but He had His reasons. Again, ask your professor when you study Old Testament in more detail. Here, we are just getting the quick trip through.

Since it is a quick trip through, let's skip ahead to the next book. Actually, we'll skip a whole book. Not that it's not important. However, we are telling the narrative here, and *Deuteronomy* is largely a repeating of things that have gone on before. Moses' teaching and instructions are very important, but the narrative moves into the next book.

In *Joshua*, the story moves on. In the first two verses, three things are stated clearly 1) Moses is dead, 2) Joshua is in charge, and 3) it is time to move in to the Promised Land. God's directions to Joshua about how to lead were to be strong and courageous, and be careful to obey God completely. God assured Joshua that if he would do this, things would go well.

First order of business was again the sending of spies. However, these spies were different than the last bunch. The first group went in to see what was there, apparently without a clear commitment to proceed.

When they saw walled cities and giants, they chickened out, except for a couple of them.

The second team of spies, forty years later, was going in with a different attitude. There was no doubt now that Israel was coming in; this reconnaissance was for the purpose of determining how. Only two were sent this time; maybe Joshua had learned from the earlier experience.

The two spies went in to Jericho, and of all places, ended up in the house of a harlot, Rahab. She took in non-john lodgers as a side business, apparently (or maybe she ran a hotel and did harlotry on the side). Her sinful occupation is, in fact, only marginally important to this micro-narrative. She hid the boys on the roof in a haystack when the locals came looking for them. In return for this she wanted a favor; their word that she and her household would be spared when the Israelites came back to conquer the city.

The people of Jericho had heard what God had done, and had no heart to fight. Rahab recognized Who was God, and saw that the best way out was submission to Him. In return for her help, the spies promised to spare her family. She snuck them out when the coast was clear, and gave them advice on how to get back to camp without getting caught.

As they left, they gave her a scarlet cord to tie in her window. This would mark her house as the one to be spared. I wonder if the spies were thinking about the Passover when they did this. Probably "just happened" to have a piece of red rope, but God knew what He was doing.

This Canaanite madam was going to save her whole family by obedience, trusting in the scarlet cord to mark them when God judged Jericho. What a powerful picture of redemption through the blood of Christ! This changed her life, and changed history. From what follows it appears that she quit whoring and "lived in the midst of Israel," becoming part of God's people, probably even becoming an ancestor of King David and of Jesus.

The lesson for redemption is that it doesn't matter how "good" you have been (or not) in the past, salvation comes from believing God when He tells you how to be saved now. In the book of Hebrews (11:31), Rahab is listed among the "famous people of faith," and her actions are identified as faithful. It says that "by faith" she did not perish with the disobedient.

But I'm getting ahead of the story. When Israel stepped into the river Jordan, the flow stopped, and they all walked across the riverbed. I think this is a good place for another typology lesson. "Crossing Jordan" has often been associated with death, and our entrance into the "Promised Land" of heaven.

You may have heard this preached, and you surely have heard songs about it. You need to forget it. Jordan is not death, and the Promised Land is not heaven.

Reasons the Promised Land is not Heaven

1. There were battles—victories and defeat there
2. There was sin there
3. There were ungodly people living there, and many were allowed to stay
4. There was death there
5. They crossed Jordan under their own power, and by their own will
6. Some chose not to live there, and God allowed it
7. They did not stay
8. There was no temple, no permanent "Dwelling place of God" for many generations yet to come
9. There was no "judgment of small and great" before entrance was allowed

So, if Canaan is not a type of heaven, what is it? It is your destiny. It is the promise that God has given you, the dream God has placed in your heart. It is what you will do for Him. It is a type of the Spirit-filled life. Remember, they were "baptized" in the Red Sea, the wilderness worked to purge and sanctify them, preparing them for their calling. There came a time for them, and it comes for us, when it's time to receive our purpose. When it's time to move into what God has called us to be. Unlike them, we may have the experience more than once, but God has given their example to guide us.

Israel recognized the importance of this event, and God directed them to build a historical marker to remind them of the day they crossed over. Sometimes it's good to have a memorial to remind us of what God has done in our lives. Next, Israel observed the Passover holiday, and every man born on the way had to be circumcised. Now that they were caught up on that, they could receive the land that had been promised. They began eating Canaanite produce, and the manna stopped.

Now they were ready to engage the Canaanites in battle, sort of. God gave orders to go to Jericho, march around it for seven days, then shout. Joshua relayed the orders, instructing the people to remain silent each day until told otherwise. So it went like this. Each day, they took the ark and the army, and circled the city once in silence, ending with a trumpet blast. This surely weirded-out the locals, who were already terrified of Israel. They did this for six days.

On the seventh day, they got an early start, and marched around the city seven times. The psychological impact of this tactic must have been great, with all Jericho watching them from the walls, waiting for what they would do next. Seventh time around, when the trumpets blew, Joshua gave the order to "Shout! For the Lord has given you the city!"

The trumpets blew, the people shouted, and the walls fell down flat. The falling of the walls probably wiped out most of the defenders of Jericho, and the Israelite army went after the rest. They killed everybody and everything, except Rahab's family, who were saved by her obedience.

While the "Rahabites" were being saved by faith through obedience, Israel was being cursed through disobedience. Joshua had ordered that no spoil be taken, and that the metals be brought into the treasury. However, a fellow named Achan had gotten greedy and took some stuff. So, when it came time for the next battle, at a little place called Ai, Israel was lacking the blessing of God, and that equals a curse. They didn't know this, so they only sent a detachment of about 3,000 men to take Ai.

Shock and awe! The 3,000 men of Israel were whipped all the way home. Thirty-six of them fell, and the rest were thoroughly disheartened. Joshua tore his clothes and fell before the ark of the Lord in despair, asking God, "Why did you bring us into this land, just to give us over into the enemy's hand, to destroy us?"

God was not patient with the grieving Joshua. "Rise up. Why are you on your face? Israel has sinned . . ." God had not deserted them at all, they had disobeyed and lost God's favor. With God's help, Achan was identified and 'fessed up to having taken some stuff and put it in his tent. The items were found and dealt with, and Achan and his family were dealt with, rather severely. Now Israel could go conquer Ai with a clear conscience. The irony is that in Ai, they were allowed to take plunder. Achan should have waited.

They took Ai, with some sneaky strategy and the help of the Lord. Speaking of sneaky, Israel next fell victim to a desperate plot by a local tribe, the Gibeonites. By deceiving Joshua and taking advantage of Israelite integrity, they managed to save themselves from destruction, ending up as servants of Israel instead of victims. This habit of not clearing the land of its inhabitants, as God instructed, became a problem for Israel later on. Incomplete obedience always does.

I was tempted to start the quick summary here, but there is another story worth telling. When the neighboring kings found out that Gibeon had struck a deal with Joshua, five of them joined to attack Gibeon. The Gibeonites yelled for help and Israel came to their defense. God really fought for Israel, sending hailstones down against the local tribes. They began to run out of daylight before the slaughter was complete, and Joshua pleaded with the Lord to hold up the sun and moon. God did, and there was never a day like that day. Joshua whipped those five kingdoms, and one more as a bonus.

This is the way it went, Joshua and the people smiting their way through the land God had given them. You might be tempted to feel sorry for the inhabitants of the land, all those "–ites" Joshua was killing. You should understand that they were wicked people, who had offended God greatly for some time with all their evil. God was using Israel as His instrument of judgment, so if Israel slacked off, which they did eventually, it would be disobedience.

The land which had been conquered was dealt out to the tribes of Israel. Some were even allowed to take land back on the other side of Jordan (one of the reasons, I told you earlier, that the Jordan is not a type of death). This caused a near tragedy when the tribes on the other side built a copy of the altar as a memorial of their unity with the rest of Israel. Israel thought they were branching out to start separate worship, and sent a delegation over to see if they needed killing. Explanation was quickly made, and the killing avoided.

By now Joshua had gotten old. His final address to the people is recorded, in which he reminds them of God's goodness to them, and exhorts them to remain faithful to God's commands. He warns them of the results of compromise with the nations around them. His warnings turn out to be a preview of the rest of the Old Testament to come.

The End of Book One

Well, this gets us from creation into the Promised Land. I hope it has been as exciting for you as it has been for me. These are the beginning of the stories you will never forget, the stories upon which all the other stories are built. More important, these are the stories upon which The Big Story is based.

These are stories which tell us about God Himself—what He is like, who He is, how He works, and ultimately what He will do to redeem us. The people in these stories were looking *forward* in faith to what God was going to do, and praising Him for it. Could you have done that? We today have the privilege of looking *back* in faith to what God has done, and thanking Him for it. Can you do that?

Book Two will take us further into the history of the people of Israel, and their interaction with the nations around them. We will see whether they were indeed faithful to the Covenant God made with them, and how God responded. Book Two takes us through the remainder of what we call the Old Testament. It will prepare us for the New Testament, in which Jesus, the Center of the Big Story, is revealed.

Book Two

The Kings, The Poets, and The Prophets

Book One Revisited

Time to stop and review. God has created everything, and put mankind in the middle of it. The prototypes failed (sinned), as He knew they would, and The Plan went into effect. Humanity increased, and so did their sin. Sin became so dominant that God was required to "reboot" the human race and start again with one family. They multiplied quickly, and after their languages were scrambled, they got with the program and began to disperse across the earth.

Out of all humanity God had a very special friend, from whom He promised to develop a nation. Abram/Abraham was faithful and so was God, so the nation of Israel (also known to us as Hebrews, or Jews) came about. Through their story, God teaches us many lessons about faith. Also, the Messiah, who will redeem us all, will be brought into humanity through this nation.

A descendant/patriarch of that nation, Joseph, got "Shanghied" to Egypt. Through God's favor and Joseph's faithfulness, he rose to second-in-command of the kingdom, and saved everyone's hide in a great famine. The famine brought Israel to Egypt, where they lived happily for a while, until things went sour between them and the Egyptians. Israel both multiplied and became slaves, until God heard their groaning and moved to deliver them. In delivering them, God would both do miracles for them and teach the rest of us many lessons about redemption.

The way He chose to do this was to send Moses. Born a Hebrew, Moses was raised as a member of the Egyptian royal family. At forty, he was exiled into the boonies. At eighty, he was summoned by God to return to Egypt and demand the release of the Hebrews. God knew that their release would be unacceptable for Pharaoh, the king of Egypt, so He planned to get involved and deliver Israel Himself.

Because of Pharaoh's stubbornness, God sent plagues upon Egypt. They wreaked misery and destruction in increasingly devastating ways until the night of the Passover. That night God slew the firstborn of every household in Egypt, but spared obedient Hebrew homes. Israel got kicked out of Egypt immediately.

As quickly as he had thrown them out of the country, Pharaoh changed his mind. He sent chariots and blood-thirsty soldiers after Israel, and things looked bad. Under God's direction and miraculous intervention, Israel fled across the dried-up seabed of the Red Sea. Driven by hatred, the Egyptian army pursued. God drowned the Egyptians. Game over.

Now on the other side of deliverance, Israel had to learn more lessons about obedience. They traveled to the Land of Promise, then balked at going in, because of their fear and lack of faith. God sent them back into the wilderness for forty years or so, and taught them (and us) many lessons about faith and redemption, until a new generation was prepared to try it again. This time, they took the land through their obedience.

This brings us to the opening of Book Two. We are six Bible books down in our journey through the Bible. Book seven is *Judges.* This unit will take us through the rest of the Old Testament, a lot of ground to cover. *Volume II* will be the New Testament story.

You will note that we do not follow the order of the English Protestant Bible as we go through the rest of the Old Testament story. I want to tell you the whole story of God's people, Israel, first. After that we will go back and pick up the stories that the Poets and Prophets tell us. Don't worry, it will make sense as we go.

Let's go.

13
Right in His Own Eyes
Judges
Ruth

There are a lot of good and/or important stories (micro-narratives) from what we call "the time of the judges" (the macro-narrative). Following *Judges* is another book, *Ruth*, which takes place during the same period. It is a sweet relief from the brutality and sin of *Judges*, so I am covering it here, also. Settle in for story time, kids.

Our story begins just after the death of Joshua. There was still more of Canaan to conquer, and the tribe of Judah was chosen to be lead conquerors. The land was taken from the Canaanites and Perizzites, and Jerusalem was captured, one of many times this city will be conquered. Unfortunately, before the first chapter of Judges is complete, a list of unconquered places begins.

The "angel of the Lord" visited Israel to deliver a rebuke for their incomplete obedience, and they mourned a little. After Joshua's passing, a generation came up who did not know God, and they turned away into idolatry. This brought God's discipline, in the form of defeat by their enemies. When they were being plundered and subjugated, they cried out to the Lord, who would in His mercy, send them deliverers. These deliverers, known as "judges," would lead the repentant people into freedom from their enemies, then govern the people for as long as that particular judge lived.

But the people wouldn't learn the lessons their judges tried to teach them, and as soon as the judge had passed, they went back into evil, starting the cycle again. This is the whole story of the time of the judges. I am going to give you some of the highlights, the way I see them. I will warn you, this story is full of brutal people killing other people—killing them in very unpleasant ways.

God turned Israel over to serve the Mesopotamians for eight years. Then they cried out to the Lord, and he gave them Othniel, Caleb's nephew. Deliverance came, and they served God for forty years. Then Othniel died, Israel backslid, and God gave them to Eglon, the obese king of Moab, for eighteen years. (Think of an ancient, fat, mafia don.) They cried out to God, and He gave them a deliverer, Ehud, the Left-Handed. (I'm giving a number of these people nicknames or surnames to help us remember who the players are. Some of the names I call them, you won't find in the text.)

When Ehud the Left-Handed went in to pay Israel's protection money to Don Eglon, he asked him for a private word in Eglon's summer chamber. Ehud said, "I have a message from God for you." I can almost hear the mandolin music.

Since he was left-handed, Ehud could quickly and easily whip out the eighteen-inch dagger that was stealthily fastened to his right thigh. He stuck the dagger into Eglon's prodigious belly. His fat swallowed up the blade and handle, and the King James translation says the "dirt" came out. (Told you this would get yucky.) Ehud locked the front door, and snuck out the back way, so Don Eglon's people thought the boss was just relieving himself in the summer chamber. I guess he was—out the side of his belly!

After awhile, they got anxious and got the key. Eglon was recently dead, and Ehud was long gone. When he got home from the hit on Don Eglon, he raised an overthrow of Moab, and they had eighty good years. This was because Ehud the Left-Handed was aided by Shamgar of the Oxgoad, who went Jackie Chan on 600 Philistines with an oxgoad, and saved Israel for a little while longer.

It didn't last, of course. Israel went back into evil after Ehud the Left-Handed passed, and for twenty years they suffered under the domination of King Jabin of Canaan, who kept them in line through his "enforcer," Sisera of the Chariots. *Pastora* of Israel at the time was Ma Deborah the Prophetess, who carried on her judge business under her own palm tree in the hill country. She sent for an Israelite fighting man named Barak the Kedeshian of Naphtali. (Yeah, I know he sounds like a *Star Trek* character.) Ma Deb ordered him to take 10,000 of his fellow Naphtalites and Zebulunites, and march to Mount Tabor. There she promised and prophesied that she would draw out Sisera's chariot army and hand them to Barak, the K of N, for thumping.

Barak recognized the Lord's anointing, and apparently knew when he didn't have it. He committed to the plan, but conditionally. If Ma Deborah the Prophetess would go with, Barak, the Kedeshian of Naphtali would go. Maybe we should call him "Barak, the Timid," or "Barak, the Skirttail Rider."

Ma Deborah was ok with this, but she made it clear that the glory for the victory would escape Barak, for God would give Sisera into the hand of a woman. They gathered the 10,000 troops, and went out from Kadesh. Sisera had a mole near there, so soon he had his 900 chariots mobilized.

By going to Mt. Tabor, Israel had apparently taken the high ground, and attacked from a position of advantage. The Lord was with them, and they routed Sisera and the Charioteers, raining down death until Sisera bailed from his chariot and ran. His whole army was wiped out, and Barak was in hot pursuit. Sisera the Chariotless ran to a safehouse, or so he thought. He took refuge with Jael, the wife of Heber the Kenite. She had called to him as he was running by, "Quick! In here!" He dashed into her tent, and she hid him under the rug.

Running for your life makes you thirsty, so Sisera asked for some water. What she had was a skin of milk, not refrigerated. You know exactly how this feels. Sisera has had a workout all day, fighting, then running. Now he's wrapped up in a warm rug, with a belly full of room temperature milk, and what he thought was a lookout. No mortal man could stay awake. Sisera couldn't. He didn't. In no time he was cutting zz's in his hiding place. He was dead tired, and soon he would be just dead.

As he was getting his snooze on, "Jael Kruger" prepared for his "nightmare on Kadesh Street." She went to the toolbox and picked up a hammer and a tent peg. She tip-toed over to the sleeping Sisera and DROVE the PEG through his TEMPLES, nailing his head to the floor. Now that she had assured that He wasn't going anywhere, she headed back outside and found Barak coming by with his posse.

"Yo! Over here! I got your fugitive!" She took Barak in the tent and showed him that Sisera was "not only merely dead, but really most sincerely, dead." As Ma Deborah the Prophetess had promised, Sisera had been delivered into the hands of a woman. From here Israel continued to go after Jabin until the Canaanite-beating was completed. Ma Deborah and Barak sang and celebrated, and Israel had a break for forty years.

After the forty good years, Israel got evil again, and God turned them over to the Midianites for discipline. This looked like the situation from Disney's *A Bug's Life*. The Israelites would plant and grow a crop, like industrious ants, then Midianites, like that grasshopper gang, would come over and harvest it, even destroying what they didn't want for themselves. This went on for seven years, and Israel got really hungry, and cried out to the Lord. Just like in the bug movie, God would find a mild mannered hero from the crowd to lead the people to deliverance.

His name was Gideon. We first see him hiding out, threshing wheat in the wine press, to save a little from the Midianites. Along came "the angel of the Lord," and sat down under the oak tree there. We don't know if he spoke immediately or sat there a while, but sooner or later he startled poor Gideon by speaking up, "The Lord is with you, O valiant warrior!" Gideon may have interpreted the angel's words as sarcasm, and returned some sarcasm of his own. "If the Lord is with us, why has all this happened? And where are all His miracles?" Gideon was singing the "Why, Where, Whine Blues." You probably know this song. I do.

The angel ignored this, and went on with his business. Gideon was to be the deliverer of Israel. Gideon was not ready. "I'm the least boy from the puniest family in my tribe," he objected. Gideon wanted confirmation of his destiny (Don't we all?) He brought a lunch offering to the angel, who received it by sending it up in a column of fire, and then the angel disappeared.

Gideon realized he had been visited by the Lord, and had to be reassured that he was not going to die. God began to speak directly to Gideon at this point, which helps to move the story along considerably. Gideon was given his first orders, to wreck his father's Baal altar and Asherah pole, and offer a sacrifice to God there. Gideon was obedient, but cautious, so he took a crew of ten men, and did it at night.

Next morning, the men of the city deduced who had done this, and came to the house of Gideon's father, Joash. They demanded that Joash bring out Gideon to be killed for his offense to Baal. I love Dad's response; it makes me chuckle every time I read it. Apparently Joash is the local heavyweight, and what he says, goes. His rebuke took all the enthusiasm out of Baal's lynch mob. "Who is going to defend Baal? Let Baal's defender die by morning! If Baal is a god, he can take up for himself." Looks like at least one guy was delivered from idol worship that day.

"Let Baal defend himself" became the boy's nickname, and he began to get a rep as a guy not to be messed with. Meanwhile, a confrontation was building with Midian and Amalek. Gideon got in the Spirit and blew a trumpet, calling his clan, the Abiezrites to report for duty. Word was sent out throughout the tribe of Manasseh to muster, as well as to the tribes of Asher, Zebulun, and Napthali.

Gideon was still feeling timid. He asked, and received clear signs from God through his legendary fleece. We still refer to "putting a fleece before the Lord" when we want to confirm His will. This is alright, if you really are trying to do God's will, and just want to confirm what that is. However, if you really know what God wants, and you are using your "fleece" as an excuse to get out of it, shame on you. You will get fleeced.

Having confirmed God's intent, Gideon led his army toward battle. God interrupted his progress to inform him that the army was too big. Gideon let everyone who was afraid go home. That excused 22,000 rational men, about two-thirds of the army. God said that was still too many, because He wanted to do a miraculous deliverance here, and wanted it to be clear Who deserved the glory.

So the task force was thinned down to 300 men. Three hundred men of Israel on the high ground, a huge army of thousands of Midianites in the valley below. In the night God spoke to Gideon. "Get up and go down; I have given these guys to you. But, if you are still anxious, you can sneak down there and listen to them, and then you'll feel better about my plan."

Gideon and his servant crept down to the Midianite camp to eavesdrop on the enemy. This seems to me to be scarier than just taking his army into battle, but what do I know? What Gideon heard was that the Midis and Amis were already afraid of him, because of the dreams they were having. When Gideon and his buddy got back to camp, they roused their troops for battle.

This battle plan has to be understood to be appreciated, because there is so much we can learn from it. Gideon instructed his men to follow his lead. They were all equipped for the battle with a torch hidden inside a pitcher, and a trumpet. Interesting choice of weapons. Had any of the troops not completely trusted God and Gideon, this would have been a tempting time to relieve the goofy Gideon of his command.

The faithful 300 surrounded the enemy camp, and on Gideon's signal, broke their pitcher, releasing the torchlight. They shouted, "A sword for the Lord, and for Gideon!" This was important for two reasons. First, the glory for the victory was given to the Lord. Secondly, the name of Gideon was shouted, perhaps because the Midianites were already having bad dreams about Gideon. Psychological warfare had been underway ahead of them, and Gideon's army took full advantage of it.

Imagine the scene from below. In the dead of night, the Midianites and friends are sleeping in trepidation. They are having nightmares about their opponent, and they have no clue where he is. Suddenly there is a crash, as the pitchers are smashed. A blood-curdling war cry is heard, as their nightmares come to life. The army of Gideon is upon them—a night time attack! They crawl out of their tents and look up. They are completely surrounded. They have no way of knowing that the 300 screaming, trumpet-blowing troops above them are not the front line of thousands. They could not have suspected that these were the entire attacking force.

The army below first started killing each other, then they fled. All of Gideon's reserves got into the chase eventually, and a great time was had by all. This got them forty years of peace.

After Gideon died, Israel went back to their old sinful ways. Gideon had seventy sons, for he had many wives. However, the son of one of his concubines, Abimelech, decided that he should be king. He murdered all of his brothers and went about doing brutal things to whoever opposed him, until one day a lady dropped a big millstone on his head, and that was the name of that tune.

There were a couple of good judges, then Israel went bad again. Each description of Israel's sin in *Judges* is worse than the one before. Now Ammonites and Philistines were oppressing them, and God threatened to leave them there. They repented, however, and God got involved with them again.

Then comes the somewhat bizarre story of Jepthah. Right here in the middle of God's Word is a *Twilight Zone* episode. Jepthah's mother was a bad girl. He was despised by family and townsfolk, and this apparently gave him a fighter's attitude. So, when his people needed a fighter to lead them against their oppressors, they came to Jepthah. Jep called up the Ammonite king, and they argued about history for a while, with little benefit. There was going to be a fight.

This brings about the strange part of the story. The Spirit of the Lord came upon Jepthah, and he moved toward the battle. To ensure victory, he believed he must impress God with his sincerity. Out of his lack of trust in God, he committed a religious act which was contrary to God's known will. He vowed that if the Lord gave him success, "that whatever comes out of the doors of my house to meet me when I return" will be given to the Lord as a burnt offering. This was a dangerous vow; Jepthah should have been more thoughtful. (Apparently he wasn't too tight with the family dog.)

The Lord did give him victory, and in two verses he is coming back home. All looks wonderful. Now comes the twist, and Rod Serling is standing somewhere close by. As Jep approaches his house in triumph, out to meet him dashes his daughter, his only child. She is all tambourines and dancing, and was probably shocked at her father's reaction to her when she appeared.

There is some disagreement about whether Jepthah actually offered up his daughter as a burnt sacrifice. As Matthew Henry says, "Jepthah's vow is dark, and much in the clouds." (*Commentary,* Judges XI:29-39) Henry comes down on the "burning" side. Gleason Archer, in his *Encyclopedia of Bible Difficulties* (Zondervan, 1982) makes an excellent case for the non-burning of the girl. Read them both to get a fuller understanding of both sides of the difficulty. It is enough here to say that she was given to the Lord from that day forward, and Jepthah was not happy about it.

The men of Ephraim got a knot in their knickers because Jepthah had taken Gilead, his people, into battle without them. This offense caused civil war between them. (These people didn't know God very well, and some of the things they fought about would be laughable, if real people weren't getting really killed.) Some of the Ephraimites got caught behind shifting battle lines, and had to come back through Gileadite checkpoints. They would deny being of Ephraim, but the crafty Gilead guards would require them to say "Shibboleth." The Ephraimites had a heavy accent, and could only say "Sibbolet." Forty-two thousand of them died because of it. There was no ACLU around to stop the profiling.

It seems things went along pretty well, until Israel got evil again. The Philistines came back for a forty-year run, and Israel got real tired of that. One day an angel appeared to a formerly barren woman, and promised a son. She was given special instructions for her pregnancy, for he was to be a special kid. He would be a Nazarite, living under a vow not to drink wine or strong drink (not even to eat grapes), or eat any unclean thing, or cut his hair. Ever.

Part of the promise was that he would begin to deliver Israel from the hands of the Philistines. The instructions were repeated later to the boy's father. Then, as promised, a boy-child was born, and he was named Samson.

The story fast-forwards to the now-young adult Samson, hanging out in Timnath. This does not look good, since his vow prohibited him from partaking of grapes, and Timnath was the Napa Valley of its day. While visiting there, Samson saw a woman, a Philistine girl, of all things, whom he wanted. This troubled his parents, but God was going to use it to pick a fight with the Philistines.

On the way down to make the marriage deal, Samson killed a lion, but failed to mention it to anyone at the time. Next trip by, a swarm of bees had set up shop in the carcass, and it was filled with honey. Samson took the honey, ate it, and shared it, without divulging the source. This is another violation of his vow, since honey eaten out of dead cat road-kill cannot be kosher, I think.

Samson made a bet with thirty local boys, in-laws, probably. He gave them a riddle based on the experience with the lion honey, and wagered new suits for everybody that they couldn't solve it. The Philistines got nasty, and threatened the bride's family with extinction unless she wheedled the answer out of Samson. She whined and cried, and Samson caved. Then the Philistines answered the riddle, as if they were smart.

Samson recognized that they had gotten the answer from his new wife. Not one to welch on a bet, however, he paid the thirty suits of clothes. He just went to a neighboring community and killed thirty guys and took their clothes. The Scripture says that "the Spirit of the Lord came upon him" when he was doing this, so we should understand that God was behind it all. These Philistines were oppressing Israel, and apparently needed killing.

This caused more tragedy, however. Since his would-be father-in-law assumed that Samson didn't want his new wife anymore, she was given to the best man. A quaint wedding custom, don't you think? Shortly after, Samson came to see the girl; he even brought a goat. When he found out that she had been given away to another, he was intensely ticked off, but as always, very creative in his dispensing of mayhem.

He gathered up 300 foxes, and tied torches to their tails (no PETA, either). When he released them into the fields, there was a huge conflagration, and crop failure. This caused the Philistines to turn on the Timnite girl's family, and they got burned up after all. Now Samson felt justified to take further vengeance. He killed a large number of the Philistines, then went and hid out in a rock.

The rest of the Philistines came to that country, and demanded that the trouble-maker be turned over to them. The men of Judah were so submissive to the Philistines, that they went to Samson to bind him over.

Samson made them promise that they would not kill him themselves, but conduct him safely to the enemy.

As soon as he got there, the Spirit came on him, and he popped his ropes. He found a fresh donkey jawbone, and butt-kicking ensued. Before you could say, "jackass-headbasher," a thousand Philistines were smacked down dead. Think Chuck Norris in sandals.

Killing a thousand guys would dehydrate anyone, and Samson was normal in this respect. He gave glory to the Lord for the victory, but wondered if he was going to die anyway, of thirst. God provided. He opened a spring on the spot, and Samson was watered. After that, Samson was the boss of Israel for twenty good years.

Samson had a problem, however. He was all about his appetites, and he had an appetite for girls, especially foreign girls. (Single believer, if you want to please God, it's good to remember what your mama told you, "Keep your eyes open and your pants closed!") *Judges* 10 opens with a visit by Samson to a harlot's house. This account seems to be given to underline Samson's weakness for skirts, and to give witness to another of his exploits. At this time, his fleshliness was getting him into trouble, and God's faithfulness was getting him out. God's faithfulness is given to us in unending measure, but we can foolishly walk out from under his protection. Samson killed thousands of Philistine men, but never met a Philistine woman he could conquer.

Samson had a girlfriend named Delilah, in fact the Bible says he loved her. The Philistines must have seen that she was more than the usual 'ho that Samson hooked up with. They came to her and hired her as a "double agent" of sorts. They paid her a significant sum to get the secret of Samson's strength, and to betray him. She was apparently talented at this sort of thing, and Samson was not much acclaimed for his wisdom.

She began with a rather direct approach, as if Samson was going to just blab away his secret. He toyed with her, giving her some baloney about being tied with green cords, then with new ropes. What he told her, she tried immediately. This should have clued him in on where this relationship was headed, but apparently no.

Delilah pressed on, and Samson was as dumb as dirt. The next lie he told her was closer to the truth. If she would weave his hair into the loom and fasten it with the pin, he'd become just a regular guy. She went to weaving as soon as he dozed off, and woke him when his new 'do was done. As soon as he awoke he got up and left, taking the loom apparatus with him, showing Delilah that she had been lied to again.

Now Delilah whined terribly, and gave Samson the "If you loved me" line. This was so lame; she had already shown what she intended to do with the information. She put up such a fuss that Sam was "annoyed to death." So, he spilled his guts and told her the whole story. Bible students like us are still scratching our heads and speculating about why he did this.

I think that Samson was more in lust than in love, and that does tend to make one stupid. I don't want to be overly crude, but apparently Delilah held on to Samson by something other than his pure heart. The reason I point this out so bluntly is that it still happens today, and many of you really need the warning. Read on and learn.

Another very logical explanation says that Samson did not really think that this attempt to steal his strength would be effective either. Perhaps he had gotten so backslidden and presumptuous that he thought the power actually belonged to him. He had apparently been a frequent visitor to Wine Country, and had handled a dead lion carcass at least once, eating honey out of it (Yum!). Both these things seem to be violations of his Nazarite vows. His strength remained, however, and perhaps this is why he was so foolish.

You see, God didn't cut him off at the first rule violation. In His mercy, God held on to Sammy, literally, by the hair of the head. When the hair was gone, it may well have been the last condition of the vow to be violated. God, in His holiness, could not indulge Samson by ignoring this arrogance.

But, we get ahead of ourselves. What the girl did was get Samson off to sleep, and call for a barber. When Sam was shorn to the skin, she tested him, and found him to be like Superman after a kryptonite milk shake. Now she called for the Philistines, and they came to the scene.

"Awake Samson, the Philistines are upon you!" she said. He did awaken, and thought that he would get up and pass out a round of whuppin', just like before. He did not know that the Lord had departed from him, leaving him bald and defenseless in the lap of that ungodly and cold-hearted woman. He found out the truth of his sad situation right away, but too late.

The Philistines grabbed Samson, and poked out his eyes. Then they took him down to Gaza, where he was bound with chains and put to work at the mill, like a dumb ox. From this experience, we get a classic outline for a message on sin, which has probably been preached for centuries in the English language.

Sin blinds, then binds, then grinds. Many a regretful sinner can testify to this truth, and the message is an effective one still today. Yet there is another good text here for your next camp meeting assignment.

Chapter fifteen, verse twenty-two says, "However, the hair of his head began to grow again, after it was shaved off." Satan always over plays his hand. Why didn't they just kill Samson when they had him? They knew nothing of the mercy of God, and of the power of grace available to us through repentance. This is a redemption story, and as Samson's hair grew back, he repented of his willfulness, becoming submissive once again to God's requirements of him.

One day the gloating Philistine bosses called for Samson to be brought to the banquet hall for show and tell. They were celebrating their false fish-god Dagon, and thought another chance to mock Samson and his God would be fun. When he came to the party, however, he was a different fellow.

The humbled hero could hear the huge crowd before he even got to the room. Something about drinking dulls the hearing, and drunks just get louder as they go. As he was led from the grinding stone to the banqueting hall, he had been thinking. And praying.

He had been a fool. He had presumed upon the power and holiness of God. God's intention for him to judge Israel in wisdom and strength into his elder years had been squandered, for the fleshly pleasures of a skank who rented her loyalty out for money.

His eyes didn't hurt anymore; the empty sockets had healed, but blindness does not get better with time. You can adjust your habits and attitudes, you can learn coping skills, but you still just can't see. There is a frustration that comes with the loss of vision that eats at you constantly. Losing vision seems worse than being born blind. Samson had been a free and powerful man, able to do as he pleased, and indeed he had. Now, he lived in blindness and captivity. It had taught him humility before God, but he was still in a downer mood a lot of the time.

Arriving at the booze-hall, Samson stood tall and straight. He could still do that much. He took inventory with the senses he still had. Full hall. Dagon party. Important big-shots of the Philistines. Upper crust of society, the people who made the city function. "The people who paid to have me betrayed and blinded!" he muttered to himself and to God. "Bored with their boozing and whoring —" The thought of their whoring caused his grief to come to an abrupt halt, in a jolt of realization.

She would be there. Why wouldn't she be? She was rich, now, and in great favor with the Philistine lords. Since she wasn't fooling around with Samson anymore, some other guy would surely have moved in, and he would have to be a rich and powerful jerk to keep a high-maintenance hottie like Delilah. Just the kind of guy that this hall would be full of.

Sam actually wasn't sure how he felt about this. He had loved her, but he was so over that now. Blinding and binding and grinding will do that to a man. Still, you never fully eradicate those soft feelings for a girl like that, even when she's poison.

As he stood there at the entrance, the guests began to take notice of his arrival, and the blasphemies jarred him from the thoughts of Delilah. This was the worst of it. Worse than the blindness. Worse than the chains, or the grindstone. His stupidity had shamed God. This uncircumcised bunch had gotten the upper hand through his foolishness, not their strength, and now they acted like they and their god had really accomplished something. "Stupid fish-heads! It would serve them right if I—"

He hadn't had a thought like that in a long time. And—Hello!—as the thought began to form, a feeling began to wash over Samson that he hadn't felt since before the shearing. In a flash of godly insight he understood it all. God had departed, due to Samson's sin, but He had never deserted His warrior. The Spirit of the Lord was upon Samson, and the man thought about what was happening, where he was, who he faced, and the immediate future. The very short, immediate, future.

Samson knew what he would do, but this time, he truly understood Who would provide the power. The fish-freaks had placed him between the pillars, in the most prominent place, for show. And a show they would get.

This time, Samson's feat of strength would not come with the old cockiness. This time there would be no statement of smart-alecky anger to tell them why they deserved to die. This time Samson wouldn't address the Philistines at all. He only addressed his God, asking for the Spirit to come once more and enable him, to avenge him the loss of his eyes, and to let him die with the Philistines.

It was not really suicide. Samson was not doing this for the purpose of killing himself; he only recognized that he would be his own collateral damage, and he was willing. He took hold of the main pillars of the house and leaned into them. Before the drunken crowd knew what was "going down," it was going down on their heads. Some 3,000 of the "best people" of the kingdom were snuffed in a terrible moment, more than Samson had taken out in his whole life.

When his soul left his body, Samson was no longer blind. He went to where the Old Testament heroes were gathered, and was greeted, not as a perfect one, but as one of the Faithful Forgiven.

And so it went. Israel wandered on, some of them falling into idolatry, and doing awful things, even to the point of losing pretty much an entire tribe. They were supposed to be the People of God, yet much of what they do in this book seems crude and bizarre. The last verse of the book closes the tragic story with a sad insight. It gives us some understanding of the situation, it clears God of the blame, and it sets the scene for what is to come.

"In those days there was no king in Israel; everyone did what was right in his own eyes."

But it wasn't all depressing. There's the story of Ruth. It is not found in *Judges,* but it happened during that time. Out of the middle of the miserable up and down time of the Judges comes one of the sweetest stories in the Bible. The story didn't start out that way, however.

The story of Ruth starts out sadly. Sort of *Les Miserables*, without the music. In the days of the Judges, there was a famine in the land. Elimelech left the country with his wife Naomi and their two sons, and beat it for the greener grass of Moab. We should take note that not everyone did this. The land of Israel had been given to God's people by

His promise, but when things got tough, Eli turned his back on what God had promised, and struck out on his own.

Life might have looked better for a while. The family assimilated into the Moabite community. The boys, Chilion and Mahlon, found local girls to marry, which would not have been pleasing to God, but couldn't have been a surprise to their parents.

Then the men all died. First Elimelech, perhaps before the boys were even married. Then eventually both sons checked out, leaving the three women to face a hard life as widows, before we even get to the sixth verse. When you married a man in those days, you really were betting your life on his longevity and success. If he did not achieve either, you were just sort of dead in the dirt.

The two younger women, Orpah and Ruth, had some assets. They were not elderly, and they were in their homeland. They could find husbands. Their situation was difficult, but not hopeless. Naomi, on the other hand, was in a miserable position. She was an old lady, and she was a foreigner, the widow of a foreigner. None of the neighbors had any obligation to be kind to her, and compassion had really not come into fashion at that time.

The girls started out making a commitment to their mother-in-law, but Naomi explained to them how impractical it would be for them to stay with her. This made sense to Orpah, who decided to go home. Ruth, on the other hand, decided that Naomi *was* her home. She proclaimed that she would identify henceforth with Naomi's fortunes, her people, and her God. She made a declaration to her mother-in-law that has occasionally been lifted out of its scriptural context and romantically misinterpreted in our times. I wonder how many brides who choose to refer to this passage in their weddings, or have "Whither Thou Goest" sung during the ceremony actually realize that these words were spoken by a widow to her mother-in-law.

But this parting of the three ladies deserves a closer look. Scripture says that "Orpah kissed her mother-in-law, but Ruth clung to her." Three very separate times, Naomi says to her son's widows, "Return." (In 1:11, 12 she repeats it twice, so you could even count four times.) Twice was enough for Orpah; she loved Naomi, but the elder woman made a lot of sense. Orpah had fulfilled her obligation to Naomi, and she went home to get on with her life.

Naomi was a "driven" woman. Circumstances had taken her to where she was, and events were driving her to where she was going. She had to follow her husband to Moab, then he died. The boys died on her, and left her alone in a strange land. This was not what she would have chosen for the particulars of her life, but she did choose to throw in her lot with Elimelech, and life had driven her since then. Naomi, just like "driven" people that you know, is all about duty.

Orpah was "drifting." Orpah is a picture of those who have an acquaintance with God, those who have "kissed" him, but do not cling—don't commit their lives. She could have gone either way, but she didn't have to. Things happened to her, she made nothing happen. She started to follow Naomi, but when Naomi explained why this was not good for her, she changed her mind and went home. This apparently ended her experience with Israel, Israel's people, and Israel's God. She was absorbed back into Moab, and disappears from the Bible, never to be heard from again.

Ruth was "drawn." Ruth was not *"driven"* or *"drifting."* Naomi had something that Ruth had seen and wanted, and the younger woman latched on to it. All Ruth knew about the place they were going was that the people there were Naomi's people, and that was enough. The presence of the God of Israel that had filtered through Naomi to Ruth drew her. She recognized that the uncertainty of life with Naomi was to be preferred to anything she knew about life in Moab. Ruth made a decision of faith, and set in motion events more powerful than she could probably have imagined.

When they returned to Naomi's people, the bereaved mother/widow gave vent to her sorrow, and showed just how depressed she was. But Naomi was humble before God, and it is mentioned, incidentally, that the barley harvest was beginning. Like Samson's returning hair, this is a hint of a comeback. The "redemption" element of this story is about to kick in. Pay attention.

That was just chapter one. As the next chapter opens, we are introduced to Boaz, a clan-brother of Elimelech. Ruthie asked to be allowed to glean a living for herself and Naomi. This was how Old Testament Israel provided for the poor. Po' folk came in and picked up what the harvesters left behind, plus, the corners were left unpicked for their benefit.

The plucky lass went to work with the gleaning crew, and it "happened" by the hand of God, that she was gleaning in Boaz's field. She caught the boss's eye, since it can be assumed that everyone usually knew everyone, and Ruth was a new girl on the job. The boss was almost certainly not an old man, although mature. Of course, about the first thing this eligible bachelor noticed when he got to the field that day was the sudden appearance of this young woman. Boaz asked his foreman whose girl this was, and as is usually the case in small rural communities, the foreman already knew. As is also the case in such small towns, Bo already knew the girl's story.

He knew of the tragedy back in Moab. He knew of this girl's commitment and faithfulness to her mother-in-law, the widow of his own kinsman. He knew that she was there because she chose to be, and that she was working hard to make the best of a bad situation. He appreciated her, and he knew that she was family.

He gave instructions to his reapers, and to Ruth, that made her practically a part of Boaz's crew. Boaz and Ruth exchanged statements of gratitude, and she joined the reapers and boss for lunch. She had a prosperous afternoon, and returned to Naomi with a good days' gleaning. Naomi noticed that someone had helped Ruth do well, and asked in whose field she had worked. When the old girl heard that it was Bo's field, she got really happy. Gleaning was insecure and dangerous work for a young lady like Ruth, so it was a great favor from the Lord that she had an invitation to stay in Boaz's field for the entire harvest. I suspect that as time passed, and these two worked in their respective places in the harvest, they got better acquainted—and "twitterpation" may even have set in somewhere along the way.

This went on through the barley harvest and the wheat harvest, and Naomi began seriously thinking about what would come next. She knew the customs of her people, and she sent Ruth on a mission that seems strange to us of another time and place. What happened here revolves around an idea expressed by a Hebrew word: *goel*. The word means "kinsman-redeemer," and normally, I'd just use English, but we don't really have this idea in our culture, so I'm using the Hebrew term. Besides, it's shorter.

Under the Law of Moses, a widow had a right to ask the nearest kinsman of her departed husband to marry her, thus "redeeming" her in the society. The guy who did this was the *goel*. Naomi looked at Boaz and his kind behavior toward Ruth, and saw *goel* written on his forehead.

Naomi's desire was security for Ruth; Ruth's motive was provision for herself and for Naomi. Everyone's motives were pure; there is nothing sleazy about this story. I used to think that Boaz was pretty clueless about all this, but in his excellent book, *Ruth—the Romance of Redemption*, Dr. J. Vernon McGee informs us otherwise. Boaz knew who he was, and had done all that he could properly do to "court" Ruth. It was now her move.

It seems that Naomi prepared Ruth very effectively. Since she was now prepared to be redeemed, she probably changed out of her widow's mourning clothes and we know she washed and anointed herself. I'll bet she "cleaned up pretty good." According to Naomi's instruction, Ruth went to the threshing floor, after the evening supper. A company sleepover at the threshing floor was the custom, due to the nature of the threshing, which went on into the late evening. The day's work was capped off with a big midnight supper, and then the whole group found spots on the floor to sleep a few hours until morning. Whole families may have been represented in the assembly of threshers, and while it was obviously dark, there was little occasion for privacy.

Ruth took note of where Boaz was sleeping, and went to his spot by the end of the grain heap. There, a highly symbolic and very touching communication ensued between Ruth and Boaz. It was all significant, and all honorable. The girl took a position at his feet, covered herself with his cloak, and waited. In a while, he woke up, and—Lord above!— there was a woman at his feet. It was Ruth, and it probably did not escape his notice that she had gotten out of her widow's garb, into a spiffier ensemble.

It wasn't Sadie Hawkins Day, or Leap Year. This all had to do with the fact that Boaz was a kinsman of Elimelech, Ruth's dead former fa- ther-in-law. His benevolence to her during the harvest had shown that he would be a likely *goel.* Her actions that night said that she was amenable to this idea, and if he wanted to make a formal offer, she was available for redemption by him.

Ruth could have done this publicly, before the whole town. How- ever, had Naomi and Ruth's beliefs about Boaz been inaccurate, they would have been putting a nice guy in a terribly embarrassing position. He was blessed and impressed by Ruth's kindness in coming to him, rather than to some young hunk, and he agreed to do his part as kins- man, because everybody knew by now what a babe of class and quality Ruth was.

However, there was a closer kinsman than Boaz, and that fellow had the first right of redemption. The fact that Boaz already knew about this indicates that he was likely thinking in the same direction as the ladies. This is why Ruth took off from the threshing floor, before anyone recognized her. There could be no question about their integrity, since the nearer kinsman had the priority claim, if he chose to exercise it. Boaz went immediately to work on this.

Right away, a meeting was arranged, and the other fellow was quite anxious to claim his property, until he was informed that such redemption would have to include marriage to Ruth. This he could not do, due to issues related to his own inheritance. The nearer kinsman is a picture of the law, which would redeem us if it had the power, but does not. Boaz was allowed to buy out Naomi's inheritance, everything from Elimelech, Chilion, and Mahlon, which aside from Ruth, amounted to approximately squat.

What Boaz did for Ruth is what Christ did for us—redemption. It differs from the Exodus story in that the deliverer didn't come to Ruth, but she came to him. She was a gentile, remember, a descendant of Lot's debauchery with his daughter. She had no claim on the covenant, but like the rest of us gentiles, she got in by faith in the Redeemer.

Her redeemer claimed her, not for what she could offer to him, but in order to offer something to her. The town probably had other young ladies from which Boaz could select a bride, but the relationship of redeemer was not possible with them. Because of the covenant within the family, Boaz chose to marry and redeem Ruth. Because of the Covenant, our Redeemer has chosen us.

They got married, and right away Ruth bore a boy. Naomi was blessed to have this baby in her old age, and his name was Obed. This was written sometime after the fact, so the writer goes on to tell us that Obed became the father of Jesse, and that Jesse was the father of David.

David. Remember that name. We'll come back to it later.

14
So, You Want a King?
1 Samuel 1-16
1 Chronicles 1-10

It so often goes badly with multiple wives. Even when some members of the marriage are happy, others are frequently not. God didn't create polygamy; He has never been in favor of it, being omniscient and all, as He is. He has put up with it, at times, but it is never wise. However, as I told you in the *Genesis* stories, it is marriage, and the Bible defines marriage as honorable.

The marriage of Elkanah to Hannah and Peninnah illustrates some of the problems that multiple spouses can generate. Elkanah loved Hannah greatly, but she had borne no children. He loved Peninnah also. Perhaps greatly, but certainly adequately, since she had children. Every year, the whole family would go up to Shiloh to worship. When passing out the portions that everyone was to offer in sacrifice, Elkanah would hand out double portions to Hannah, to reassure her of his love for her.

Peninnah, on the other hand, took the annual opportunity to provoke Hannah, rubbing in the fact that, while Hannah was barren, Peninnah was poppin' 'em out like twinkies at the Hostess plant. Hannah would get all sad and lose her appetite. In time, Hannah had enough. She got up from the feasting table and headed to the House of the Lord. (Yeah, that'll preach!)

At the entry to the tabernacle, Hannah poured her heart out to God. Eli, the priest was sitting nearby, and to him, Hannah just looked like another crying drunk. I have seen drunks that react that way. They get all religious and weepy, and often want to get saved, if they're in church. Eli knew the type, and rebuked this woman cynically.

Hannah answered humbly and sincerely, and Eli saw that she was no drunk, but a woman with a great need. He spoke with encouragement, "Go in peace, and may the God of Israel grant your petition. . ." Hannah received faith in this, and went her way. She even started eating again, which was good, because before long she was pregnant.

Hannah had been desperate in her prayer. Desperation is often a good thing, because it takes us into serious petition and conversation with God. Not negotiation and deal making; those do not move God's heart. Hannah made a promise to God, not a deal. The child that would come would be given back to God's service.

Hannah had come to God with more-than-the-usual prayer. He would respond with more-than-the-usual results. This boy would be special, and the boy would become a special man. His name was Samuel, and he is rare among those whose story is told in these pages. He was obedient to God without failing, while those around him, even those who served God, would behave in very fallible ways. You want to "give birth to a Samuel?" Then pray like Hannah.

I don't remember ever seeing a movie about the life of Samuel. If somebody would give me a whole lot of money for the project, I'd write one, and produce it. He is well worth it. He spans the time between the judges and the kings, and directs Israel through a crucial time in its history. His life was full of drama, including direct communication with God, political intrigue, and big battlefield scenes. If Hollywood or TBN is not interested, at least Ken Burns should be.

Remember Eli? He had gotten old and fat, and couldn't see well. He had two rowdy boys that he wouldn't control. They grew up into a couple of real jerks. Problem was, they were in the position of priests. They ignored what the law said about taking the priest's portion of the sacrifices, and they just took what they wanted. Aside from being rude and arrogant, this inhibited the people's obedience in worship, and God was displeased. The boys also were presumptuous with the young ladies, using their influence as an opportunity for horizontal "body min-istry," right there in the church house. Again, God was displeased. So were the people.

But as for Hannah and her house, things went well. When Samuel was old enough, Hannah fulfilled her vow to the Lord, bringing little Sammy to the Temple. She brought him a new little Junior Priest outfit each year when they came to sacrifice. Eli blessed her and her husband annually for her faithfulness, and Hannah bore five more kids. Guess that pretty much shut Penninah's mouth.

The boy Samuel was raised in the Temple, and became Eli's second chance at boy-raising. Samuel ministered in temple service as he grew up, and was faithful at it. He had these wicked foster brothers, and that must have been challenging, but instructive to the boy. Kind of like Cinderella, except Samuel was real.

Eli did speak to his nasty boys, but took no action to protect the integrity of the Lord's house. This displeased God more, and a man of God was dispatched to pronounce a whammy upon Eli's house and descendants. Right after this visit, God came to young Samuel by night and began the transition.

First Samuel, chapter three sets the scene carefully, telling us 1) the Word of the Lord was rare in those days, and visions were infrequent, 2) the "lamp of God" had not yet gone out, and 3) Samuel did not yet know the Lord. The Lord called out to Samuel, and the boy answered, think-ing it was the old man, Eli. He went to Eli, who must have been both-ered to have been awakened from a sound, old man quality slumber by the kid. He sent Sammy back to bed, but the Lord called the boy again.

This teaches us so much about the passing of the presence of God between generations. God will call out to the young ones, even before they know Him. He skips over those who neglect and despise His ways, and chooses those who are dedicated to Him. The older ones are often slow to recognize God's calling to the next generation; they just want them to go back to sleep and not bother anyone. But it is God Who has awakened the chosen of the next generation, and those whose hearts are experienced and tender towards God will, like Eli, eventually figure out what is happening.

Three times this calling happened, and Eli was finally awake enough to realize that God was calling the boy. He sent Samuel back to bed, this time with instructions to answer the next call by saying, "Speak, Lord, for your servant hears." This is an important responsibility of the elder generation, to tell the younger ones how to respond to God's calling. When God spoke again, Samuel obeyed the boss's instructions. God began to tell Samuel what was coming for Eli and his kin. This began a long, close, relationship between God and Samuel.

Next morning, Eli asked what God had said. This also illustrates the dynamic which should exist between the generations. As Eli had instructed Samuel in how to hear and respond to the Lord, so Samuel was expected to share the fresh word from God with his elder. Samuel was at first afraid to tell what he had heard, but Eli insisted.

Samuel was learning to faithfully deliver the Word of the Lord, a skill for which he would become famous. Eli received that Word of the Lord, which is what the elder generation must do, if we expect the flow of God's Spirit to continue. He would accept God's judgment and wait for its (and his own) execution.

Samuel grew, and so did his reputation. Before long, all Israel knew that the Word of the Lord was back, and that Samuel was hearing it. That must have given hope to those who were tired of the evil behavior of Eli's sons.

The current campaign against the Philistines was going poorly. When Israel sought to determine what was wrong, some brainiac suggested that the presence of the Ark of God would be a "good luck charm" to aid them in their battle.

This wasn't "Noah's Ark," but the big, gold, ceremonial box, upon which the Presence of God dwelt. It had been with them since Moses' time, in the holiest place of the Tabernacle. It had been given near-idol status by the Israelites.

This is the way religion thinks. Israel was focused on having the Ark of God on hand, more than they were concerned about whether the God of the Ark was with them in battle. He wasn't, really. They brought the Ark in for a big pep rally, and hyped themselves into an enthusiastic state, illustrating for us the difference between noise and worship. They made so much noise that they scared their enemies into desperation. The desperate and surprised Philistines waxed Israel pretty badly, killing *beaucoup* Israelites and taking their Ark home as a trophy. Hophni and Phineas, Eli's evil boys, took for themselves the "important position" near the Ark. This probably got them killed. Well, something got them killed, for dead they were.

Eli was back at home base awaiting news, and he was nervous. He took the news about Israel's defeat pretty well. He took the word about the death of his sons well, because God had already let him know it was coming, and he knew they deserved it. The news about the capture of the Ark he did not take well. When the messenger told him that the Ark was lost, he fell over backwards and broke his neck, for as I may have told you, he was ninety-eight years old, and fat.

God had allowed this defeat of Israel, but that didn't mean he was now backing the Philistines. The Ark, a means of blessing to Israel, was a channel of curses in the wrong hands. The Philistines brought the Ark into the house of their god, Dagon.

Remember Dagon from the "Samson" story? A real loser of a god. Our God has patience with the ignorant, but He was not going to tolerate the disrespect of having the Ark put in some other god's temple, and being treated like a regular old idol. The next morning, Dagon was on his fishy stone face before the Ark. They set him up again, and the next day, there he was on the ground again, but with his head and hands cut off!

For this insolence, the people of the town were touched by God with judgment. Many were killed outright, and for others, there was an outbreak of "tumors" (NASB), which the KJV translates, "emerods," and Matthew Henry plainly describes as "piles," an archaic description of hemorrhoids. Much suffering for their disrespect of God's Ark. Being the religious, idolatrous type, they were not interested in repenting and making a covenant with God, but only with ridding themselves of this (to them) pain-in-the-butt Ark. They put an apology offering with the Ark, consisting of golden hemorrhoids and golden mice, and sent it back to Israel.

(I know what a golden mouse would look like, but a golden hemorrhoid? Well, let's just not go there.)

The Ark came back to Israel, but 50,000+ Israelites died, because some looked into it, in disobedience. It sat for twenty years out in the boonies, and then Samuel called the people to repentance and revival. They got right with God, then He delivered them from Philistine oppression. Things were good for a while.

Samuel rode a circuit and judged Israel for many years, but we all get old, if we live long enough. Ministry is not a family business. You can't pass your relationship with God on to your children. They must have their own. Samuel had no Bible to teach him this. He appointed his two sons as judges over Israel, but they turned out crooked. This irritated all Israel, and a "We want a king" movement began.

The elders met with Samuel and demanded that he appoint a king for them. This hurt his feelings at first, but God assured Samuel that the people were just treating him the way they had always treated God. It was God who was being rejected, not Samuel. The old judge was to anoint the man God showed him to be king, but he was to warn the people that this "king" thing was not all as good as advertised.

Samuel told the nation all that a king would demand of them, and how unhappy they would be. They still wanted to "be like other nations" rather than trust in the Lord, so Samuel proceeded. A regal-looking, tall young man named Saul was identified and called out to be King. Samuel anointed Saul, the Holy Spirit anointed him, and most of the people, the good ones, anyway, recognized him as their new King. Samuel gave a farewell address to the nation, and stepped back. From now on, he would address the King, not the people.

The new king went home after his coronation. There never being a king before, there was no real job description, or even a place dedicated for him to live. So, he went back to the farm. Meanwhile, a bully besieged one of the cities of Israel, and demanded the right eye of all the men as a payment for their lives. War was kind of polite in those days, so a seven day waiting period was allowed, to see if anyone would come to the rescue. This was enough time for Saul to get the word, and the kingliness in him rose up.

Saul sent pieces of ox carcass throughout Israel, and very forcefully put out the notice that anyone who did not come out for the battle would end up like the oxen. This raised an army, and the bully was routed. The new king had saved the day.

Saul now looked good, but had trouble immediately. He picked a fight with the Philistines, and those guys brought an army that outnumbered Israel twelve to one. Saul was waiting for Samuel to come and offer a proper sacrifice before the battle commenced. Samuel took a while. Samuel took seven days, and that was all Saul could endure. He took it upon himself to offer the sacrifice, which was improper. Saul was a prophet and king, but not a priest. He was out of order, and Samuel showed up as soon as the sacrifice was offered. Busted!

Saul offered lame excuses, but Samuel cut to the heart of the issue. Because of Saul's foolishness, God was not going to allow his line to remain upon the throne forever. In fact, Samuel tells Saul that his successor has already been chosen. He does not name him, but describes him as "a man after (God's) own heart."

Saul continues to be unwise. His son, Jonathan, was quite a young warrior, but Saul was not as quick with his faith. While Saul had the troops in "wait mode," Jonathan was making like the Terminator with the Philistines. After the rest of the army got into the battle, a great victory was shared by all Israel. However, Saul had the army on a fast, not an example of great commanding. For goodness sake, feed the army; tell the folks back home to fast!

Jonathan had not gotten word about the fast. He found some honey, and ate it, and felt good about it. Probably killed more Philistines because of it. When they told him about his dad's order, he was not impressed. His logic persuaded the people, and the next enemy outpost that got raided, the poor enemy soldiers were fortunate not to have been eaten themselves, in the rush of hungry Israelites.

Saul wanted to know who had caused the people to disregard his order to fast. They took lots and the lot fell to Jonathan. Saul was ready to kill his son in obstinate, religious stubbornness, but the people intervened.

Samuel brought orders to Saul to go and completely annihilate the people of Amalek. Not one living creature of that nation was to be spared alive. This they did—almost. Worthless stuff and people were destroyed but good livestock, and the king, were preserved. Samuel knew this right away.

Notice, the Prophet shows up when the King disobeys. Even today, this is a characteristic of prophetic leadership. When kingly leadership needs support and direction, or outright fails, the prophet is often called upon to step up, not to usurp or disrespect leadership, but to speak God's word to the leaders and the people.

Saul, as he tended to do, made more excuses, but Samuel was not buying. Now a stronger rebuke than the first was given. Earlier, when

Saul improperly offered the sacrifice, God sent Samuel to tell him that his dynasty would not last forever. This time, Samuel told the King that God said, "You're fired!" Saul was rejected from being king over Israel.

Samuel mourned, God showed regret, but eventually, Samuel was sent to anoint the next king. God instructed him to go to Bethlehem, ostensibly to make a sacrifice, but really to anoint a son of Jesse as king. Samuel came into town, which initially caused a stir, but he assured the people that he had come in peace.

The sons of Jesse were brought in, eldest to least, and Samuel was less impressed with each one. Samuel was looking at their outward appearance, but God said that He was looking at the heart. All the boys in the house came and went by, and God said, "Nope" to each one. The confused Samuel asked, "Are these all you have?" He was told, "The youngest is out with the sheep." Says Samuel, "Get him; we won't eat until he gets here."

He was a good-looking kid, with "beautiful eyes and a handsome appearance," but he was after all, a kid. Samuel was likely both surprised and amused when God said, "Arise and anoint him." The Prophet took the horn of oil and anointed the youngest boy in the presence of all the older brothers. His name was David.

15
David: The Shepherd Boy Becomes King
1 Samuel 17-31

Saul was really going bad. Scripture tells us that the Spirit of the Lord departed from him, and an "evil spirit from the Lord" came and troubled him. Commentators and scholars have interpreted this in various ways, but what you need to know is that this is a bad thing. A very bad thing.

It was thought that good music would lessen the evilness Saul was exhibiting, so it was suggested that a skillful harpist be found to play for him. One of the guys hanging around the King said he knew a son of Jesse who:

1. Was a good musician
2. Was a mighty man of valor—one would have to be to hang around this wacko
3. Was prudent in speech—no blabbermouths in the throne room
4. Was a handsome man—in their culture and time, this was not as fruity as it sounds to us; apparently, ugly people need not apply for palace work, however.
5. Had the Lord with him—this turned out to be his most important attribute

So, once again, David was called from the flock to center stage. He came bearing produce from home, and soon had won the king's favor. David took the position of "armor bearer," a kind of "caddy to the King." He moved into the palace, for at least a time, although he apparently traveled home occasionally to tend his aged father's sheep.

On one of these trips home, Jesse gave David a donkey-load of groceries and sent him back to the battle front. Israel was engaged with the Philistines in one of their frequent wars. David got loaded up and went back to the fight. When he got there, apparently things had changed dramatically.

The Philistines and Israelites were at a standoff on opposite mountains, looking at each other across a big valley. For forty days, a monster named Goliath had been stomping out into the valley and issuing a challenge to Israel: One of Saul's army could come and fight him, one-on-one, winner-take-all. The loser's nation would serve the winner's. Goliath was huge—over nine feet tall—and one bad, very bad, man.

Now myself, I would have had about a half-dozen of my best archers hidden out by dark, behind the rocks somewhere, waiting. When the old boy came out to yell at us the next morning, they could pop up and take target practice on his freakishly huge target, or perhaps lure him into a twelve-foot hole. I'm a child of the Vietnam era; I guess I think differently than Old Testament warriors. Maybe they just didn't do sneaky back then.

David did not understand this challenge at all. I mean, he did not understand why it had gone on for so long. He started by asking innocent questions. What was the bounty for the man who was up to the challenge? Who is this uncircumcised Philistine who dares defy the army of the Lord?

The people told David what he wanted to know, but David's oldest brother Eliab told him something else entirely. Eliab snarled at David like a jealous big brother, questioning his motives, and belittling his place in the family and the kingdom. Compare *1 Samuel* 16:18 with 17:28 to see how much the opinion of our worth can vary between those who know "of" us and those who "know" us.

With seven big brothers, David had heard that stuff all his young life, and he didn't really seem to care. With intentional cluelessness he said, "What? It was just a question!" And he kept asking. Apparently getting a consistent answer, and finding no one else interested in "cage-fighting" Goliath, the boy stepped up.

Saul heard that David was inquiring about the job of giantkiller, and sent for him. David came with words of assurance to the King, but Saul was incredulous about this kid from the country who was going to deliver them all. To the King, it looks like Pee Wee Herman is picking a fight with Jet Li, and a nine-foot Jet Li at that. But David had things Pee Wee would not, like a pure heart, and a word from God.

And a resume. When David was out with the sheep, they had been assaulted by wild predators—lions and bears and such. David had killed lions, and killed bears, and did not see this goon as being significantly different. Additionally, faith was operating in David's heart. True faith in God doesn't make us goofy, and shouldn't be used as an excuse for squirrelliness, but God often gives His people extra information which changes the situation.

This would have been a suicide mission, except that God had let David know that He would be involved. And besides, sometimes you have to do the right thing, instead of the "wise" thing. As Goliath roars his challenge, we can almost hear David whisper to himself, "That's just *wrong*!" (If he had been a native Texan, like me, he would have said, "Thatain'tright!") It seemed perfectly logical to David, that since this heathen had challenged the armies of the living God, Goliath would have to be killed. If no one else would, he would. He would rather get killed defending the honor of Israel's God than to hang out with an army that wouldn't.

Why do you suppose the King didn't "do the right thing?" I think it was because he knew that God's favor was gone. Saul knew that he had been fired as king, and was just "waiting for the other shoe to drop." He wasn't going to "throw that shoe down" by running out on the field and offering himself to Goliath, when he knew God's anointing was gone.

Saul tried to be helpful, however. He offered his armor to David for the fight. David couldn't be David in the King's gear, which he had not tested. Better to do what you know than try something new at the last minute. I'll bet a good first baseman wouldn't wear a new glove straight out of the box into the World Series. David was a shepherd, and he would fight in shepherd's armor.

Time for the Smackdown. Out into the valley went "The Kid." From the other corner came "The Monster." On the opposing hillsides stood their respective armies in battle array, but doing no battle. It must have gotten really quiet. Maybe some "spaghetti western" showdown music was playing somewhere. I hear it, anyway.

Goliath strode forcefully out to face his opponent, probably curious as to what kind of champion Israel could put forth. His shield bearer went before him, and they expected a victorious, but conventional effort. Then the giant saw the "warrior" who would oppose him. David, the shepherd boy, stood there looking much like a shepherd boy, staff in one hand, strap of leather in the other. Apparently alone. No shield bearer—no shield to bear.

We can learn things from examining the words that passed between the two fighters. Goliath mocked the "Hebrew champion," and cursed him by his Philistine gods. Then he threatened, the method by which one would intimidate an adversary. "Come here, and I will feed you to the birds and the beasts!" There is a kind of formal "battle rhetoric" going on here, and God uses it to His glory.

David wanted everyone to know Who was really fighting this battle, so he answered the giant's curses and threats one by one. Goliath mocked David for bringing a "stick" to the battle, so David told the soldier that victory would not come by a "sword, a spear, and a javelin." Since Goliath had invoked his gods to curse David, David declared that he would defeat Goliath "in the name of the Lord of hosts, the God of the armies of Israel." Just as Goliath boasted that he would feed David's flesh to the critters, David told Goliath that he would not only take his head, but give his whole army to the wild animals for lunch. I can almost hear David say, "I'll spank you. . . and the horse you rode in on!"

Goliath lumbered toward David, and David ran to the battle. A good tactical move, and another good sermon title. No sense standing there waiting for Goliath to take his best shot. David intended to kill him before he got started. As he ran, David loaded his sling with one of the stones he had picked up for ammo. In one swift verse, he loads the sling, unloads on the giant and watches as the stone sinks into the big boy's forehead, bringing him face-down to the ground. Imagine the stunned silence across the battlefield, as the giant champion of the Philistines went splat in the dirt.

So now David had killed Goliath, but he still had no sword. Not to worry, the giant wouldn't be needing his anymore. Standing over the fallen bully, David pulled Goliath's own sword out and took off the Philistine's head. Upon this confirmation of defeat, the bad guys fled the field. Now every man in Israel felt like being a hero, and the Philistines were routed. David took the big ugly head to Jerusalem, but took Goliath's weapons back to his place.

Thus began David's career as a soldier prior to being installed as king. He did well, but Saul was unhappy. It must be miserable, just waiting to be replaced, when God has already rejected you. Saul was bad enough off, but then that "evil spirit" thing was going on, also. Saul's son, Jonathan, was tight with David, and this caused even greater resentment by the King. Saul was coming apart, but he took a good long while to do it.

Every good thing David did made Saul nuttier. His murderous rage and jealousy poisoned the King's thought processes, and he turned against his own children. David had married Saul's daughter Michal, and she wouldn't sell him out to crazy old Dad. Jonathan was his best bud, and helped David escape. Little by little, a civil war of sorts was developing, but it was not because David was in rebellion. He and those who were with him just wanted to stay alive.

Saul chased David all around the countryside. David and his crew were helped by the people, with the exception of those loyal to Saul. Those folk would squeal, and Saul got just enough information to keep him crazy and in the hunt for David, just a step or two behind.

David had opportunities to kill Saul, and be named king, but he would not. He knew what was right, and trusted God to make him king, in His own time. No one could say that David had achieved the kingdom by his own hand.

He and his posse had many adventures, enough to fill a book of their own. Like the time David had to fake being crazy himself, and the time they spent being wanna-be Philistines. I think the story of David and his mighty men is a good one, as exciting as the stories of Robin Hood or anyone else of legend or fiction. But this story is a true one, a story that will teach us the way to live, not just get a prize in Sunday School. Read it for yourself.

Meanwhile, Saul just got more hateful, and goofier. The last straw was when the King got lonely for his old mentor Samuel. The king went to visit a witch in order to find the prophet. This is messed-up on so many levels, since Saul knew that Samuel was dead. Something extraordinary happened, and when Samuel came up from the "under-world," he had one more piece of really bad news for Saul. "Enough is enough, tomorrow you and your sons will be with me!" As I said, Samuel was now dead, so this was particularly disturbing for Saul to hear.

As Saul was "bottoming out," so was David. He had said to himself, "One day Saul is going to get me." So, he and his entourage went over to the land of the Philistines, and even pretended to raid their old neighborhoods. This worked for a while, but when the time came for the big final battle with Saul's army, the Philistines didn't trust David, and sent he and his guys home. When they got back to the place they had been given as a home town, it had been raided by the Amalekites, those rascals. These were the same Amalekites whom, as you may remember, would have been all dead—had Saul obeyed God.

Their stuff, their wives, their children—all taken away, and their village burned. This was demoralizing, the low point of the story. Grieved, they discussed how best to satisfy their rage. As it always seems to, attention turned to the leadership. Some decided that this was David's fault, and that perhaps it was time to make him accountable for dragging them all over the region. They spoke of stoning, and David heard it. He wasn't sure he didn't agree.

But rather than succumbing to depression, David took a time out with God, and was transformed. First, he strengthened himself in God. He probably did this by directing his focus on to the greatness of his Lord, instead of the awfulness of his troubles. Next, he inquired of the Lord, and when he had been assured of God's promise to restore everything and everyone that had been taken, he came out of his "time out" a changed man. One look at his face and the way he carried himself stopped all the talk of stoning. God's word was to go, overtake the adversaries, and take it all back. That's what they did.

While David's low point was a turning point, bringing him back in line with God's purpose, Saul's low point just kept getting lower. The battle began the next day, and just like Samuel said, Saul and his sons died. The Philistines nailed their corpses to a wall, to admire them as trophies. Except, perhaps, for Saul's head, which may have gone on tour.

Saul's line was ended, and David's began. The king who had looked like a king had failed. The kid who was chosen by God from the flock, the man after God's heart, would take the throne. But not automatically.

16
David: Being King is Harder than it Looks
2 Samuel

After the massacre of the Amalekites and the return of the wives and families, David waited in Ziklag, his location while in exile, for just two days. To David's HQ came a bedraggled fellow with a sad story. The refugee was quick to tell David how Saul had ended up, assuming that this would be good news to Saul's enemy.

The guy was up on Mount Gilboa, just passing through, I guess, when he came upon the mortally wounded King Saul. Saul had leaned on his own spear in an attempt to kill himself before the Philistines got there. The King pleaded with the passer-by to finish the job before the enemy army arrived. Being a cooperative sort of fellow, he complied, and, he told David that this is how he knew that Saul was dead.

The wanderer's account of the battle did not get the expected result from the new "King-elect." David had the guy terminated on the spot, and explained the action by commenting that the helpful stranger should have been afraid to lift his hand against the King. This story is sad because the stranger has informed both Saul and David, "I am an Amalekite." Yes, the same Amalekites that Saul was supposed to kill off—but didn't. The moral of that story is that what you leave alive in disobedience to God will someday come back to finish you off.

David sang a moving song to honor Saul and Jonathan, particularly Jonathan. Proponents of homosexuality have tried to convince us that there was a gay relationship between David and Jonathan. There is no reason to believe this. The rhetoric describing their friendship comes from another culture and century, and those who claim to see homoerotic elements in it are just exposing their own ethnocentricity. Call it a "bromance," perhaps, but nothing gay.

David's home tribe, Judah, anointed him as king, but the rest of Israel was of another mind. The remnants of Saul's regime were still loyal to his house, making his son, Ishbosheth their king. There was war between Israel (Saulists) and Judah (Davidites).

This war gets a little like a soap opera, or the plot of *Lost,* or *Fringe.* One needs to take notes to keep up with who's on which side doing what. In addition to the political loyalties, there were also family blood feuds, and tribalism, and even disputes about women. A good man on the wrong side got murdered by a shady guy on the right side.

Eventually, two old boys snuck in to Ishbosheth's bedroom during siesta and took off with his head. They brought the head to David, who was very consistent about this sort of thing. He reminded them that the Amalekite who had brought news of his "enemy's" death had been immediately put down. They were, too.

Nonetheless, David was now king over all of Israel. He had been thirty years old when he became king over Judah. Seven years later he was made king over all Israel, and would be king for forty years total.

David began to do the things that kings would be expected to do. You might be a good king, or an evil king, but some things just came with the job. Like picking up wives and concubines, and procreating with them. (This shows us that even people like David, who had a faith relationship with God, even people who intended to obey God in their lives, were drifting quite a bit from God's best.)

And they kept having war with the Philistines. After David led Israel in yet another rout of the Philistines (kind of a Yankees-Red Sox thing they had going there), he decided it was time to bring the Ark home. They got together a big parade, and put the Ark on a new cart, and away they went. As the oxen jerked and the Ark wobbled, a man named Uzzah reached to steady it. When He touched the Ark, he died immediately.

In all their zeal, David and his parade crew had pretty much ignored the way God said He wanted His Ark handled. You can't treat God's power and holiness just any old way. David was scared by this response from God, and the Ark stayed with some blessed people along the way for a while. As David realized how much those folks were getting blessed, he determined again to bring the Holy Box back where it belonged.

This time, they did it in a more respectful fashion. After they had gone six paces without anyone dropping dead, they offered a sacrifice. Then they started for the city, with David dancing along the way.

It's hard to dance in royal robes (I've heard). To really get his praise on, David shucked his kingly duds and danced in the clothes he had on underneath. He wasn't dancing naked, in the way we understand that term. That would be way past casual. It was more like someone taking off his jacket and tie, in order to really get down to business.

David's wife Michal saw this and was unhappy. Remember that she was Saul's daughter, and had been raised in the palace. She had a strong sense of protocol and position, and she saw David's dancing as undignified and improper for a king. When he came home she rebuked him for this behavior telling him that he had made a fool of himself before the servant girls and all of Israel.

David's response was like this (paraphrased), "I was dancing before the Lord, who, by the way, chose me over your father and all your family to lead His people. I will be even more undignified and humble than that, but as for those servant girls—they understand a king who worships with all his might!"

David just answered for his own behavior, and did not react to Michal's prideful disrespect and spiritual cluelessness. But it appears that God did. The next verse pointedly informs us that she had no child until the day she died. And I don't think she gave birth on that day, either. It looks like God shut up her womb. Those who despise sincere worship will always tend to be unfruitful.

The King wanted to build a house for the Lord. Nathan the prophet heard from God and delivered a message to David. God said that He would do many great things for David and his descendants. It would be David's son, however, who would build the temple. David took this very well and gave glory to God. Then God really turned on the blessing, and Israel subdued the Philistines and everyone else within reach. Loads of gold and stuff were coming into the kingdom, and David dedicated it all to the Lord.

David asked his research people if anyone was left of Saul's family. Not to get rid of them, but to bless them. There was one guy, Mephibosheth, Jonathan's son. He had been injured as a little boy and was lame. David called for him and the poor guy was probably scared for his life. The King quickly assured him that he had no need to fear, and explained that it was David's desire to bless him, because of Jonathan, his father. Mephibosheth was a bit self-effacing, but grateful, and became part of the King's household from then on.

There are redemption lessons to learn from Mephibosheth. First, God's blessings to you are often not about you at all. Second, if you receive God's favor, accept it. You may not deserve it, but who are you to say that God is wrong to bless you? Mephibosheth is a picture of those who have received grace. We sit in the presence of The Ultimate King, only because He desires for us to be there.

But sometimes grace gets spit upon. After this sweet interlude with 'Phib, the king of the Ammonites died. This fellow had been good to David, so David decided to return a kind gesture to that king's son, Hanun. He sent men to deliver his condolences. When the messengers got there, suspicious advisers to Hanun decided that these were actually spies.

The Ammonites got smart-alecky with David's men, shaving off half of each man's beard, and cutting their clothes off up to the hip. I suppose they had to leave the Ammonite headquarters bare on one side of the face, and with their hineys hanging out. This was a huge humiliation, and David sent word for them that they could stay away until their beards grew back. (And, perhaps, they should pick up some Wranglers at the Ammonite Wal-Mart.)

To quote Bugs Bunny, "Of course, you know, this means war." When the Ammonites saw what they had stepped in, they hired help from the Arameans, and a few other kings. Israel whipped them all, and the Ammonites learned a lesson. So did the Arameans. They were afraid to help the wimpy Ammonites anymore. You have to pick your battle buddies wisely.

After that triumph, David hit a bump in the road. Okay—he crashed and burned.

Hollywood has tried to glam-up this story, and put a romantic tinge on it, but we will not put lipstick on this pig. This is an ugly, tragic story.

During the battle season, David stayed home. That is where the problem starts. If you are fighting the battle God has given you to fight, you are less likely to fall into "skirt trouble." Or, in David's case, "neighbor in the bathtub" trouble.

While idly strolling on his rooftop one night, David noticed a neighbor lady taking a bath, and she was apparently very easy on his eyes. He asked questions and found out that she was Bathsheba, the wife of Uriah, who was one of David's soldiers, one of his "mighty men," in fact. The king sent messengers over and brought her to his place, where they spent at least a night together. There is no appearance of compulsion in this, so they were really in it together.

When you sow seeds, you reap their harvest. Bathsheba sent word to David that she was pregnant. The King quickly had a plan. He called Uriah home from the battle, expecting that the soldier would come home with the natural desire for his own wife, satisfy that desire, and unknow-ingly make it look like the coming child was his.

Uriah was too much man for that. After reporting to David about the war, he stayed just outside the door of David's house, with the King's servants. He did this even though his own place (and his wife) were apparently within sight of the palace. When David asked why, Uriah explained that with the ark in a tent, and "my lord Joab" and his men sleeping in the field, how could he go home and eat, drink and be merry with his wife?

David hadn't counted on this, an incredibly honorable soldier with deep convictions about faithfulness to the cause. This would require ex-tra measures. This would require alcohol. Second night, Uriah had din-ner with David, and the Bartender-in-Chief kept the soldier's glass full. Uriah got drunk, but not so drunk that he forgot who he was and what he believed. (Maybe he just forgot where he lived.) Again, he didn't go home. If Bathsheba had come over to David's back porch where her husband was, maybe things wouldn't have gotten so sordid, but she didn't.

Now David decided to employ the final solution. He wrote to Joab, giving instructions that Uriah was to be put into the fiercest part of the battle. While Uriah was fighting out front, Joab was to withdraw from him, so that he was killed. Sort of a "homicide by combat." And, how cold was this? He gave the note to Uriah to deliver to Joab.

This plan worked, because it depended on Uriah's own faithfulness to get him killed. (For instance, that he wouldn't sneak a peek at the note to Joab.) Killed he was, and word came back to David and Bathsheba. After the mourning period, she moved in with David, and I guess they were planning to tell everyone that the baby was premature when it came. (Would serve them right if it weighed ten pounds, and nobody believed them!)

But David belonged to God, and God was not going to let His Chosen King act like that. God told all to Nathan, and Nathan came before David with a story of his own.

"Hey David, I just heard about these two neighbors out in the countryside. One was very rich, with great flocks and herds. The other was a poor man with nothing but a little home and family. Somewhere the poor father picked up a little lamb, and the kids took it on as a pet. This little ewe lamb was all the family had, and it was hand raised by them all. It ate right there from the table with the family, and even curled up to sleep with dad and the kids at night. To him it was like another daughter.

"The rich guy had company, and wanted to put on a good supper for him. But instead of taking one of his many sheep or fatted calves from his own stock, this low-life stole the poor man's little lamb and slaughtered it to feed his guest."

This story was simple genius. The crisis with Bathsheba's pregnancy was past, or so the king thought. He was not on guard now. It was David's nature to be fair and do right, and he expected the same from all his subjects. We are much better at seeing the ungodliness of others, especially when our spirit is dulled by our own sin. And it was a lamb story. David had probably grown up with lambs like the one in the story, and Nathan might have known this. Anyway, the king bit hard and was white-hot-angry.

David declared, "This man deserves to die, and must pay back the lamb four-fold because he did this thing and had no compassion!"

As soon as David spoke his angry judgment, Nathan opened up on the king with all his prophetic authority and force. "You are the man! Thus says the Lord, 'I made you King of Israel, I saved you from Saul, I gave you his house and his wives, I gave you Israel and Judah—and I would have given you more. Why have you despised the Word of the

Lord like this? You have killed Uriah with the sword of the Ammonites, and have taken his wife.

"Therefore, violence will never leave your house. I will raise up enemies from your own family. I will take your wives from you and give them to a companion in broad daylight. You did your sin in secret, but I will do this thing in front of everyone!"

David repented of his evildoing immediately, and Nathan continued his message. "The Lord has taken away your sin, you won't die. But because you have given God's enemies a reason to blaspheme, the child will die."

All this happened. David had grief and violence for most of the rest of his reign. The baby died. David's own son, Absalom, rebelled against him and David had to flee. To add insult to injury, Absalom even pitched a tent on the palace roof, so everyone could see that he was taking his father's concubines in broad daylight. There was civil war and David had to flee the city. When it finally came to an all-out battle David's side won, but his rebellious son was killed.

Seems the boy had long thick hair, which got caught in some low branches as he was fleeing. There he hung, helpless in the oak tree. Joab came along, and in disobedience to David's orders, killed Absalom. David almost lost the kingdom when he went into grief for Absalom and disregarded his own faithful men who had fought to save his kingdom and his head.

But God was merciful. David had another son with Bathsheba, Solomon, and that child was blessed. He would become king. David got very old, and would finally die in bed, which would be a blessing in itself. As we will see, this is often not how the future kings would end up.

17
Solomon and the Cracked-up Kingdom: Riding the Royal Roller Coaster
1 and 2 Kings

When David was very old, there was another attempt to take over his throne. The King had already made the decision that Solomon would succeed him. But as the old man entered his declining days, a son of David, Adonijah, decided that he wanted the job. He gathered a small entourage of chariots, horsemen, and runners to travel around with him. Made him look regal, I suppose. If David knew what Adonijah was planning, he never let on, didn't even ask questions.

Adonijah had conferred with two of David's close associates, Joab and Abiathar, and was lining everything up for his coronation. These two men of David's were very loyal to the aging king, but a continual source of trouble. They had David's back, but not his heart.

The wannabe king had a big sheep-killing feast, and invited all his brothers to it. Well, not all. Solomon wasn't invited. Also not invited was anyone in the kingdom who might be loyal to David's intentions. The purpose of this ceremony and barbecue was to declare Adonijah king.

It was Nathan who was on the ball again. When he heard what was happening, he went to Bathsheba with a plan. They had to be subtle, because even elderly David did not like to be pushed around, and after all, Adonijah was his son. This was not just about who would be king. If Adonijah's attempt to grab the throne succeeded, Bathsheba and Solomon, and anyone else suspected of being a rival would be toast. This stuff didn't start with the Sicilians, it's been happening a lot longer.

Bathsheba and Nathan came to David, tactfully letting him know what had happened, without insulting his kingly sensibilities. He renewed the vow to Bathsheba and reaffirmed his choice of king. Then he called in his guys, and gave orders to fix the problem. They would take Solomon, on the royal mule, to a public place and anoint him king. Blow the trumpet and make the proclamation, so that all Israel would know who the rightful king was. Since David was not yet dead, there could be no argument. After this they would bring Solomon back, and put him right up on the throne, making a real slam-dunk of it.

All the people got into this when the orders were carried out. There was much trumpeting and shouting and celebrating, and the earth shook from the noise. Meanwhile, over at the barbecue, they heard the noise and wondered what was up. Soon a full report came to them, and it pooped the whole party. When the guests heard that they were hanging with a usurper, they scattered like cockroaches.

Adonijah ran to church. He went into the Tabernacle and took hold of the horns of the altar, and cried for a promise from Solomon that he would not be killed. The new king sent word that, if he behaved well, Adonijah could live. He was brought before Solomon, and fell on his face, promising not to do anything like this again. We'll see.

After this Solomon had a long talk with his father. Kind of a king orientation. David told him how to be a king, and who to trust, and who probably needed killing. There were people like Joab, who had never betrayed David directly, but were not always faithful to his directions. (Remember Absalom?) Again I say, they had his back, but not his heart. They could not be trusted once David was gone.

Take for instance, Adonijah. To understand how he ended up, first I have to tell you about Abishag. When David was old, he apparently got cold a lot. They kept him covered up, but he could not get warm. A young lady, Abishag, was brought in to share her body heat. A walking bedwarmer, she was. There was no sexual relationship. She just stayed really, really close to the king, and took care of some of his simple needs, especially when he shivered. She must have been a real sweet girl.

After David died, Abishag was out of work. She may have gone back to her home, or found another position in the royal household. Dr. Delmer Guynes has speculated that Abishag and the young woman of Song of Solomon are one and the same. That would explain Solomon's behavior in this story. Regardless, she was well known by the royals of Israel by the time David expired.

Now back to Adonijah. Shortly after David had his talk with Solomon, he died. Right after that, Adonijah came to a cautious Bathsheba with a request. He started his pitch with a couple of lies; 1) that the kingdom had been his, and 2) that all Israel had expected him to be king. He tried to make it sound as though his attempt to grab the throne had been just an awkward misunderstanding, which he had settled by yielding to Solomon. Based on this, he wanted a consolation prize. He wanted Bathsheba to ask her son to allow Abishag to marry Adonijah.

Bathsheba made no comment but agreed to ask. Maybe she knew what would happen, maybe not. There was not a lot of persuasion exerted in her request. When she did ask, Solomon went off. "Why not ask for the throne for him? And for Abiathar and Joab!" Apparently, Solomon had feelings for this Abby girl, and she was exactly the wrong thing for a convicted usurper to ask for. She had been the intimate servant and literal bed-partner of David the King, and for Adonijah to end up with her would communicate all sorts of things that Solomon didn't want communicated.

See also that Solomon sees these three—Adonijah, Abiathar, and Joab—as a group. Their fortunes were linked in his mind, and he still resented their attempt to steal his throne. This seemingly innocent request of Bathsheba's (actually, of Adonijah) set off the round of killing that had been coming for a while. It had been gathering like a thunderstorm, and Solomon rained all over his enemies.

Adonijah was executed, and Abiathar was fired and exiled. He got to live because he endured all the hardships alongside David. Looks like you don't kill old family friends as quickly as you do your brothers. Joab ran to the Tabernacle, like Adonijah did earlier, but Solomon pronounced judgment on him for being a sneaky murderer, and he was executed right there at the altar.

Solomon soon started a practice which would later deeply damage his kingdom. He struck a deal with Pharaoh and married one of his daughters. It looks like Solomon did this a lot, and each foreign wife brought foreign gods. The growing idolatry in the palace was not pleasing to God, but more about that later.

God came to Solomon in a dream, and said, "Ask for what you want." Solomon was feeling pretty inadequate, so he asked for wisdom to know how to be king. This pleased God, and because Solomon didn't ask for long life, riches, or the life of his enemies, God gave him his desire for wisdom, and threw in the other things too.

We know Solomon as the wisest and richest man who lived. He became fabulously wealthy, and all Israel was blessed with him. It was a great time, and a great kingdom to live in. Solomon knew all about almost everything, and wrote thousands of proverbs and songs. It was a high point in Israel's history. People came from the ends of the earth to visit Solomon. People like the Queen of Sheba, who left very impressed after her visit. (By the way, those legends about an intimate relationship between Solomon and the Queen of Sheba, and her subsequent pregnancy, are just stories made up much later. There is nothing in the Bible to indicate anything of the sort.)

David had begun stockpiling materials for the Temple, and Solomon continued to get things from everywhere. He also began construction, bringing craftsmen and contractors from far away for the project. The temple was rather fabulous, with lots of gold and other expensive materials and elaborate work. It looks like the whole thing was overlaid with gold, and it took seven years to finish. Solomon built himself a big house too, and that took thirteen years.

The Ark was brought in and the Temple was dedicated. God showed up in a powerful way, and it was a wonderful thing. God made promises to Solomon, and Solomon blessed the people. Twenty-two thousand oxen and 120,000 sheep were sacrificed, so you know it was huge.

God makes the promise to Solomon that if he and those who follow him will be faithful to the ways of God, God will be with them, and they will be on the throne of Israel forever. However, if they are not faithful to God things will not go well at all. This is worth remembering for the rest of the story.

Solomon had many collections. He got gold and silver, ivory, animals, spices and many other things. And he also collected wives. He had 700 of them, and 300 concubines. Many of them were foreign, all those "-ites" whom God had commanded Israel to destroy, then have nothing to do with. They were evil nations whom God had judged, and idolators of the worst sort. But Solomon loved them.

I don't think he loved them as persons so much as he loved having them all as a group. He loved having all these wives, but he really couldn't know many of them very well. It was not a bad deal for the girls. If you were one of his 1000 women, and if he systematically slept with a different one each night (which I doubt), it would be over two and a half years in between visits. Meanwhile, you were taken care of.

The older the King got, the more he drifted from the worship of God, into idolatry with all the imported gods. God spoke to Solomon about this, and told him how displeased He was. Solomon ignored God's commands, so God gave him bad news. The kingdom would be taken from Solomon, and given to a servant. But because of the faithfulness of David, this wouldn't happen to Solomon, but to his son. And it wouldn't happen completely; there would be one tribe left for Solomon's son to rule. God is faithful to His promises and His friends, even when He has to correct us.

For the first time, God now raised up enemies against Solomon. He struggled against them from then on, and finally died. Solomon's son Rehoboam would be king. All Israel came together to make him king. But some came to town for other reasons.

One of the enemies that God raised up was a fellow named Jeroboam. He had been a leader under Solomon, but the relationship had soured, perhaps because the prophet Ahijah had anointed Jero' as King of Israel, and Solomon wanted to kill his intended successor. God offered Jeroboam the same deal He had offered Solomon. Be faithful to God and His ways, and you and yours will stay on the throne for generations to come.

When Rehoboam was crowned, Jeroboam decided to come back home. Jeroboam and an assembly representing the people of Israel came to speak with the new king. They had a suggestion.

"Your father, Solomon worked us very hard. If you will just cut us a little bit of slack, we will work hard and serve you faithfully as king." Reho' sent them away so he could think about it for three days. Then he asked the elders who had served with his father what they thought. The elders, who still retained some of Solomon's wisdom, counseled him to listen favorably to the request. "Be a servant to them now, and they will be faithful to you forever."

Apparently, wisdom in this family stopped with Solomon. Rehoboam asked his peers what they thought, a bunch of young bucks who had just came in, and knew no more than their fresh, new boss. They counseled rejection of the people's suggestion. We can almost hear their collective "good old boy wisdom."

"Now is when you have to show the people who is in charge! You're the King—act like it! Tell them that your father was hard on them, but they ain't seen nothin' yet."

When Jeroboam and the people came for Rehoboam's response, he acted in the "wisdom" of his buddies. "I'll be harder than my father ever was!"

The people of Israel had no use for this. They walked out on Rehoboam and declared that they would have nothing to do with David's house. Reb still didn't get it; he sent out his foreman to put the people to work, and they stoned the guy. The people, all but the tribe of Judah, made Jeroboam their king. Rehoboam gathered a good army of Judah, and was about to enforce his will on the rest, when God told him to back off.

Jeroboam had good potential, with that promise from God and all, but he didn't perform well. He got worried that if his people went to the Temple in Jerusalem, which was in Judah, they would once again give their allegiance to Rehoboam. He consulted with some losers in his government, and the bright idea they came up with was to make two golden calves and set them up in convenient locations. They would tell Israel that these were now their gods. Amazingly, Israel bought it!

I need to break in here to introduce an important group of people to The Story. I want to do that by way of comparison. I want to compare something from this section of the Bible with something you may know about already.

The spirituality of *Star Wars* is not biblical. It is a new ageish, pantheistic philosophy based on belief in an impersonal "Force" rather than a living, loving, and personal God. I had to say that before I tell you what I am about to say, to minimize confusion about where I stand on the subject. However, I want to show you something from that series of movies, to help you see what we are looking at now.

Throughout that whole story there is a class of people called Jedi. They didn't simply decide to be Jedi, but were born with a high degree of the Force, which determined their destiny. They had to be trained and disciplined, in order to maximize their Jedi potential. Having been ceremoniously certified as real Jedi knights by the order, they are unleashed on the universe, to do right. The Jedi seem to have an inherent code of right and wrong, and they go about enforcing it from one galaxy to another.

Enough about that; let's get to the point. Whenever I see the Jedi in a SW film, I think of some folks I know from the Bible. Through much of the Old Testament, there are people who move about the land under great authority and power. They do things similar to what the movies depict the Jedi doing. Like the Jedi, they see scenes of the future. They don't know everything, but they know way more than regular folk. They also act on what they know, to confront injustice, oppression, and general evildoing. In the *Star Wars* mythology, the Jedi are "knights," because they also fight, like traveling marshals in an old western. In the Old Testament, our heroes are "prophets," different in some ways from Jedi, but in many other ways, very similar.

Our prophets didn't just choose their lifestyle, but were called and commissioned by God. They have His power at their disposal, but unlike Jedi, prophets don't practice with it, or do demonstrations. All prophets train for is hearing God better. Then they obey what they have heard, and God backs up their courageous obedience with His miraculous power.Prophets don't own the power, they just cooperate with it obediently. Jedi get killed, and so do prophets, but because they are under God's commission, prophets never get killed early, but right on His schedule, when it fits His purpose. Like Jedi, they may be loners, or they may travel with an apprentice or servant.

The stories of prophets often seem like fiction. Not just fiction, but fantasy. You may notice that the way I describe the action will sound somewhat like a comic book. (BOOM! POOF! WHOOSH!)

If you take a suspicious or negative view of media and the *Star Wars* films, you may scoff or be offended at the comparison. If that is the case, read on and get over it. It was not written to teach *you* anything much. However, for many readers of our generation, this comparison will resonate with you, and give you a more vivid picture of the prophets. If it helps, use it.

Now, back to our story. One day a prophet came from Judah to Bethel, while Jeroboam was worshipping at his cow-god altar. The prophet had been sent by God, and cried out against the false altar, declaring that a day would come when a descendant of David would come, named Josiah, and destroy the altar, killing its priests and burning human bones on it. King Jerry got mad, and gave a royal order to "Seize him!" but when he pointed to the prophet in anger, his hand "dried up" and was just stuck out there, paralyzed. Awkward!

The altar split apart, and the ashes in it came pouring out, a pretty convincing sign to go along with the prophecy and the king's stricken hand. The king's attitude did a 180-degree turn at that point, and he asked the prophet if he would please pray for the king's hand to be restored. When the prophet prayed, the king's hand was healed. You would think that might cause repentance and a turn from idolatry right then, but unfortunately, no.

Worship centers for false gods were put in the high places, and unqualified people were made priests. Jeroboam started substitute feasts, and led the people in sacrifices to the cow-gods. Rehoboam was no better than Jeroboam. He led the people into idolatry, and they worshipped false gods, with idol houses all through the land, and with male cult prostitutes, and other abominations. Reho' and Jero' fought their whole lives. Rehoboam died first, but eventually they were both gone.

Now starts a part of the Bible consisting of one micro-narrative after another. There was a divided kingdom, which went on for generations. There were kings in both Judah and Israel, and God sent them prophets to tell them when they were out of line, which was often.

God warned them, and sometimes good kings, like Asa, would arise and lead the people back to God. But then wicked kings would come along and lead both Israel and Judah into idolatry. It was kind of like the time of the Judges, but these people had kings, and they knew better than to get into the things they did. But they did.

Rehoboam and Jeroboam, and their successors, took God's people on a roller coaster ride, up and down between faithfulness and disobedience. While Asa, a good king, was in Judah, Ahab became king in Israel. Ahab was awful. He followed the evils of those who were evil before him, and got worse than that. He was into the worship of the false god, Baal.

Ahab married a particularly ungodly broad named Jezebel. We still use her name today, when we want to really insult a woman, especially a woman in leadership. This pair wasn't just naughty, they were EEE-viiil.

Right at this point, one of God's Great Ones is introduced. Suddenly, in the middle of this wicked kingdom, Elijah the Tishbite walked in and declared to this evil king that the rain would not come anymore. Not until Elijah says. For years. Then Elijah walked out and went to a place God sent him to wait. He got water from a brook, and ravens brought him food. When the brook dried up, it was time to move on. God directed him to a widow, whom God had commanded to feed him. She was on her last meal, but when she started feeding God's prophet in obedience, her supply never ran out.

The widow's son got sick and died, which was about the worst thing that could happen to her. Elijah took the boy upstairs to where the prophet lived and laid him on his own bed. Then he stretched out over him and asked God to bring him back. The kid came back, and Elijah gave him to his mama. This is the kind of thing that happened with Elijah.

Three years passed. Three very dry years. Strangely, Ahab had an assistant, Obadiah, who served God. The two of them went out to scour the countryside in separate attempts to find grass for the starving animals. Obadiah found Elijah, and the conversation gives us some insight about how the people of God regarded the prophets.

Elijah said, "Go tell Ahab that I am here, and I am going to send rain."

Obadiah complained, "What sin have I committed, that you would send me to my death? I'm on God's side! Don't you know that Ahab has been searching for you everywhere, and cannot get you? Yeah, right— I'll go tell the king that you are here, then the Spirit of God will swoop you up and take you who knows where, and I'll get killed for lying, when it's not my fault at all!"

Elijah promised that he would indeed appear before Ahab, so Obadiah delivered the message. Ahab came out to speak with Elijah, and of course, blamed the prophet for the suffering that his own wickedness had brought upon his kingdom. Elijah reminded Ahab who was actually EE-vil, and said, "Get 850 of your false prophets (450 for Baal, 400 for the Asherah, another form of false worship) and meet me on Mount Carmel."

When they all got there, Elijah addressed the people of Israel, who had come to watch the showdown. "How long will you waffle? If the Lord is God, serve Him. If Baal, follow him." The people said nothing. They were confused; that's why they were worshipping Baal in the first place.

Elijah went on. "I am the only prophet of the Lord left. Baal has 450. Let's make two altars, and offer two oxen as sacrifices, one to the Lord, one to Baal. The one who answers by fire will be the one we serve."

Elijah let the Baalies go first. They put their sacrifice on their altar. They called upon Baal to send fire. No fire. They jumped up on their altar. No word, no fire.

Elijah was not respectful of their "world religion." (There may be times for that; this was not one of those times.) He hooted at them, "Shout loud! He is a god, you know. He may be busy, or gone somewhere. Perhaps he is taking a nap!" The New Living Translation (NLT) says "maybe he is relieving himself." Very disrespectful. "Maybe your god is in the can!" Elijah was enjoying this.

They yelled loud and cut themselves, which was their custom, until they were all bloody. They wailed all morning, then they carried on all afternoon. When it was the time for the evening sacrifice to God, Elijah was ready to call the game. First, he rebuilt God's altar, which had fallen down. If you want fire to fall from heaven, you have to rebuild the altar. The fire has to have a place of sacrifice upon which to fall.

The true prophet put the wood on the altar, then prepared the ox. Next, he poured water on it all. Lots of water. This was pretty nervy, since it hadn't rained in three years. Then Elijah prayed. He prayed that the people would know that the Lord was God, and that He would turn their hearts back to Him.

Then BAM! The fire of the Lord fell, and burned up everything that had been offered —the ox, the wood, even the water. The people began to shout, "The Lord He is God!" Elijah said, "Grab the prophets of Baal—don't let one get away!" They were rounded up, and Elijah killed them all. He did it down at the creek, so it wasn't so messy. Remember, although he acted kind of "Jedi," Elijah didn't have a light saber.

Elijah prayed some more, and it rained. The victory was total. Then, Jezebel threatened Elijah, and he went into total depression. Ran and hid. God came and found him, though, and renewed his faith. Sometimes, when you want to die, you really just need a good dinner and a long nap, and that's what God gave Elijah. Then God gave orders for what to do next. There were two kings to anoint, as well as his own successor.

Israel was in a funny place at this time. The people were more faithful to God, so He was blessing them. But their king and his old lady were awful. Ahab was greedy and idolatrous, and Jezebel was a witchy old murderess. She made him even worse than he would have been alone. God finally pronounced judgment on them and their line. They would die badly.

When *2 Kings* starts, this is where we are: Ahaziah is king of Israel, and Jehoshaphat is king in Judah. Elijah is still God's ambassador to Samaria, Israel's capitol. Life was still interesting for the man of God.

Elijah told the next king's people that their boss was going to die, because he consulted Baal when he was injured instead of the true God. Ahaziah sent a captain with fifty men to get Elijah. The guy was kind of rude, and Elijah called fire down from heaven to burn up the captain and his fifty men. The king sent another captain, and he was more rude than the first. So—POOF!—more fire came down and toasted him and his fifty men to death. Again, a captain with fifty more men was sent to haul the prophet in to the king.

The third captain was wiser and more respectful than the first two. He humbly pled for the lives of he and his men, and the Lord instructed Elijah to go on in with this group. He did, and told the king to his face what God had said—"You're going to die." Next verse, Ahaziah is dead, and a fellow named Jehoram takes over.

So it went, in both Israel and Judah. Good kings and bad kings. Now Elijah, as I told you earlier, anointed a replacement for his tired self, named Elisha. (You can remember who came first because they are in alphabetical order.) Elisha accepted his role and began to follow Elijah.

Word was out that Elijah was going away. It was strange. Everyone seemed to know that God was going to take the senior prophet away on that very day. Knowing this, Elisha followed him diligently. Where

Elijah went, there was his shadow, Elisha. At each point Elijah spoke to his apprentice, "Stay here, while I go on." Each time Elisha refused to allow Elijah to leave him behind.

At the Jordan, Elijah took his mantle and parted the waters with it. They crossed the riverbed, and went on, leaving all the other apprentice prophets on the other side. Just like in the exodus and *Joshua*, the Jordan is the River of Destiny. After they were across, Elijah turned to Elisha and asked, "What can I do for you before I am taken away?" Elisha does not seem to have hesitated to put in his request to his mentor. "I want a double portion of what you have."

Elijah acknowledged that he had asked a hard thing. But if he saw Elijah when he was taken away, the thing would be done. They went on, talking together as they went, and in the next verse—WHOOSH!— a chariot and horses of fire separated the two, and Elijah went up to heaven in a whirlwind. After the dust settled, and Elisha recovered from the spectacular experience, he took up Elijah's mantle which had fallen from him, and headed back toward Jordan.

When he got to the river, he had to get across somehow. Notice that he did not moan, "Lord God, where's Elijah?" Instead, he proclaimed, "Where is the Lord, the God of Elijah?" He struck the waters, and they got out of his way. Elisha was the "top-prop" now, and he began doing miraculous things right away. His ministry was a lot like Elijah's but more so. The "double portion," you know.

Judah and Israel kept fighting with one another, and with their other neighbors. Elisha finished his long, powerful life as a prophet, then died and was buried. Much later some Moabites, of all things, were burying a buddy when they were interrupted by some enemies. They dumped the corpse in a handy grave, in haste. It was Elisha's grave. When the dead guy hit the bones of Elisha, he came back to life.

More rulers came to both Judah and Israel; there was even a Jeroboam II. Eventually came catastrophe. Hoshea became king of Israel, and in his ninth year, Assyria came over and took them all captive into exile in Assyria. There is an explanation in the Bible of why God did not rescue them this time:

1) Israel had become followers of other gods
2) They had begun to behave like the Canaanites whom God had driven out before them
3) The people had willingly followed the ways of the kings of Israel, when those kings took up ways that displeased God

God had warned them all about this idolatrous behavior. He sent prophets to tell them to return to God, but they did not. So, they were taken away. Nothing was left but the tribe of Judah.

Hezekiah was king in Judah. He was a pretty good guy, and served the Lord. The king of Assyria, Sennacherib, couldn't make Judah serve him, and Hezekiah beat back the Philistines as well. (I always thought that it would be cool to open a barbeque place with a Bible theme, and call it "King Snatch-a-rib's." But, I digress.) Later, Hezekiah tried to buy off Assyria, but the Assyrians just got bolder and wanted more. They came to Jerusalem and made threats, because that's what bullies do. Sennacherib said awful lies about Hezekiah and about God. They tried to win by intimidation, without actually having to fight.

Things looked really bad for Judah, because they knew that Assyria could do all the things they were saying, militarily. Hezekiah got serious with God. He went into the house of the Lord and called for Isaiah, the prophet. Not to yell at him, like Ahab used to do, but to get his help in pleading for a miracle. Isaiah assured the king that God would take care of His people, and give the Assyrians what they had coming.

Isaiah gave this message to Judah, and that night, the angel of the Lord went out and killed 185,000 Assyrians in their camp. When the survivors woke up the next morning they decided to go home. Sennacherib was worshipping in his idol temple later and got assassinated to death. Serves him right.

Shortly after, Hezekiah took sick, and Isaiah broke the news to the king that it was going to be terminal. Hezekiah didn't take it well, and begged God for more time. God gave him fifteen more years, and at first, this looked like a good thing. However, some unfortunate things happened during the "overtime."

A delegation from Babylon came to visit, and Hezekiah opened the palace to them, showing them everything, even the treasure house. When Isaiah found out how naïve the king had been, he informed him that these guys would come back and carry everything away. Even the king's sons would become their servants. Hezekiah eventually died, and his son, Manasseh, became king.

Manasseh was another tragic thing that happened during Hezekiah's extra fifteen years. Actually, Manasseh was probably the worst thing that came out of that time. He was twelve years old when he became king, so he would have been born after his father got the extension. He had a fifty-five year reign of almost complete evil. Everything Hezekiah had cleaned up, Manasseh messed up. He reinstituted all the old idolatries and Canaanite habits, and in fact, was worse than the Canaanites.

God sent prophets to Manasseh, to rebuke and warn him, but the boy wouldn't listen. So, God sent Assyrians to him. They chained him up, and took him to Babylon. That adjusted his attitude. He repented and cried out to God, and God brought him home. Then he behaved much better. When he "slept with his fathers," his son Amon took over.

Amon got killed by his own staff, and then the people rose up and killed the assassins. Amon's son, Josiah became king. Did you think Manasseh was a pretty young king at twelve? How about Josiah at eight? Of course, there were other, older officials to operate the government and watch out for the minor king, and as a ruler came of age, he would take on more and more authority. The people charged with watching over Josiah must have been good ones, because he turned out pretty well.

Under Josiah, the temple was repaired, and a lost book of the law was found. Idols were smashed, and their worship places destroyed. All over Judah, things got cleaned up, and Josiah even had the altar at Bethel destroyed, the one that Jeroboam had made 300 years earlier (Remember the golden calves?). You may remember that this had been prophesied to Jeroboam's face right after the false altar had been built, the prophet even calling Josiah by name! Passover had not been observed since the days of the judges, and Josiah had it started again.

Unfortunately, Josiah was just putting off God's judgment, not preventing it. God had called Judah, "over" during the reign of Manasseh, and He was going to follow through on His promise. Pharaoh Neco of Egypt was muscling in on Judah. He killed Josiah, and kicked Josiah's son off the throne after three months. Pharaoh put another son of Josiah on the throne as a puppet ruler of Israel. Things were going downhill fast.

A bigger gangster than Pharaoh came—Nebuchadnezzar, king of Babylon—and he started running things. He placed kings over Judah (all bad) and then came to besiege Jerusalem and take them all into exile. Jerusalem was finally sacked and burned, and the book of *2 Kings* concludes with all of Judah in exile in Babylon and an appointed governor over Judah. The books of *First and Second Chronicles* follow. They repeat a lot of this, but give additional details also, some of which I have been including in this story all along.

The people of Judah get off the train in a strange land. They have forsaken their God, and He has allowed them to receive the natural consequences of their behavior. The long royal roller coaster ride rolls to a stop in Babylon.

18
Jeremiah: When Nobody Wants to Listen

Jeremiah

Lamentations

Jeremiah's story begins back in the time of King Josiah, king of Judah. It continues in the reign of Jehoiakin, Josiah's son. This is before the Exile. You can see the history of these kings in *2 Kings* 22-24, and *2 Chronicles* 34-36.

God came to Jeremiah to recruit him as a prophet. Jerry was reluctant, claiming that he was just a child, and didn't speak well. God reminded him that He knew and approved Jeremiah before his conception, and it was God Who made his mouth, so if He wanted to claim it for His service, so be it.

Jeremiah was commissioned, and began to see things right away. God would ask, "What do you see?" and Jeremiah would answer that he saw an almond tree, or a boiling pot. Then God would tell him the meaning of what he was looking at. God would just talk to the prophet about His unfaithful people, and how He longed for them to return to Him.

God gave vivid word pictures of the spiritual harlotry of His people, then informed them of the coming judgment. Another nation would subdue them. God said that because they had forsaken Him and served foreign gods in their land, they would serve strangers in a land that was not theirs. Judgment was coming from the north.

Jeremiah was not a happy prophet, nor a prophet of happiness. His message was troubling. Judah was sinful, they had forsaken God, and He was hurting. It may seem strange to think of God hurting, but read the things He said to Jeremiah, and you will understand that this is a Person in pain. There is true grief expressed in these words, and even today, when someone delivers a speech about how we have fallen away from the right way, it is called a "Jeremiad."

Jeremiah is known to us as the "weeping prophet." He says things like, "Harvest is past, summer is ended—and we are not saved." He bares his soul, saying, "Oh, that my head were waters, and my eyes a fountain of tears, that I may weep day and night for the slain of the daughter of my people." This was not depression, like Elijah got into, this was grief. Depression is internal, and may have nothing to do with what is happening. Grief comes from what is happening around you. Jeremiah was truly sad for his people.

The people were not just unfaithful to God, they were deceitful with each other. They were filled with greed, and Jeremiah wanted to get away from them. He dreamed about just opening a motel on the high-way somewhere. God gave warnings to Jeremiah for His people. Judg-ment was coming, for both Israel and Judah.

Jeremiah was sent to the temple gate, to stand there and proclaim repentance. By repenting and changing their ways, they could avoid this judgment. They wouldn't. Jeremiah delivered a satire on the foolishness of fearing inanimate idols, and proclaimed the greatness of God.

The prophet indicted the people for their unfaithfulness to the cov-enant. For his service to God, Jeremiah was rewarded with a plot against his life. God informed His servant of the conspiracy, and promised judg-ment upon the plotters. Jeremiah prayed and asked God why these wick-ed ones prosper, and God replied that He was through with them.

However, He was not through with them forever. God told Jerry that He would uproot His people for their sin, but also bring them back. In the midst of this proclamation of judgment is the promise of mercy. God may be leaving His people without help, but He is not leaving them without hope.

God occasionally has His prophets act out the messages He sends. Jeremiah was sent to buy a linen waistband, and wear it around his waist. Then he was instructed to go to the river Euphrates and bury the waistband in the rock there. Many days later, God sent him back to dig it up, and of course it was ruined.

God interpreted His object lesson. Israel and Judah were made to be close to God, just like a linen waistband is made to be close to its wearer. God was going to take Israel and Judah away from His side, into captivity on the banks of the Euphrates. They would be ruined, just like the linen cloth.

Shame was promised. Jeremiah prayed prayers of sorrow, but knew that God would have to act against his people. Jeremiah pointed out to the Lord that other prophets were prophesying that the sword and famine would not come, but that peace was ahead. God replied that these false prophets were not speaking for Him, and they would die by the sword and famine that they said was not coming.

Jeremiah asked God if this disaster could not be averted, and God answered that judgment must come. Jeremiah asked God to please vindicate him among his persecutors and to remember that Jeremiah was not unfaithful. God promised that Jeremiah would be a "wall of bronze" to his people, and that God would deliver him.

God ordered Jeremiah not to take a wife of this doomed people, for death was coming to small and great of them. He should not go to comfort them in their time of mourning because this was the work of the Lord, and it would be done all across the land. But again God promised to bring them back from captivity. We tend to think of Jeremiah as a "prophet of doom," but he consistently prophesied the return, as well as the exile.

God gave specific orders about keeping the Sabbath, then sent Jeremiah on a field trip. The prophet was to go to the potter's house for a message. While there Jeremiah saw the potter making a piece on the wheel. The vessel was ruined, and the potter started over, making a different vessel out of that clay. God said to Jeremiah that this was how He would deal with the house of Israel. He would make of them what He wanted.

Another picture story. Jeremiah was sent to get a clay jar and gather a committee of leaders of the people, to go with him to a prescribed spot. Then Jeremiah was to smash the vessel, and tell the leaders that, just as the jar was broken beyond repair, so would Judah be also.

After that, Pashur the priest had Jeremiah beaten and put in the stocks. As soon as he was released, Jeremiah went back to foretelling doom. He complained to God that it was a real bummer to have to proclaim this bad news all the time. But, Jeremiah admitted, when he tried not to preach this message, it was like a fire shut up in his bones, and he had to speak.

He was not happy, though. In fact, he wished he had never been born. He cursed his birthday, and the man who delivered the good news to his father. If he were around today, what would we do with him? He wouldn't sing patriotic hymns with us, would he? He loved his nation, but God wasn't giving him a message about how great it was. I don't think he'd get far on talk radio, either.

God sent bad news to the king of Judah, and He got very specific. Nebuchadnezzar was coming, and God declared that Judah would be handed over to the king of Babylon. Those who tried to stay and defend the city would die, but those who went out would be captured and escape with their lives. Not a pleasant set of options.

More messages about the fall of Jerusalem were given to Jeremiah for the king and people, then a prophecy was given which referred to the coming of the Messiah, the Ultimate King of Israel. God declared Himself against the false prophets.

This story jumps back and forth in time, and it's only by taking note of who the king is that we can keep up. Here, we fast forward to a vision Jeremiah received after Nebuchadnezzar had arrived. He saw two baskets of figs, one very good and one very rotten. The good figs represented God's people who had gone away into captivity in the land of the Chaldeans. God would bless them in their captivity. The rotten figs were those who stayed in the land with their sinful king. They would be destroyed.

After this, there was a flashback to an earlier prophecy. Jeremiah reminded the people during the reign of Jehoiakim that he had been telling them about their evil ways for twenty-three years. Because they had not listened, judgment would come. But after seventy years in Babylon, God would punish their punishers. The nations which God would use for judgment against His people would themselves be judged.

Jeremiah told the cities of Judah that they must repent or be destroyed. The priests and the prophets and the patriotic people of Judah seized Jeremiah and cried for his death. The civil authorities got involved, and heard both sides. Jeremiah repeated his story, but submitted to the princes' judgment. The princes told the mob that Jeremiah should not die, and they quoted historical precedent to make their case. At least one other prophet got killed for delivering this kind of message, but Jeremiah was spared to accomplish all God intended.

God said a strange thing to Jeremiah. He instructed the prophet to make bonds and yokes for himself, to illustrate the coming bondage. Then he was to tell all the kings of the surrounding lands that God said they had all been turned over to Nebuchadnezzar. They were to serve him and his descendants until his number was up, then other nations would come and take over Buck's place. God promised to punish any nation or king that would not submit to Nebuchadnezzar, His appointed instrument of judgment.

God warned the local kings that their prophets, soothsayers, diviners, and the like would try to tell them not to accept the "Yoke of Buck." He clearly told the rulers that those who did not submit would be dragged far from their land in slavery. Those who would surrender their sovereignty to Nebuchadnezzar would get to stay in their lands.

Jeremiah delivers this message to the king of Judah. He is called to a confrontation with another prophet, Hananiah. This guy prophesied doom to Nebuchadnezzar, proclaiming that within two years, all the vessels would be back in the temple, and the people would be safe at home. Hanny broke the yoke from Jerry's neck, the one that God had told him to put there. After that, God said to Jeremiah, "Tell Hananiah that he's a liar, and I am removing him from the earth." That is what God did; Hananiah was dead within the year. The rule for Old Testament prophets is, "You lie—you die."

After the king and all his court were taken away, Jeremiah wrote an open letter to the people of the exile from Jerusalem to Babylon. The gist of the letter was, "Settle in; you are going to be there for a while." He counseled them to go on with their lives and be good citizens. Plant crops and get married, pray for God's blessing on the city to which they had been taken. Be good figs, remember?

Again Jeremiah warned the people about the false prophets. God promised that it would be only seventy years until He would release them. Those who would submit to His discipline would be blessed. Those who would not, God declared, would get the "SFP" treatment— sword, famine, and pestilence.

Shemaiah was another false prophet. Whether blinded by pride or patriotism or greed, we can't tell, but we can read that he sent letters to the people in Jerusalem and to the priests, calling on them to shut Jeremiah up because of his prophecies. A copy of one of these letters was passed to Jeremiah, and God told him that He was going to put an end to Shemaiah's whole family line. Ironic that the fellow who refused to accept anything but "good news" prophecies was not going to see the real good things that God was going to do.

God directed Jeremiah to collect all the things He had said into a book, because this captivity wasn't going to last forever. Jeremiah recorded a lengthy prophecy of repentance and restoration. It even included God's promise to establish a "new covenant" with His people. This is all about their redemption, for the present age, and in the future. Later, Daniel would read the prophecy of their release in seventy years, and begin to pray for its fulfillment.

When you read *Jeremiah*, you should see that it is a bit episodic, from chapter to chapter. He's pretty good about telling us when things happened, but we have to pay attention, if we are going to follow. Take notice of chapter 32. It starts with the historical setting, then tells you the story.

In the tenth year of Zedekiah, king of Judah (the eighteenth year of Nebuchadnezzar), the Babylonian army had Jerusalem under siege, and Zedekiah had Jeremiah in jail. The king of Judah thought Jeremiah was guilty of treason or something, because Jeremiah continued to prophesy that Babylon would take Judah into captivity. Sometimes we are misunderstood because our first allegiance is to the Kingdom of Heaven, not our earthly nation.

Meanwhile, Jeremiah did an interesting thing. A relative came to visit him in jail, with a piece of land to sell. This doesn't look like a good deal to us, since they are all about to go into exile. Jerry bought the land, to show his belief that God's people were coming back to this land. He did have the deed sealed up really well however, because it was going to be a long time before anyone came looking for it.

God and Jeremiah had conversations about what was about to happen, and why. God made it clear that Israel and Judah had it coming. In the land that God gave them, they committed abominable idolatry, even sacrificing their children to the god, Molech. This discipline was righteous, and was being promised for their redemption. God indeed promised that they would be redeemed and restored. That's what God is always up to, and that is why it is the Big Story of this book, and His Book.

The Ultimate King was talked about by God to Jeremiah. This descendant of David, whom we know would be Jesus, was to be the fulfillment of God's promises to the houses of Jacob and David. At Jeremiah's time, it looked like maybe God had reneged on these promises. God says, "Not so!" and promises that His Righteous Branch will sit upon the throne forever. Just not yet.

First, there was business to take care of. One of the dirty deals the people of Judah had done was particularly annoying to God. God had ordered that every seven years, all Hebrew slaves were to be given their freedom. This command had been given centuries before, but by the time of Zedekiah, it had apparently been forgotten. Under Zed's reign, a decree was made and carried out that these servants would be freed, like God had originally instructed. But then, they all took their slaves back, and put them in bondage again. Their "freedom" turned out to be just a cruel vacation. God was upset.

God sent Jeremiah with a word for Zedekiah. His kingdom was going to be destroyed; his city burned. The king was going to come face-to-face with Nebuchadnezzar, and although he would die in peace, he would die a captive. God seems to be keeping him alive just so he can see who's really in charge, and admit that Jeremiah was right, all along. God even gets sarcastic. Because of the way they "released" their Hebrew slaves, God says, "I will 'release' you all—to the SFP!" (Actually, "SPF" in this passage.)

Strangely, God told Jeremiah to invite the Rechabites into the temple for a wine tasting. When he served them wine, they politely declined, explaining that they had been commanded by their forefather Jonadab not to drink wine or build houses in Israel. All the time they had been there, they had been living in tents, drinking a lot of milk and water, I suppose. Now, Jeremiah saw what God was up to, and heard Him saying, "These Rechabites obeyed for generations, after being told just once! My people have been told over and over how to obey me—and continue to rebel!" More justification for the Exile.

The rest of Jeremiah's macro-narrative plays out in several micro-narratives. They are episodes in a continuing saga that will take us right into the Captivity. The first one is about "the scroll." God told Jeremiah to record His words on a scroll, as a complete record. God's idea was to give Israel and Judah the opportunity to hear the full judgment against them, so they could turn from their evil and be restored.

Jeremiah couldn't go to the Temple; the text doesn't say why. His scribe, Baruch, went to read the scroll. This writing and reading did not happen over a weekend; it took the better part of a year, it seems. Eventually, word of the message worked its way up through the government to the king, Jehoiakim. The scroll was brought into the throne room to be read to the king by Jehudi the scribe.

Jehoiakim was not very receptive, spiritually. Jehudi had just gotten started with his reading, when "King Jerkim" called for the scroll. The king cut the scroll, then pitched it in the fire, against the advice of everyone who mattered around him. A royal "skip tracer" was put out to bring Baruch and Jeremiah in, but God hid them. God told Jeremiah to get a clean scroll and write it all down again, including some additions about what bad stuff would come down on Jehoiakim, His Royal Rudeness.

Jehoiakim passed, and his son ruled for three months, before Nebuchadnezzar replaced him with a relative, Zedekiah (2 Chron. 36). Pharaoh Neco came over from Egypt with his army, and the Chaldeans/Babylonians retreated from besieging Jerusalem. Seems like this business of taking over another kingdom was not too clean and tidy; Zedekiah was king of Judah, and was asking Jeremiah to intercede with God about the Egyptians, but Jerusalem had not yet fallen to the Chaldeans.

God then spoke to Jeremiah, to straighten things out. The Egyptians would go away, and the Chaldeans return. Even if the Egyptians cut up the Chaldeans pretty badly, they could still come back and conquer Jerusalem, because that was what God had decreed.

While the siege was lifted, Jeremiah decided to go down to Benjamin county for a land deal. He got stopped at a Border Patrol checkpoint, like we do when we go across country in the Southwest U.S. An accusation was made that Jeremiah was defecting to the Chaldeans, and he found himself in a bad local jail, mistreated by the local law.

King Zedekiah got him out, and when they met secretly at the palace, the king asked, "Have you heard from God?" Jeremiah had indeed received a word from the Lord. "You are going to be taken by the King of Babylon." Zed kept Jerry in the guardhouse prison, a considerable upgrade from that provincial hole he had been in; Jeremiah knew he'd be killed if he went back there. He almost died anyway.

The guys in the kingdom who disrespected Jeremiah went to the king to get control of him. They lowered him into a cistern, a hole in the ground for retaining rainwater. There was no water there, only mud, and Jeremiah was sinking deep. He would have starved had a friendly eunuch not gone to the king to intervene. The king ordered him taken out. Zedekiah was interested in what God had to say. He had interest, but little courage or faith in God.

A long conversation went back and forth between the prophet and king. It looked like negotiation. Jeremiah assured the king that if he would surrender his government to Babylon, he and his household would be spared. Zedekiah was reluctant, since everything he knew about running a kingdom said to stand and fight until God brought the victory. God, however, had made it clear that he was the One sending the Chaldeans, and He would be sitting out this battle.

Jeremiah stayed in the guardhouse cell until Jerusalem was taken captive. Things went badly for Zedekiah. When the wall was breached, he tried to flee, but got caught. The Chaldeans killed all his sons, while he was forced to watch, then he was blinded and taken to Babylon in chains.

Nebuchadnezzar had some regard for Jeremiah, and the prophet was given his say about where he would go next. Neb had left some of the poorest of the people behind in Judah, so that the land would not be empty. Gedaliah was put in charge of them, and Jeremiah decided to attach himself to this community.

Jews came from the surrounding territories back to Judah when they heard how Babylon was treating the remnant. Some of these Jews came with a story about a conspiracy to kill Gedaliah. They had heard that the Ammonites were planning something, and one guy even offered to go kill the enemy who was plotting. Sort of a "first strike" murder. Gedaliah declined. He didn't believe anyone was plotting to kill him.

He was wrong. Dead wrong. A nasty fellow named Ishmael led a bloody overthrow, killing everyone who could have opposed him. He was sneaky. A guy named Johanan came and rescued the hostages, but the leaders were afraid to go home, since Gedaliah had been the appointed governor from Babylon, and they didn't know how Nebuchadnezzar would respond. They planned to flee to Egypt instead.

Before they took off, they asked Jeremiah to inquire of the Lord about their plans. What they really wanted was for Jeremiah to go along with their plan to run to Egypt. This would make things easier for them with the remnant. Jeremiah went to God as he promised, and God said that there would be compassion and blessing for them if they went home and submitted to Chaldean rule. If they went to Egypt? You guessed it—SFP would follow.

This was not what the leaders of the remnant wanted to hear, and Jeremiah was falsely accused of being everything but a child of God. The bosses took everyone, including Jerry and Baruch, down to Egypt. God spoke to Jeremiah there. He promised that Nebuchadnezzar would come and trash Egypt. God's will would not be thwarted.

There followed an argument between Jeremiah, as God's representative, and the people, who stubbornly refused to submit to God. They
declared their intention to continue the life of idolaters in Egypt. God
said they would all die by SFP, except for a remnant (now a remnant of
the remnant).

Egypt, Philistia, Moab, Ammon, Edom, Damascus, Kedar and
Hazor, Elam—a long hit list of prophecies were delivered by Jeremiah
against the whole region. Finally, God's judgment against Babylon was
delivered. They would pay for their sins against God and Israel.

Jeremiah is followed by the short book of *Lamentations*. It is attributed to Jeremiah, and contains sorrowful poetry about the terrible fate of
Jerusalem and God's people. It does contain some hope, however, telling us that God's loving kindnesses will never cease, and that He does
not hurt His people willingly. It ends Jeremiah's story with repentance
for the sins of the people, and the hope of restoration, which you and I
already know is coming.

19
Daniel: Stories too Good to Rush By

Daniel

We are now in the time of the Exile, in the Captivity. Daniel and his friends were among those taken captive by Nebuchadnezzar. "Ol' King Buck" ordered that some of the cream of the Judean crop be drafted into the king's service. These boys had to look good and be healthy, they had to be smart and be teachable. They would go to Babylon University for three years, then have a career in the Royal Service. I am pretty sure that they were made eunuchs, too, but that detail is left out of Daniel's book, so I'm not dwelling on it in mine.

This story focuses on Daniel and three of his colleagues, Hananiah, Mishael, and Azariah. When they became subjects of Babylon they all got new names. Daniel was named Belteshazzar, which sounds pretty cool, but we don't ever use it. On the other hand, his three friends were renamed, and those are the names by which we know them. Hananiah became Shadrach, Mishael was renamed Meshach, and Azariah was Abed-nego.

The boys were all treated well, because the Babylonians wanted the end result to be impressive. Along with the King's schooling came food and wine from the royal kitchen. This would look good to us, but to our heroes it was a problem. Daniel and the guys wanted to remain pure and pleasing to God, and the King's kitchen wasn't kosher. To eat Babylonian groceries would defile them.

They expressed this objection to the commander, who was not impressed with their convictions. He had a job to do, and if he didn't deliver these young men in top condition physically and intellectually, he would likely be fired. Being fired could be tragic, since the only sever-ance package they probably had was to sever his head.

But Daniel was wise, and he had that favor of God thing going for him. So he spoke to the guy who was actually handling them and talked him into a test. For a trial period of ten days, they would eat veggies and drink water, ensuring that they did not defile themselves with the wrong stuff. After that he could check them out, and if they were what my East Texas relatives would call "all poor lookin,'" they would submit to the Babylonian food regimen.

Ten days later they had gotten shiny and fattened up nicely on the salad and water diet. They looked better than the others, so they were allowed to eat, and not eat, as God had taught them. That was trial #1.

Trial #2 began after they had won their jobs at the palace. They con-tinued to impress after the food test, and they learned better than all the rest of the captive boys. In fact, they were known to be better than all the magic crew and counselors that hung around the throne room. Daniel was even known to interpret dreams by the help of God. This brought them through their second trial.

The King had a dream and it upset him. When he woke up, he couldn't remember the dream, and that upset him some more. He ranted to all his "wise men" and threatened them all with death, if no one could tell him the dream and the meaning of it. Daniel and crew didn't hang with the rest of the sorcerer crowd, so it took a while for the word to get to them.

When the magician killer came around to get Daniel and his friends, Daniel asked, "What's the big hurry?" The situation was explained to him, and he went to see the king. All they needed was a little time, and they would bring the dream and its interpretation to the king. This was a different approach than the pagan magicians had tried; they were just stalling for time, perhaps to get away. Daniel actually gave the king hope, if he could just wait a short while.

The Hebrew Crew went to prayer, and shortly a vision was given to Daniel in the night. Much glory was given to God, and Daniel's praise is recorded in chapter two, verses twenty through twenty-three. Soon Daniel was before the king, telling him "There is a God who reveals mysteries." And He did.

The dream was a picture of the future, which God gave to Nebuchadnezzar as a great king. It was also for the purpose of showing Neb Who was the Great God. After Daniel delivered, the king was thoroughly impressed, and the boys all got promotions. The king promoted Dan, and Daniel promoted his buds.

King Buck was a little unclear on the concept of worshipping God. In the next verse, he orders an image built, based on the dream, and gives orders for everyone to bow before it. All the officials of the kingdom were gathered and told that, when the music starts, you bow before the image or go into a fiery furnace. Bow or burn—a classic dilemma for the people of God.

Shadrach, Meshach, and Abed-nego knew they couldn't bow. The thought of burning was unpleasant, but the idea of bowing before this image was worse. So, when they struck up the band and everyone bowed, there were the three of them, standing tall and sticking out like a ballerina in boot camp. Here we see the appearance of "certain Chaldeans," fellow leaders, magicians within the government. They were of the jealous type. They came in as tattletales, and the boys were brought before the now angry king.

You would think that this king would know better, but no. He knew that these were Daniel's friends, who served the same God. He knew that it was that God Who had showed him the mystery of the dream in the first place. But Daniel wasn't there—we don't know where he was—so maybe Buck thought God wasn't looking either. In any event, the king thought perhaps he could bluster the boys into submission. He threatened them, then offered them a second chance to bow. Then he said something important. "What god is there who will be able to deliver you out of my hands?" God, as we see throughout the life of Nebuchadnezzar, is interested in this king. When Buck asks this defiant question, God will be there to answer.

The boys weren't surrendering to the threats. In fact, they replied, they didn't need time to think, and there was no reason to waste time on a second chance. The result would be the same. They respectfully told the king, "God can deliver us, but if He doesn't we still won't bow." This is a powerful picture of faith. We believe God for deliverance, but even more, we trust Him in obedience.

This really chapped the king, who ordered the furnace stoked up to a heat seven times beyond normal. I think he was just being dramatic. I don't think they had the technical ability to measure the heat that precisely, or perhaps even to create that much heat. What we do know is that the men who put S, M and A into the oven were killed in the effort. That's a bodacious blaze.

But our heroes were bound and tossed into the furnace. It must have been some experience. I want to ask them about it sometime; to hear their story firsthand. This is one of the things we will do in Heaven. We will tell each other how great God is, and how he brought us through our stuff.

Nebuchadnezzar and his staff watched from a safe distance. The escorts who were scorched by the furnace were carried away discreetly. Then the king turned his attention back to the middle of the oven. And he blinked. Then he rubbed his eyes to clear them. Then he blinked some more.

"Didn't we throw three men, bound, into that furnace?" It was sort of a rhetorical question; he very well knew what he had done. "Look! I see four men, unbound (and unburned) walking around in there!" Then the king got eloquent, as he was occasionally prone to do. "And the appearance of the Fourth Man is like a son of the gods!"

He stepped over to the furnace, as close as he dared, and called the boys. But this time his tone was completely different. No bluster, no threat, just a recognition that his question about "what god" had been completely answered.

"Shadrach, Meshach, and Abed-nego! Come out, you servants of the Most High God, and come out here." You can almost hear him say, "Please?" Then the guys came out of the oven. Apparently the Fourth Man excused Himself.

All the officials in the house gathered around and examined the subjects of this wonder. Other than burning the ropes off, there were no visible effects of the fire. There was no singeing, not even a smell. Buck got into one of his proclamating moods.

"Blessed be the God of Shadrach, Meshach, and Abed-nego! He has sent His angel to deliver them when they trusted Him, disobeying the king's command. Anyone who says a bad thing about their God will be torn apart, and his house made a rubbish heap." Nebuchadnezzar seemed to like this particular threat; there were probably rubbish heaps all over town, wherever someone had crossed him. Our heroes got more promotions.

One would think that this would be enough for one book, but the book goes on. The king had another dream, this time about a big tree that got chopped down. When Nebuchadnezzar got around to asking Daniel about it, Daniel was appalled. He didn't want to answer, but the king insisted, so Daniel delivered. The tree was the king himself, and God was going to bring him down. Nebuchadnezzar had been using the services of the servants of God, and giving homage to their God, but he had not been recognizing that this God had sovereignty over the king himself. God was tired of this.

Daniel warned the king to repent, so that he might put this judgment off for a while. That might have helped, but it only lasted for a year. Nebuchadnezzar got full of himself again, and was strutting around on his rooftop, proclaiming his own glory. A voice came from heaven and said, "You will be driven out from the company of people, you will eat grass like oxen, and sleep under the stars, until you recognize that the Lord is sovereign over the rulers of men."

At that, King Buck seems to have gone slap dilly-dab crazy. He was run out of the palace and had to live by himself in the woods. His hair grew long like feathers, and his nails like claws. He went about like a human version of Warner Brothers' "Tasmanian Devil."   This lasted for seven years, and then he got his right mind back and praised God. At that time, He recognized that God had the say-so over himself, not just over the Hebrews.

That closes the book on Nebuchadnezzar, and Belshazzar enters the picture. This king was more blasphemous and disrespectful than his predecessor. Belshazzar ordered that the vessels taken from the temple be brought to his wine party. Using the vessels that had been consecrated to God for worship for his drunk-fest was a great insult. God called an end to his reign.

A hand appeared and began writing on the wall. This pretty much killed the wine-buzz. Belshazzar, badly unstrung by this apparition, called for someone to interpret the few words that were written. Of course, the call came to Daniel. He arrived, and Belshazzar, who does not seem to have known Daniel previously, offered him riches and promotion for the interpretation of the wall-writing.

Daniel had no use for the king's rewards, and told him so. I think Daniel recognized that promotion in a kingdom that was coming down was not really a good thing. Dan reminded the king that Nebuchadnezzar had his faults, but he finally recognized God as Lord of all. Belshazzar knew this, but refused to honor God. He insulted the God of Heaven, and praised the false idols. Daniel showed proper respect, but little personal regard for this king, unlike the personal concern he clearly had for Nebuchadnezzar.

Daniel then interpreted the three words written on the wall. Note that Daniel didn't need to *translate* the words; they were clearly understood. The quote was something like this: "Numeration (counting), numeration, weighing, division." What Daniel did was to interpret the message, the meaning of the words. The message was bad news. This kingdom had been counted, or measured, and had come up short. It had been weighed, and found to be insufficient. It would now be taken and divided.

Belshazzar follows through on his promise, and gives Daniel the rewards, including a gold chain as a symbol of his authority, and the rank of third in the kingdom. Perhaps the gold chain looked nice (should he have changed his name to Danny-L, and started rapping?), but the promotion was no big deal. The king was dead that night, slain by the incoming power. Darius the Mede was boss now.

Darius recognized a good man in Daniel, and made him one of the top three rulers in his administration. Daniel was good and honest, and this made the crooked politicians around him angry. They looked for some dirt to get on Dan, but there was none. He was a man of complete integrity, who honored the king and honored God.

That gave someone an idea. Perhaps he remembered the story of the friends of Daniel and the big statue. Anyway, they realized that the one non-negotiable in Daniel's life was his worship of God. If they could make that against the law, they would have him. A decree to that effect was written, and with flattery, they brought it before Darius. They threw in the famous "Medes and Persians" bit (See *Esther*, also.) just to make sure that the king couldn't back out of it. Darius bought the scam, not realizing who it was really aimed at.

For thirty days, anyone who prayed to or petitioned any God or man other than the king would be thrown into the lion's den. That was a stupidly impractical decree. You could have been thrown to the lions for saying, "Pass the butter, please." Perhaps you could have said, "On behalf of the King, would you pass the butter?" You see, it was not going to be enforced on the people, only on Daniel.

When Daniel saw the decree, he knew what it was about, and didn't waste any time wondering how he was going to get by. He did what he had always done, and he left the windows open, so everyone could see, if they wanted. Daniel was in the habit of praying three times a day, and he kept on. Sometimes you just have to provoke the thing. Soon the conspirators had the evidence they needed to throw Daniel to the lions.

They brought their accusation to the king, who was sorry immediately that he had made the law. Darius had taken a liking to Daniel, and was now distressed that these sneaky blokes had tricked him into a situation in which it appeared Daniel would be lion lunch. He tried the rest of the day to rescue Daniel from this predicament. At sunset the creeps were back, insisting that the king honor the law of the Medes and Persians, and put Daniel to the lions.

The miserable king had Daniel brought to him, so the king could apologize to him, I suspect, and then to be taken off to Kittyland. Darius says something remarkable here, "Your God, whom you constantly serve will Himself deliver you." Compare that to King Buck's blustering threat at the furnace. Darius had hope in God, but it was still a long night. The king stayed up all night fasting. No food, no girls, no nothing.

As soon as the dawn came, Darius hot-footed it down to the lion quarters. Breaking the royal seal, looking into the dark den, Darius anxiously called, "Daniel, has your God been able to deliver you?"

What would you have said, if you had been Daniel? "Yes, king—no thanks to you!" Or maybe, "Okay—YOUR turn!" Daniel was not like this. His first words from the den were "O, King live forever!" The king was overjoyed that, 1) his friend had made it through the night, and 2) his death was not on Darius' conscience, and 3) apparently Daniel wasn't mad at him. An angel of the Lord had spent the night there also, and had shut the mouths of the lions. The cats just weren't hungry that night, you think? God is in control.

Darius had likely been thinking all night, along with his prayer for Daniel. This king, while he did honor God, was still pretty much a paganesque king. Not restrained by godly ideas of fairness and mercy, he ordered the guys who conspired against Daniel to be brought, along with their wives and children, and all of them tossed into the lions' den. Guess what? The lions were hungry, after all. Before the bad guys hit the bottom of the pit, the lions caught them and munched them.

Darius made a proclamation to glorify God, and Daniel served him for the rest of his reign, and then served into the time of Cyrus, who came next. Daniel received more visions of the times to come, and of what would happen to his people. He also had some interesting conversations with angels, and this gives us some insight into how things work in the heavenlies.

Daniel's story shows us how to live in a hard place. He and his friends teach us that no matter where God's hand takes us, His face is always before us, and His eye is always upon us. God miraculously intervened in these men's lives, but it was to get them out of situations that their obedience to Him had brought about! He got them into trouble— and He got them out. The lesson for us? Do right and trust God.

20
Esther: the Book and the Babe
Esther

Esther has her own book. She deserves it. Her story is a good one, as good as anything you will read, literarily speaking. There is a beautiful, virtuous woman, there is an EE-vil bad guy, there is a wise old man, and treachery, and suspense, and a happy ending. Everything you want in a great story.

Read this one from the Bible; don't just take my version. You can do it—it's short. Modern readers like it because the "damsel in distress" is saved, not by a hunky hero, but by her own courage and smarts. This story is just begging for Disney animation. (Hey, they did *Hunchback*, and everybody's dead at the end of that book.) But I get ahead of myself.

The story does not start very nobly. King Ahasuerus invited all the cool people to a six-month party at his place. Sounds kind of like a World's Fair. At the end of that, there was a seven-day wine banquet with the King. We discussed this before; much wine = little wisdom. People do dumb things when the booze starts talking. First, the King gets full of pride and wants to ceremonially show off his trophy wife.

Queen Vashti had other things going on. One of the themes of this book is the dignity of women, or lack of it. I didn't get that from the "Liberal Feminist Commentary;" I can see it for myself, and you will, too, if you read with an open heart. Now, maybe she should have swallowed her dignity and submitted to her knuckle-headed husband. That can be debated elsewhere.

Vashti refused the King's summons. She was busy with her own event, and it was important, at least too important for her to interrupt it for a trip to the King's winefest, just so she could be ogled by a bunch of liquored-up politicians. Her refusal jolted the party. Anger was mixed with pride, and maybe a little lust, and fueled by alcohol; a volatile combination. The King had to save face, but how?

When one has a perplexing domestic issue to resolve, it is best to sober up first. Add to that the political and social ramifications of this problem, and we see how important this gets. You would think a king would call off his drinking and think about this a while. Not this king. He turns to the good ol' boys all around him, to get "wisdom" from a bunch of guys no wiser than him—and perhaps drunker.

"You can't let this go on!" they counseled. "If the other wives of the kingdom find out that the Queen refused an order from the King, all our wives will become unmanageable." You can see whom they really cared about. They had visions of a terrible (for them) kingdom in which all the women locked up the kitchens and crossed their legs. This was a thorny problem, to be sure, and I don't want to minimize the trouble Vashti was causing, but it truly was not handled wisely. The King just summarily dismissed the Queen— "You're fired!" That he didn't have her killed shows us that his heart was not as hard as his head, and that is what will save him later.

When he woke up from "drinking wine, spo-dee-o-dee," he remembered what happened, and then he started thinking. Actually, this probably didn't happen overnight, but pretty close to it. When his anger subsided, he realized he was alone. He couldn't even change his mind and have the Queen back, because his order had been given "according to the Law of the Medes and Persians," and couldn't be revoked. This dumb law is important to this chapter's story, and the "Daniel" one.

No queen. Not a good thing. All those "counselors" who talked him into firing his wife went home to their own wives, and were still happily married the next morning, if perhaps hung-over. The King did have those around him who seemed to be professional "suggesters." They suggested that every beautiful young virgin in the province be rounded up and brought to the King, so that he could pick a replacement queen. He went with this suggestion—wouldn't you?

The scene changes to introduce Mordecai, a Jew of the exile. You remember foreigners coming and hauling all the people away into exile, right? That's how Morty got to Susa province. He had a beautiful young cousin named Hadassah, or Esther. Esther's folks had died, and Mordecai had taken her in to raise as a daughter. We know that she was "beautiful of form and face," a real looker.

Chapter two, verse eight of *Esther* just hints at some things that we should think about. Many young ladies "were gathered" to the capitol city, "into the custody" of a eunuch of the King, named Hegai. Esther also was "taken" into his custody, and he was "in charge of the women." There is no reason to be sure that this was a voluntary thing; in fact it seems rather compulsory. A draft of all the honeys in the province. Not a fancy ball to which all the maidens of the kingdom were invited, like Cinderella. "Don't care what you had planned, don't care who you were engaged to, you're coming to the palace!"

Esther and the rest of the girls were swept up in the dragnet, voluntary or not, and placed in the care of Hegai, an important eunuch. This means we ought to talk about eunuchs, because they are important to the story. A eunuch is a castrated man. This was done in order to have the advantages of a man's size, strength, education and social standing without having all that testosterone to get in the way.

Many servants of the kings of that time were eunuchs; castration seems to have lessened ambition and that made the eunuchs more trustworthy. It certainly made them more trustworthy around the king's women. While all these women were in the custody of Hegai, it was still clear to whom they belonged.

We don't have many eunuchs around us today. Even if you lose your testes through accident or disease, you can have them chemically replaced, so you are not inclined to appear neutered. Eunuchs were not homosexual, a misunderstanding that people of our time sometimes have about them. They were not "girlie-men." They were more asexual, or non-sexual, if you prefer. With a little imagination, you can see how useful a non-sexual man might be, if you can imagine such a thing.

The King trusted Hegai to keep the royal interests in priority, and the women were likely pretty comfortable with him as overseer, since he was neither a competitor nor a threat around the harem. He probably got a lot of "Heggy, can you tie this strap?" "The sandals or the heels—waddyathink, Heg?" and "Heggy, does this skirt make me look too trashy?" (Remember, it was a competition for the King's attention and favor, so that's not really a stretch.)

Hegai took a liking to Esther in a brotherly, eunuchly, sort of way. He gave her cosmetics and food, and a staff of girls to assist her, and the best room in the harem complex. She had just arrived there and already she's being treated like the queen. How did she score this? There are a few reasons.

First, she was obviously a world class darling. Not just from the way she was described, but by what follows, we gather what a sweetheart she was. She was as attractive on the inside as she was on the outside. Hegai was just charmed. (Thousands of years later, I think I have a little infatuation with her, myself.) Also, a happy king meant a happy eunuch, so Hegai did his best for the king.

But there was something else working here. There was a palace full of charming girls, but Esther had something going for her that the others didn't—the favor of God. He is not mentioned by name in this whole book, but His fingerprints are all over it. Esther is being positioned to do a great thing for God and His people, and His purposes are served by her rising to the top of this beauty pageant.

There has been a lot of prejudice and hatred against Jews for a long time, and this was the case in Esther's time. Being a minority in a foreign city, she kept quiet about her heritage at the advice of Mordecai.

Morty, by the way, checked on his girl every day by visiting at the gate of the palace.

This process of queenly selection is confusing to us, who have modern day ideas about biblical morality and westernized views of romance. Don't be distracted by the details. The Kings of Israel—David, Solomon, and those who followed—had wives and concubines galore. This was a pagan king, and as I told you before, I don't think this was a completely voluntary activity. Morals have developed over time in the Kingdom of God. You just live by the ones we have now, and do your best to understand the way ancient people saw things. Give the girl a break. Whether you would submit to this or not is absolutely not important to the story.

When girls were brought in, they got cleaned up and softened up for twelve months. Country girls, foreign girls (like Esther) and peasant girls had to be instructed in how to act around the palace. After they were fit for presentation, they were brought to the king for an overnight interview, or perhaps we should say, tryout. They could bring whatever they requested with them; this was their big night with the King, and everyone wanted them in the best mood possible. They were put in the custody of the eunuch in charge of royal concubines, and brought in to the King for presentation. They spent the night there, and the next day they went back to the sorority house.

When it was Esther's turn, she requested nothing but what her mentor in the harem, Heggy, instructed. After Esther's visit, the King closed the competition. For the same reasons I mentioned above, Esther won the heart of the King immediately. She was a keeper, and the Boss put her on the Queen's throne. There was a big banquet and a holiday. And they all lived happily ever after? Well, not yet.

Still nobody knew that Esther was a Jew. Although he was a Jew from out of town, Mordecai was an important and respected man, apparently. Remember Jeremiah's vision of the good and rotten figs? Mordecai was a very good fig. He spent time with other important guys of the city around the king's gate. While there he got wind of a plot by a couple of the King's disgruntled employees to kill him when he wasn't looking. Morty told Queen Esther, and she told the King, and there was an investigation. The plot was uncovered and proven, and the plotters hanged. This was recorded in the King's chronicles, a journal of important things that happened. More about this later.

Ahasuerus had an eye for great women; for good men, not so much. He made this fellow Haman his Prime Prince. Everyone bowed to Haman when he came by, everyone except Mordecai. When the other princes inquired about this behavior, Morty told them he was a Jew. Jews of that day would not bow to anyone or anything except God—the exile had taught them that lesson.

Hate is a twisted, evil thing. It often makes no sense. When you get it into your heart, it goes to your head, and you can get stupidly mean. When Haman heard the story of this fellow Mordecai, who wouldn't bow to him because Jews didn't do that, he decided to kill not just Mordecai, but all the Jews in the province. No reason for this except hatefulness. Esther, the "stealth Jew," had been Queen for just over four years.

Haman went to the King with his plan. He told lies, and he gave the King a bribe. The result was that a date was set later in the year, and on that day it would be open season on Jews. Anyone in the kingdom could kill Jews and take everything they had, sort of like Nazi-land (Satan is not very creative, and his people tend to not be very original.)

The decree went out, that on the date determined by "chance" or "Pur," this awful thing would happen. The date set was much later in the year. I think maybe Haman was superstitious, and this worked against him. Otherwise, why wouldn't you just decree this killing to begin as soon as possible? Then the Scripture says that after the decree was posted, Haman and the King sat down to drink, while the city was in confusion. That's a real picture of bad leadership.

When Mordecai heard about this, he went into mourning. As they did in those days, he fasted, put on sackcloth and smeared himself with ashes, as a symbol of great distress. He went to the area just outside the king's gate, for that was as far as he was allowed to go when mourning. Word of this got to Esther, and she was disturbed.

What Esther heard about was Mordecai in sackcloth out in front of the house. She apparently was clueless as to why he was acting this way. She sent some good clothes out to him, so he could get out of that sackcloth, but he refused. Next, she sent one of the eunuchs out to see what was up. He came back with the story, and with a copy of the edict, to show Esther. Mordecai suggested that she go in to ask the King's favor in this, since it involved her and her people.

Esther's reply was cautious, not courageous. "I have not been summoned." It was true enough. She had not been called for thirty days. Looks like the honeymoon was over. The Queen was still living under those same macho-kingdom rules as her predecessor, and had no privilege of coming to the King's office unsummoned. Anyone who interrupted the court, including the Queen, would be dragged out and executed without question. The exception was that if the King wished, he could recognize you by extending his scepter. Then you would get to live. Guess you had to make enough noise to ensure that the King knew you were there, but not so much noise that you annoyed him.

When Esther sent this word out to Mordecai, he didn't seem to care much about the royal rules. They all had their heads on the block. He did give wise counsel to his young cousin, however.

"If you don't speak up, the Jews will get by somehow, but your family will end. And who knows but that you have come to the kingdom for such a time as this?" With these words believers have gained courage and faith in God for centuries. Mordecai reminded Esther, and all of us, that God gives favor for His purposes, and we really don't know what all those purposes are, so we'd better do the right thing. In fact, God still had a covenant with these people, and He wasn't going to let them get annihilated just because Haman wanted his pride stroked.

Hearing this, Esther had her attitude adjusted. She asked Mordecai to call a three-day fasting prayer meeting for all the Jews in town. She and her crew would do the same. After that, she would go in to the King, and the law be hanged—maybe the Queen be hanged, too.

Esther got royally dressed up and stepped into the throne room. The King saw her, and she received his favor. She stepped forward and touched the extended scepter, acknowledging his sovereignty. The drama was over. Or was it?

The King was in a loving mood, sounds like. "What is troubling you? What can I do for you? Even half the kingdom is yours for the asking."

Esther had been thinking during her fasting and praying. She had also been preparing. Her request was simple, at first. She did not want this showdown with Haman in the open court. That was his territory, and she could not be sure how things would go there. She had to get the adversary on her home court, to deal with him on her terms, where she had the advantage. Her response to the King was brief, but brilliant.

"If I have found favor with you, and you don't mind, let the King and Haman come for a banquet that I have prepared for you both tomorrow. After that, I will tell you what's on my mind." This was genius. Count 'em, four "yous" and one "the king" in that request. Esther wanted something, but notice that her words were all about the King's feelings. By now she knew him, and although he was a pretty good guy, he was still all about himself.

The King sent for Haman, who of course cleared his calendar, and the banquet was on. Haman was a happy villain when he left the palace. Imagine! The queen asks you to a private banquet with just her and her husband, the king! You are important, indeed!

Then he comes up on Mordecai. No bowing, no fear, he just looked at Haman as if Mordecai were as good as the Prime Prince himself. All the good feelings about the Queen's invitation evaporated, and he was filled with rage. This Jew would die for his nerve!

Haman went home, and gathered his flunkies and his wife around him. He whined to them all about how important he was, and how the Queen invited him—just him—to dinner with the royal couple. Yet he couldn't enjoy all his importance while that Jew just sat in the gate and refused to bow to him. "Poor me!" you can hear him thinking, and "Poor you!" all his sycophants said to encourage him.

The friends of Haman had an idea. They at least knew how to make this whiner happy. "Have a really high gallows built, and in the morning ask the king to have Mordecai hanged on it. Then you can enjoy the banquet when you go!"

"Sweeeet!" thought Haman, and that night, he had visions of Mordecai hanging, swollen and twitching, with himself standing proud, next to the gallows. Everyone would say, "Haman is the MAN! Don't mess with him, or you'll end up like poor pitiful Mordecai!" He went to sleep consoling himself that tomorrow he would have his vengeance on that impudent Jew, Mordecai. In fact, Haman was up extra early the next morning, so he could be first in line to ask the King about hanging Mordecai.

Ahaseurus meanwhile, was not sleeping. Counting sheep wouldn't do it. Warm milk wouldn't work. Something was keeping him awake. He ordered the chronicles to be read to him. You can do that when you're the king. Maybe he was just starting to relax when the story of the earlier assassination attempt was being read.

I don't know that this was actually a good idea. "You can't sleep, Your Majesty? Let me read to you about the people who tried to kill you!" No wonder he was still awake in the morning when the palace opened.

However it came out, the King had a thought. "What did we do to honor Mordecai for blowing the whistle on those guys?"

"Nothing yet."

At just that time, Haman was coming in, bright and early, to get Morty hanged. As the King heard his Main Prince, he asked, "Who is that coming in?"

"Haman is waiting for you."

"Bring him in." Haman knew about these things. The King wanted to make a big hoity-toity deal of this, and Haman was as hoity-toity as they came. He would know just how to honor Mordecai.

Haman was feeling pretty important as he stepped in. Right straight in to see the King in his chambers. No line, no waiting. But you still don't speak until you are spoken to, so Haman waited for the King to ask his usual, "What can I do for you?"

But that was not the question the King asked. Instead, he asked something strange. "What should be done for the man whom the King desires to honor?"

Now, maybe the King was drowsy from being up all night. Maybe the Starbucks hadn't kicked in yet. Perhaps it was because Haman had just showed up while the King was thinking, interrupting his thought process in mid-cogitation. For whatever reason, Ahaseurus neglected to say WHO he wanted to honor.

Haman was left to surmise that this was just a subtle way for the King to greet him, and to find out how Haman would like to be honored, since, he figured, no one was more worthy of the King's honor than himself. Okay, he would play along, and pretend to be overwhelmed with surprise when the King revealed the subject of such honor.

"Uh, bring a royal robe that the King has worn, and put it on him. Then put him on a horse which the King has ridden. Next, have an important man lead him through the city square, saying to all the people, "This is what is done to the man the King wants to honor!"

"Let Mordecai refuse to bow after *this*!" Haman thought. He would put off the hanging until after the honoring, so that Mordecai would have it as a last memory before he swung on the gallows. Haman was really enjoying this fantasy when the King's voice startled him and crashed his world.

"Great! Go and do all that for Mordecai the Jew who sits at the city gates. And since there is no one more important in the kingdom than you, you lead the horse yourself! Oh, Haman—did you need something?"

"Nothing important, Your Majesty."

It was the longest morning of Haman's life. Somehow he got through it without choking Mordecai with his bare hands, his hatred for Mordecai only overcome by his fear of the King. When it was finally over, Haman slunk home with his humiliated head covered. He had to explain to his wife and friends what had happened, and that just made it happen for him all over again.

His wife was sympathetic, but not optimistic. "If he is a Jew, you will not succeed. You will fall before him." Newsflash! Did the old girl just find out about Mordecai's heritage? Before he could get any more of her "advice," the eunuchs were there; it was time for the banquet.

At the end of his horrible morning, Haman was going to just try to enjoy the luncheon. Soon he was seated, along with the King and Queen, and it was very nice. After some wine, the King asked Esther, "What is it that you want—ask, up to half the kingdom— it's yours." Esther's answer was a shock to both the King and Haman.

"If I have found favor, and you don't mind—may I have my life, and the life of my people? That's all I want. For you see, we have been sold as slaves, to be destroyed and annihilated." She still remembered to stroke the King's ego in the middle of this, begging pitifully, "If we had just been made slaves instead of scheduled for killing, I wouldn't have said anything, for that would not have been worth troubling the King."

The King, being rather thick, said, "Who would try to do something like that?"

Now the girl could have quoted Nathan, and replied, "Thou art the man!" but she was wiser than to do that. This was not the place to get points against her gullible husband. She fingered the real culprit.

"A foe and enemy is this wicked Haman!" There. We've been waiting for that the whole story, and now it's out. Everybody knows. Haman was now terrified, and the King left the room, perhaps to sign a death warrant. He stomped into the garden to clear his head, and think about this string of revelations. He had just learned that his wife was a Jew, and that Haman was plotting to destroy her and her people. However, he has learned from his past about making rash decisions. After a few moments reflection, he headed back inside. When he returned he could scarcely believe what he saw.

Haman had taken the opportunity of the King's absence to beg for his life from Esther. He knew his case was weak, but he was a slimy one, and would try anything, even groveling, to save his sorry skin. Maybe the Queen would have some pity, and he could use that to stay alive. In his groveling, he stumbled and fell on the couch where the Queen was. Remember, he'd been drinking. That's when her husband walked in.

"Will you assault the Queen here in front of me?" Palace security was right there, and they didn't even need orders. Haman was apprehended, and his face was covered immediately. You're dead meat when that happens.

Eunuchs have been friends to Esther and her family through this whole story, and now one of them spoke up. "Haman has a gallows built at his house on which to hang Mordecai, who spoke well of the King." That was an understatement; Mordecai had saved the King's life, and this Haman was planning to kill him. Even the dense King had to enjoy the irony when he said, "Hang him on it." The King felt better after that.

Had he known what was to happen after his death, Haman would have been really angry. Esther got his house, and Mordecai got his job. Esther turned the house over to Morty, too, but the girl still wasn't happy. The order to kill and plunder the Jews was still in force.

Remember that "Law of the Medes and Persians" stuff. The King himself couldn't repeal the law, so a balancing law had to be enacted to fix the mess. Mordecai was given the job of writing this law, and it said, in effect, that if anyone attacked the Jews, their rear end was at the mercy of Morty's Mob. Normally you wouldn't allow such violence in your kingdom, but this was a one day thing. As the law went out, the Jews were joyous. It was such an impressive victory that many who were not Jews converted.

On the appointed day of killing, there was a great slaughter. Actually, they had to get an extra day's extension from the King to get all the killing done. The Jews went through the land and destroyed their enemies. They did not take their stuff, however. It wasn't about the stuff, but about the right of the Jews to defend themselves against the people who hated them. It still is.

After this, the Feast of Purim was established as a memorial for all time, and the Jews still observe it. Esther and Mordecai became greater and greater, and *then* they all lived happily ever after.

21
A Jerusalem Makeover
Ezra, Nehemiah

There were some pretty good guys out there in Gentile Land. Even though they were not Jews, and not in on the Covenant, they respected God. Cyrus was one of those. After the people of God had spent sufficient time in exile in Babylon, Cyrus from Persia came along and took over. He decreed that Jerusalem should be rebuilt, and the Jews should go home. That's the end of *Second Chronicles*.

A new book starts to tell the story of how this happened. As *Ezra* opens, Cyrus' declaration is repeated in more detail. The Jews got their stuff together, and good ol' King Cyrus had all the temple vessels that Nebuchadnezzar had hauled away brought out for the trip home. God had instructed Cyrus to rebuild His temple, and the king was doing his best to obey. The Jews took a head count, and started out.

As soon as they got back to Jerusalem they started offering all the sacrifices that the Law called for. They were back home, but they were very vulnerable to the people surrounding them, who might not be so happy to have them back in the neighborhood. It seemed smart to please God. The sacrifices were restarted before the temple work had even begun. Worship is the first step of work.

Before too long, however, the temple was started. The foundation was laid with much shouting and fanfare, and building was underway. Not everyone was glad about this. Judah's enemies first asked them if they could participate in the rebuilding. We suspect they really just wanted in so they could slow things down and mess things up.

The wise men of Judah declined that offer, so the enemies started open opposition. They lied about the Jews and fought them in court right through Cyrus' reign into the administrations of his successors. They wrote a nasty, lying letter claiming that the Jews were rebuilding the city for rebellious purposes. The king (not Cyrus, but now a different guy) checked his records and saw that Jerusalem had once been a mighty city that had collected tribute from its neighbors. This spooked him, and he ordered the rebuilding to be stopped. The sneaky enemies of the Jews ran right out and made sure that the order was enforced. Building stopped until the reign of Darius.

When Darius was king, men of God prophesied to Judah, and they started rebuilding again. Of course, their enemies questioned it, and the Jews appealed to Darius to search his records and confirm that Cyrus had indeed approved the project. He made the record search, and found that Cyrus had not only approved rebuilding the temple of God, but had committed his kingdom to pay for it! Building went on, the enemies got out of the way, and the temple was finished. They dedicated the house and observed the Passover, and they all had great joy that they were back home worshipping God.

Ezra was a scribe. He was very knowledgeable about the Law of Moses and the covenant God had with His people. This was important because, as you recall, they had all been dragged away to Babylon/Assyria for seventy years, and many of them didn't remember much of anything about life in Jerusalem. They had not been faithfully serving God when they went into captivity—that was the whole point of the exile. So it is a good thing that somebody had stayed true to God's Word, or they would all have been lost.

It's a little confusing to keep up with *who* did *what*, and *when* in this story. This is complicated by these facts: First, Israel and Judah were under the rule of different kingdoms, and second, ancient Assyrian kings of this time may have all called themselves Xerxes or Artaxerxes. This is why I will lose a little historical specificity in telling the story. Later in your Bible study career, you will get the details more in order.

Also, Bible writers were of another culture and time, and they don't tell stories quite the way I do. (Yeah, that would kind of be the point of this book.) Here's the "executive summary." The Jews went back to Jerusalem and rebuilt the temple. Cyrus decreed it, Darius followed through on it, and another king sent a big bunch of people and supplies to equip it. There were enemies who tried to stop it, but God vindicated His people, and they got the job done.

Ezra was taking people and supplies back to Jerusalem. There was real concern about being attacked on the way. Ezra could ask the king for protection, but he was embarrassed to do so, since they had just received the king's decree saying how great God was. They decided to trust this great God to get them safely home. He came through for them and they made it.

There was one more thing the people of the exile had to do. It came to Ezra's attention that many of the exiles had married local girls, women of the nations from whom God had said to stay away. The people of God had been unfaithful, and this had to be corrected. Ezra was appalled and wept before God at their disobedience. Others repented as well, and the big crowd gathered in the rain to hear Ezra's instructions.

They agreed to put away their foreign wives, but there were a lot of them. So, an investigation was conducted, and records made, and within a few months the people were all purged of this unholy thing.

What has this all got to do with our Big Story? It shows us the faithfulness of God to His Covenant. Even though they were idolatrous and disobedient, God was faithful to His covenant partners. Although their city had to be destroyed and they had to be carried away for a time, God allowed them to return.

Wherever your disobedience may have taken you, there is a road back. It may not be an easy road, and you may have a city, or a life to rebuild, but God is with you the whole way. His correction may be upon us for a while, but His love endures forever.

The book of *Ezra* tells us about the rebuilding of the temple. *Nehemiah* is the story about the rebuilding of the walls. It is all the more interesting because it is told in the first person. It is Nehemiah telling us the story, himself.

Nehemiah had received news from home, and it was not good. Jerusalem was pretty much wrecked, and its walls were gone. For the walls of a city to be destroyed was about as bad as it got, because there was then no defense. Any old bunch of marauders could just come along and have their way in your town, if there were no walls to defend you against them. (Think about El Guapo in *The Three Amigos.*) You might be a little village, or an insignificant town, but you could not call yourself a real city if you had no walls. It was a reproach, an embarrassment upon Jerusalem and all those who loved her.

When Nehemiah heard of the condition of the hometown he was heartbroken. He wept for days. He fasted and prayed for God to come to Jerusalem's rescue. He repented on behalf of his people for the unfaithfulness that had gotten them into trouble, and claimed God's promise that if they would repent, He would return to them. Then Nehemiah slips an important fact into his story.

"Now I was cupbearer to the king." (Neh. 1:11)

This was a bigger deal than it at first appears. Nehemiah was in an intimate and trusted position in the king's court. It was not appropriate that one appear sad in the king's presence, but Nehemiah had been mourning and fasting for days, and it showed. Artaxerxes noticed and asked about Nehemiah's sadness. Fearfully, the servant told the king about the state of his city and its people. Artaxerxes recognized that this was something he could do something about, and asked for Nehemiah's suggestion. With prayer, Nehemiah presented a bold request.

"Send me to Judah, to the city of my father's tombs, so I can rebuild it."

"How long will it take?" The king wanted to know. A time was set, and Nehemiah had a further request. He had been thinking about this in advance, it seems.

"I will need letters to the governors on the way, guaranteeing safe passage, and I will need wood from the king's forest." All this was granted, and Nehemiah was on his way. In moments, Nehemiah had gone from despair to hope, and from hope to action. But not everyone was going to be happy about this.

Sanballat and Tobiah were not happy. They were local officials in Jerusalem, and they liked things the way they were. They cared not for the welfare of Jerusalem, and resented anyone coming along who did.

When he got to town, Nehemiah did not tell everyone what he had in mind. He first slipped out in the middle of the night and surveyed the problem. After that, he told the people what was on his mind. Sanballat and Tobiah objected immediately, but Nehemiah told them it was none of their business.

The people all took sponsorship of a piece of the wall and rebuilt it. (Don't know if they put their name on their sections, but that would have been cool, huh? *This wall section provided by Uzziel Bar-Har-haiah and sons, available for all your goldsmithing needs. Call for appointment.*) Gate by gate, wall by wall, it was all restored. S and T were there to mock the project, but Nehemiah and the people just turned them over to God, and kept working.

When they saw that ridicule and discouragement weren't working, and the job was about half done, the enemies of the Jews began to plot an attack. Nehemiah and his people got wind of it, and armed their workers. When the bad guys realized that the Jews were armed and ready, they chickened out because they were only interested in a sneak attack, not a fair fight. From then on, there were guards among the workers, and the men worked with a weapon handy.

It seemed that the people were in unity all around, but there was a problem. Some of them had loaned money to others, and took advantage of them in these hard times. (In AD 2011, this looks really familiar.) Now, sons and daughters were being taken into bondage because of the debt. This was dividing the people and destroying their united community. Nehemiah gave the leaders a good chewing out, and the people agreed to stop the usury. Unity was restored.

It was time for Sanballat and Tobiah and Co. to try another tactic. This time they called for Nehemiah to come down and talk with them. Four times they sent messages for him to meet them, and four times he was too busy. They meant to harm Nehemiah, and he knew it.

On the fifth try, they sent an open letter accusing Nehemiah of conspiring to become king. It was a ridiculous accusation, and he told them so. They hired false prophets and counselors to give bad advice and to frighten Nehemiah, but none of that worked. He just stayed solid and God led his steps. Then the wall was finished.

Next, it was time to count everyone and see who was there. *Ezra* records this count, too, and when you put their numbers together, they balance. Speaking of Ezra, he was priest and scribe, and he showed up at this point to read from the book of the Law. The people were moved by the reading of the Word, and it was a great and holy day. After that, they reinstituted the Feast of Booths that had been let go during the exile. The comeback was continuing.

It was time to get serious with God. The people gathered together in sackcloth and repented to God for all their faithlessness to the covenant they had with Him. They rehearsed the long history of Israel, and how they had been brought into the land, then lost it. Now they cried out to him that they were back, but "slaves on their own land" because they were under the rule of others. Because of this they were renewing their covenant with God.

They had an actual document, and their leaders signed it on behalf of the people. It was a solemn oath to live under God's law, and to do the things they knew would be pleasing to Him. They said they had learned their lesson. We'll see.

There was not room for everyone within the walls, so there was a lottery of sorts, to determine who got/had to live in town. Nine-tenths of the people lived in the surrounding countryside.

The wall was dedicated, and the temple purified. And here Nehemiah found an irritating thing. Eliashib, a priest who was in charge of arrangements in the temple, was related to Tobiah. This priest made a big room available to his relative, right in the temple. It was a room in which God's stuff was supposed to be stored, and when Nehemiah found out who was staying there, he threw his junk right out and rededicated the place to God.

Next, Nehemiah found out that the priests had not been receiving their rightful portions from the people, so some of them had to leave priesting and return to farming. Neither God nor Nehemiah were happy with this, and they corrected it. The tithe had to be restored to God's house.

There were a lot of things to get used to again as God brought His people back from exile. They were ignoring the Sabbath, and there were those mixed marriages we discussed earlier. But when we are redeemed, we must live like we are redeemed. God had been faithful to bring them back, and now they wanted to please Him with the lives they were living. Maybe they had learned their lesson, after all.

Poets and Prophets

22
God (and David) Wrote a Songbook
Psalms

This story will be different in style than what has gone before. This is because we are summarizing and sampling a songbook, a collection of worship songs and hymns. The story of the Psalms goes along with the story of David, often giving us insight into his thoughts and feelings as the events of his life occurred. Not all the Psalms were written by David, but as a singer and musician, it seems he had a lifelong interest in collecting and preserving the best music of his people.

It is not entirely accurate to say that nothing happens in this book. True, being a songbook, it won't make it as a novel, but the things that happen are events of the soul. Here we hear the thoughts and feelings of David, for the most part. When we link the psalms to the historical narrative, it deepens the story.

First, an overview of the collection. This is poetry, but perhaps not the type you are used to. Your first impulse may be to say, "This ain't poetry; it don't even rhyme!" Well, there are at least two reasons for that. First, it wasn't composed in English, so even if it did rhyme for David, it wouldn't for you. Rhyming words in one language don't rhyme in another.

Next, rhyming isn't what this poetry is all about anyway. Hebrew poetry is about *parallelism.* For instance:

The heavens are telling of the glory of God;
and their expanse is declaring the work of His hands.
—*Psalm* 19:1 (NASB)

You see how the first line is restated in the second. That's a form of parallelism. Another form contains a contrasting thought in the second line (*Prov.* 13:6). Sometimes a thought is continued in the second line (*Ps.* 27:1), and sometimes there is a comparison between two things in the two lines (*Prov.* 26:11). In much of the poetical books, you get parallelism, and when you learn to see it and enjoy it, you will enjoy Hebrew poetry.

So, what is a psalm, anyway? The Hebrew name for this book is *Book of Praises.* Most psalms are very praise-oriented. They are about how great God is. Sometimes they are about how great it is to be on His side, and how awful it is to be wicked. These songs are of varying length; number 117 is two verses long, then two psalms later, 119 is 176 verses long.

As music tends to be, these psalms are emotional. Great joy is expressed in high praises, and David sometimes sings the blues. In all cases the psalmist gives glory to God. Identified by content, there are seven recognized psalm types.

Messianic Psalms: These are prophetic psalms relating to the Messiah, God's Anointed Redeemer. They may speak about Him, or they may contain words spoken by Him. A whole psalm may be messianic, or just a part of one. These psalms look forward to Jesus. Some examples are *Psalm* 2, 16, 22, and 110.

Historical Psalms: Psalms which have their basis in the great things that God has done in the history of Israel are known as historical psalms. They speak of the greatness of God shown through His mighty acts. Their message is that God has delivered us in times past, and can be trusted to do so again. Many of the verses of these psalms recount the Exodus of Israel from Egypt, and how God brought them out with a mighty hand. You can see this type of writing in *Psalm* 77 and 78, and in 105 and 106.

Penitential Psalms: Not everything went well for David, remember? Sometimes he was guilty of wrong, and had to repent. These times are commemorated in penitential psalms. When we know the occasion for the repentance, it gives us insight into the emotions and spiritual life of the composer. *Psalm* 32 and 51 are samples of this type.

Imprecatory Psalms: These psalms are unsettling to some readers. David was a singer, an artist, and a shepherd, but also he was a warrior. The battle life does not yield sissies. Some of this comes through in his writing, as he prays violent destruction upon those who oppose him and oppose God. These are the desires of his heart, which the Holy Spirit has preserved for our understanding. *Psalm* 35 gives us a taste of this.

Acrostic Psalms: There are just a few of these, and in most translations you will read right through without a notation to tell you about it. *Psalm* 119 is an acrostic. I think you know that the chapter and verse divisions were not a part of the original inspired writing, but sometimes, as in this psalm, they seem to work well, following the natural divisions. This psalm is special. It goes like this:

At the beginning of each of twenty-two sections is a letter of the Hebrew alphabet, in order. There follows in each section eight verses, all beginning with that same letter of the alphabet. The message of the psalm exalts the "law of the Lord," beginning with the first verse, and throughout the psalm, the joys of adherence to God's Word are extolled. This song of Israel is truly in a class by itself.

Theocratic Psalms: *Psalms* 93 through 98 are a good sample of this genre. In them, the psalmist declares the majesty and lordship of the Lord over all the earth and heavens. God is presented as the Magnificent Ruler of All, and we are described as His submissive subjects who rightfully bring Him worship. Reading these psalms is high praise, and listening to our own reading of them can bring us to a point of pure worship.

Praise Psalms: This is how the *Book of Psalms* concludes, with psalms of praise, and with calls for the entire universe to rejoice in Him. These praise songs can be seen elsewhere in the book (33, 66) but *Psalms* 146-150 are a section of "hallelujah" psalms, so called because that word in Hebrew is literally translated "Praise God." When you then look at the English translation, and consider that each repetition of "Praise God" was originally written as "Hallelujah," you see why they are called "hallelujah" psalms.

Now, let's go back and pick out a few psalms which have a particular connection to the stories, and to The Story.

Psalm 1: The *Psalms* open with a pleasant comparison of the godly and the ungodly. Of note is verse three, which speaks of the root, fruit and branch of the godly man. This man is compared to a well-planted tree. May each one of us be such a tree.

Psalm 2: The second psalm is about Messiah, all about Messiah. Some have taken verse eight out of its context, and have appropriated it to the Church. This makes a great missions text, but it is not accurate. It is our promise *in Christ*, and coupled with *Matthew* 28:18-20, becomes our promise *through Him*. You can preach that in a missions service. What *Psalm* 2 does make clear above all is that Messiah will be Lord of all nations, not just Israel's deliverer.

Psalm 22: This messianic psalm looks toward Christ's suffering on the Cross, and it is likely that it was on Jesus' mind as He was crucified. His words, "My God, my God, why have you forsaken me?" are a cry of anguish from His soul, and are a direct quotation from the opening of this psalm. If we were hanging on a cross, we should hope that we would be quoting psalms also.

Apparently, on one of David's days of anguish, the psalmist broke through to the prophetic, and the Holy Spirit led his soul into a taste of Messiah's despair. Not only do the words of this psalm speak of Christ's feelings, but events of His death are prophesied as well. The mocking words of the onlookers, the piercing of Jesus' body, and the gambling for His clothes are all found in this psalm. It is a prophetic picture of the Crucifixion, given centuries in advance.

***Psalm* 23:** One of the first psalms to which many of us are introduced, is a song from the heart of a shepherd which extols the shepherding nature of God. It recognizes the Lord's desire to provide for the one who trusts in Him, and affirms our total dependence upon Him.

***Psalm* 32:**It is a joy to be forgiven! *Psalm* 32 gives an insight into the misery David endured when he was caught in the interval between sin and forgiveness. Redemption is not only right; it feels good. While no specific event is cited, we can easily imagine David feeling this way after things had happened with Bathsheba, Uriah, and especially Nathan. In verses eight and nine, there is a response from the Lord, calling us to submit to His teaching

***Psalm* 34:**I believe this psalm must have been loud. It praises God for His deliverance, protection, and provision. Like meat in a sandwich, it contains an admonition to pursue good/God, and it is implied that this is the way to the promised deliverance.

***Psalm* 51:**Now we get to some of the "grit" of the psalms. *Psalm* 51 is directly connected to David's sin with Bathsheba against God and Uriah. After being busted by Nathan, David cried out in repentance to God, and this is some of what he said. Note the following:

First, David appeals to God for forgiveness based on God's greatness and righteousness, not any work or attribute of his own. This is how redemption works; it's not about us. *God redeems us because He wants to.* That is the nature of grace. When we talk about receiving "grace we don't deserve," it is a redundancy. All grace is undeserved.

Second, David feels spotted and dirty. Follow his language in the next few lines. "Blot out," "wash me," "cleanse me." "My sin is ever before me." Again in verse seven and ten, David returns to the language of washing.

Third, the cleansing must occur before David can sing of sacrifice. In verses 12-14 he begins to sing of restoration and deliverance. Only after that (v. 15), can the psalm conclude with praise and sacrifice. Humiliation and submission before God, cleansing, restoration and deliverance, praise and sacrifice offered with now-made-holy hands. That's the way it goes when you have sinned and need redemption. It's the story of life. It's the story of our life.

I often work with music playing. On one of my many re-writes of this chapter, I arrived at the *Psalm* 51 paragraphs as Eoghan Heaslip began to sing the song, "Lord, Have Mercy." It speaks of our tendency to drift from God, but also of His eternal "mercies ever flowing." Steve Merkel, the composer of the song, gets Psalm 51.

Thousands of years later, we still know exactly what David meant here, and how he felt. Thousands of years later, the mercies of God are still "a river of forgiveness, ever flowing without end." My soul, and your soul, still cries out with David, and with Eoghan and Steve, "Lord, have mercy!"

Psalm **52, 54, 56, 57:**These psalms are all supplications for deliverance, with the expectation that God will soon come through for the psalmist, and bring judgment to the wicked evildoers who oppress him. If you were an Old Testament saint, perhaps you sang these songs on your bad days. Today, under the New Covenant, we still pray for deliverance, but we have kind of spiritualized the "destruction of the wicked" part. "Love your enemies" and all that, you know.

Psalm **69:**Depression rises from within, often without good cause. Despair comes for a reason. For that reason, I call this psalm, not a psalm of depression, but of despair. Life is tough, and David is singing the blues for a reason. This is not like our blues, in which it "feels so good to feel so bad." The king is truly unhappy. He cries out for bad things to happen to his enemies. As usual, however, he finds a way to give praise to God in the last chorus.

Psalm **106:**A praise song to God, and a historical psalm. This one does not so much recount God's acts of deliverance as it does His acts of mercy to rebellious Israel. Throughout their journey to Caanan, and after their arrival, they disobeyed God. "Nevertheless," David says, "God remembered His covenant . . ." Psalm 106 is all about the faithfulness of God to His people and His promises, in the face of severe testing.

Psalm **126:** This song of return from captivity was especially meaningful when the nation did go into captivity and returned. We see it as the promise of answered prayer, a reminder that our hard times will not go on forever, because God is merciful. Sowing in tears does bring a harvest of joy, so go on and sow, if you trust Him.

Psalm **137:** Along with *Psalm* 126, this imprecatory psalm indicates that material likely was added to the collection in the generations after David. There was loneliness and bitterness in the time of captivity in Babylon, and this blues song expresses it well.

Psalm **149:** Here is a "Hallelujah" psalm. As you can see, it is a high praise, a warfare praise. It is all about victory, past and present.

Psalm **150:** The next psalm is a command to praise God, directed at everyone and everything. It calls for total, absolute praise, and is the best possible psalm with which to conclude the book. Praise the Lord!

23
Books of Wisdom, More or Less
Proverbs
Ecclesiasties
Song of Solomon

I placed these chapters here because I wanted you to have the historical background (Chapter 17) before you got into *Psalms* and Solomon's writings. They'll make better sense this way. There's still a story or two to tell, but for now let's enjoy some more literature.

The poetical books are often referred to as "Books of Wisdom." That's a little misleading. Not everything in them looks like wisdom, and some of it looks downright unwise. There is much wisdom and beauty in these books, but in some places they serve primarily as a negative example.

This chapter will digest *Proverbs*, *Ecclesiasties*, and *Song of Solomon* (also called *Song of Songs*). *Psalms* you just read, and *Job* is yet to come. Those books make up the Books of Wisdom, the "poetry section" of the Bible. The texts discussed in this chapter are the work of Solomon, part of an apparently huge amount of scholarship and writing that he did in his lifetime.

Proverbs

You will remember from Solomon's story that he was given extraordinary wisdom by God. We have some examples of this wisdom in the text of his story, but while at the height of his smarts, Solomon seems to have collected a book of "Wise Things for Young Men to Heed." We know the collection today as *Proverbs*. It is a book which just drips with wisdom. If you read and heed its principles, you will have a better life.

Proverbs starts with opening remarks about the purpose of proverbs and the value of wisdom. The reader is warned to stay away from sinners and their ways. Wisdom is personified as a woman, who calls out to whosoever will hear her voice.

Much of *Proverbs* is addressed to "my son." It does not appear that Solomon was writing with a particular son in mind, but rather to all young men who would come after him. He continues to make the case for seeking wisdom, understanding above all. Seeking wisdom, and acting wisely, will bear fruit in a good life. Solomon says that his own father gave him good instruction in wisdom, and he exhorts his own sons to "take hold of instruction" as it is given.

There are both positive and negative lessons to be learned. The king does not hesitate to declare the foolishness of immorality. He seems determined to paint word pictures of "the adulteress" that will frighten any young man into staying away from her. Solomon does not deny her attraction, but tells us that the end of her dealings with us will be bitter, if we yield to her flattery. She may look enticing, and say sweet sounding things to you, but if you fall into her trap, she will suck the life out of you, leaving you sad and sorry.

Solomon also has practical wisdom about debt and the value of work in the early chapters, but he really has an aversion to adultery. Kind of makes you wonder, doesn't it, whether there were some long private talks with his father, or even his mother, about the grief they experienced through their own failure. For whatever reason, Solomon writes plainly and convincingly about the plight of the "young man who lacks sense," and who gets himself tangled up in the web of whoredom, to his great regret. The harlot seems to be evil, personified, and is contrasted more than once with Wisdom, whom Solomon presents as a virtuous woman, calling out to all who will hear, pleading with them to follow her paths and live.

As I was being raised, I had health issues from time to time. In almost every doctor's office in the land during those days were copies of *Highlights* magazine. I was in a prosthetics/orthotics shop just last week, and there it was, still keeping children occupied after all these years. Along with the stories and puzzles was always the feature "Goofus and Gallant," my favorite part. The character Gallant was a nice, polite, careful young man. Goofus was a booger-pickin' moron.

In each installment of G and G, bad manners and unwise behavior were contrasted with examples of how you should act. *"Goofus runs around with scissors, sharp point out— Gallant holds them carefully, by the sharp end, and walks." "Goofus talks with his mouth full, and spits food all over his friends—Gallant swallows before speaking, and uses a napkin."* Things like that. I think the writer/illustrator of "Goofus and Gallant" may well have been familiar with Solomon's rhetorical style. Over and over, principles of wisdom are presented by Solomon as contrasts, and these go on for chapter after chapter. "The wise man does *this,* but the fool does *that.*" I hardly ever read *Proverbs* without thinking about those boys, Goofus and Gallant.

Toward the end of the book, Solomon has quoted some wisdom from a couple of other sources, one an oracle, the other a king. It is in the section attributed to King Lemuel that a famous description of "an excellent wife" is found. You will hear this read and preached on during many special occasions in church, whenever we want to honor women. Maybe you heard it at Grandma's funeral. It's good stuff.

The message of *Proverbs* is, "This is how life is." Coupled with *Ecclesiastes*, it is a good source of wisdom and understanding about the mysteries of life. Sometimes the king is giving us advice on how to behave or think, and sometimes he just makes observations. Whichever, they are consistently smart and wise. No wonder the Queen of Sheba was so impressed.

Ecclesiastes

Back in the eighties, I saw a man with a t-shirt which said, *"He who dies with the most toys, wins."* He had obviously not read *Ecclesiastes.* Later, I saw a bumper sticker with the "rest of the story." *"He who dies with the most toys— still dies."* That, boiled down to a bumper sticker, is the message of *Ecclesiastes.*

As you may remember, Solomon did not adhere closely to the principles taught to him by God and by Solomon's father, King David. He married many foreign wives, and began to worship many foreign gods. Among other results, this had the effect of turning Solomon a bit sour. His cynicism is recorded in *Ecclesiastes.*

The book starts out declaring that "All is vanity!" What good does it do to work? Everything is as it was. Generations come and go, the sun goes up and down, the wind keeps blowing, the rivers keep running into a never-full sea, then they end up back where they started. There is nothing new under the sun. This is a man who has known the bite of boredom. Knowledge without adequate purpose will do this to a guy.

Not only is work useless, but so is wisdom, apparently. Solomon has learned more than any man on earth, but calls learning, "striving after wind." Minnie Pearl said of one acquaintance, "If ignorance was bliss, he was the happiest man alive!" Solomon says "increasing knowledge results in increasing pain." Minnie and Solomon knew some of the same truths.

Next on the vanity "Hit Parade" (or hit list), are pleasure and possessions. Solomon tried laughter, drinking, hobbies, building, and getting rich, and found it all to be "vanity," "striving after wind," and of "no profit." Solomon makes an interesting observation: It is better to be wise than to be a fool—but at some point, both will be just as dead and forgotten, so there! Wisdom is as useless as anything else.

Solomon complains that all he has spent his life working for will be left to someone else, who may just be an idiot. What's the point of that?

(As it turned out, he did leave the kingdom to Rehoboam, who quite possibly was an actual fool.) The king counsels the reader to eat and drink and work hard, for God will bless that, but in back of this is the knowledge that all this is useless, too. You're gonna die, anyway.

Solomon seems to have a very cyclical world view at this point in his life. There is a time and season for everything, he teaches, and it all comes back around again. What is, has already been, and what has been, will be again. When Solomon's eyes are only on earthly things, as they are sometimes, he seems to teach doctrines that we know are false, ignoring the eternity of the human soul, for instance. However, he is just calling things the way they look on the horizontal plane. You die, your dog dies, you both rot. You are not all that special, in that respect.

Because there is evil and oppression, says Sol, all is vanity. He gives principles that are helpful in living this life, but after a little practical teaching, the king will sigh and say, "But, you're going to die, anyway, so it's all vanity." He reminds us, however, that there is a God above us, so try not to be a fool. Not being a fool seems to be important to Solomon.

Here is a paradox. Those who love money, and really care about stuff, will never have enough money, nor will they be satisfied with their stuff. So, don't be all about your stuff! Solomon thinks that a man who eats, drinks, and works well, will sleep well, and be as happy as a guy should expect to be. He says that it is better to be miscarried, and never live, than to live a thousand years twice, and not enjoy it. In the end, both will be at the same place, and one was unhappy for 2,000 years before he got there!

In some parts of *Ecclesiastes*, Solomon sounds like Eeyore, the donkey from the Winnie the Pooh stories, especially the Disney versions. Can you hear his voice as you read? *"When you are happy—you know you're gonna get sad later. And when you're sad—you can look forward to being happy. So, sad is better. Not that it matters—all is vanity."*

Solomon said very little about understanding women in this book. This may have been because he was the wisest man who ever lived, and knew when to keep his mouth shut. He does describe as bitter the woman "whose heart is snares, and whose hands are chains." He claims that he can't find a woman. We certainly know he looked. *Ecclesiastes* gives us a little insight into Solomon's habit of collecting women like other kings collected horses.

"Vanity, vanity, all is vanity." These words are the theme of the book. Solomon's message to us is that nothing is worth anything outside of the exhortation he gives us in verse 12:13 at the very end of the book, *"The conclusion, when all has been heard, is: fear God, and keep His commandments, because this applies to every person"* (NASB). Other than this, all is useless.

I used to think *Ecclesiastes* was a pessimistic, depressing book. It is not. I have lived some life since I first tried to understand it. Every time I go through it, I understand it better. Solomon says to us, "Live your life! Live it now! Don't hold anything back for later, because you might not get a 'later!' Give this life your best shot, because this is all you are going to get. Live loud, live completely, but live wisely, because you are going to die, then you will answer to God for the life that you chose to live. One life, then you will be dead for a really long time. One game, so leave it all on the floor. One dance, so even if you can't dance well—dance hard!"

Song of Solomon

In his beautiful worship song, "Oh, How He Loves Us," John Mark McMillan describes God's love as a "hurricane" which blows against me, a mere "tree." It is a song which speaks of the passion of God's love. Beyond passionate, God's love is fierce – even violent. This is the spirit of the Song of Solomon, and that worship tune captures it accurately.

This is a book like no other in the Bible, for a number of reasons. First, there is the content. Pure mush. Two lovers going on and on about each other, in sometimes blushingly frank language. Next, there is the literary form. It's a musical, as the title suggests. It seems to have been intended as an opera, or at least a choral production. You think an opera is tough to watch or listen to? Try reading one. (Actually, that might work better.) Another issue is the question of how this fits into the Bible itself, and what to do with it.

In doing my homework for this chapter, I saw some interesting things related to *"SoS."* Commentators treat it in different ways. Matthew Henry recognizes that it is an allegory and a parable, then seems to ignore the story itself, wanting only to discuss the spiritual application. Adam Clarke denies the spiritual application altogether, stating clearly that he does not see Christ and the Church in it at all. Perhaps he was never in love.

One of my favorite treatments is that given by Dr. Delmer Guynes. He speculates quite convincingly that the young lady in the story is none other than Abishag, of *1 Kings*, chapters 1 and 2 (*Queen of the Realm,* Calvary Church Press, 1986). I want to avoid plagiarism, so let me state clearly that the discussion of the narrative which follows owes much to Dr. Guynes. While recognizing the validity of the "face-value" parable, he goes on to explain the wonderful illustration of redemptive grace which is behind the story.

Other scholars choose to identify the woman as the daughter of Pharoah, whom we know Solomon married fairly early in his royal career. *Song of Solomon* is linked with *Psalm* 45 by some, but that psalm specifically mentions the "king's daughter." If you are holding to the "Abishag" theory, there is less of a connection to that psalm, perhaps.

Other interpreters tell the story as a "love triangle." In this interpretation, King Solomon attempts to make the young lady his queen, but she is in true love with a local shepherd boy. True love wins out, and eventually, Solomon concedes. All of these interpretations are consistent with what I think is the eternal point of the story, the love of God. This connects it to the Big Story.

To follow the text of *Song*, we have to let go of some ideas that we are used to holding while we read. The first idea to let go of is linear chronology. That does not happen here. There are not just flashbacks, but the whole story is a bit of a "flash around."

Another adjustment we have to make is to recognize that the text switches from one speaker/singer to another without warning. Context is everything in understanding what we are hearing at any given time. Modern translations (NASB, NIV, NLT) will tell you who is saying what; some King James Versions give explanatory notes at the start of each chapter, which may or may not help. The Amplified Bible is interesting here. It begins with a note explaining that "positive interpretation" is not possible, then gives it a very creative try, anyway.

There are three main views of interpretation of the book. They are:

Allegorical —"It's all about God's love for Israel, and Christ's love for the Church, so don't you be thinking about anything else while you are reading it—you understand? Why else would it be in the Bible? It ain't about nothing else, so get your mind out of the gutter!"

Literal— It is what it is. In the Greatest Book of Love Ever Written, certainly we can make room for a volume extolling marital bliss. Some interpretations make *SoS* to be a sort of "God's Sex Manual."

Typical—Yes, what is written, is written, but there is more. It is a description of actual events in the life of Solomon. Interpretation must recognize that, but there are typical applications beyond the literal. If you remember our discussion of "type" back in *Exodus* (Chapter 10), you will know what I mean. If you don't remember it, go back now and review. We must interpret the text in a way that is faithful to the author's intent, but we recognize it as an illustration of much bigger themes.

Another adjustment the reader must make is to accommodate ancient eastern frankness, expressed in "lover-talk." The two lovers in the song complement one another's physical attractiveness in a way that seems to us a bit of an overshare. We should evaluate this tendency, if we must, through the lens of their culture, not ours. Theirs is a pure love, and to the pure, all things are pure. Just blush, and read on.

I would love to tell you this story in chronological order, starting with, "Now it happened that . . ." and ending with, ". . .and they did just that." However, with such time and distance between us and them, the exact sequence of events is not that clear. What I can do is point out the importance of the story, and explain how this relates to The Big Story. (The following account is written in the present tense, since we are describing a work of literature that is designed to be performed. It "is," not "was.")

Picture in your mind a stage. On one side is a small choir. To the other side, slightly back, is a young man, obviously a king. We happen to know that he is Solomon. Front and center is a beautiful young woman, and she begins to sing.

"Let him kiss me with the kisses of his mouth—for your love is more delightful than wine." She rapturizes about him, and identifies the object of her affection as the king, asking to be taken into his chambers—a complete surrender of herself to him. The girl is answered by the choir, then she continues with an apology for the darkness of her skin, a sign of her forced life of outdoor labor.

Soon the two lovers are exchanging verses about the beauty that they see in each other. This goes on through what appears to be a dream sequence, and through a brief separation brought about by the bride's slowness in response. This is instructive because the type/parable, as you remember, is about Christ and His Church. We are thinking about Him, even when He is not physically present. We look for His return tomorrow, yet when He calls us to "come away" with Him tonight, we complain that it is inconvenient, and we miss the opportunity of His presence.

The King and His bride are enraptured with each other. A couple of our "old church" titles for Jesus are "Rose of Sharon" and "Lily of the Valley." These expressions come from this passage (2:1), but are perhaps meant to apply to the bride, making them a typical description of the Church, not the Lord. We are not too distracted by that, because the big point is that we (the Church and our Lord) love each other, and may well use interchangeable expressions of affection.

At times, the young man appears to be a local shepherd; in other passages, he is revealed to be a king. This contributes to the interpretation by Guynes that Solomon comes first in disguise, wooing and winning Abishag as himself, then later being revealed as the great King Solomon. This typology is consistent with the coming of Christ first as "one of us," before He is to be revealed as King of Kings.

The Bride of Christ, the Church, has fallen in love with Him as the Son of Man (the Shepherd), and will reign with him at His revelation as Son of God (the King). Meanwhile, His love has redeemed us, and when He comes, He will not be coming for the barefoot country girl, but for His Queen. There is no real deception involved in Solomon's behavior, if indeed he is coming as a local shepherd, because he is being himself—just not all of himself—in shepherd's clothing.

This love story tells us some things about the nature of God's love. It is intense, violent, even. We are loved much more by God than He is by us. This thought is worthy of some time to digest. It is because He loves us that He created us, not the other way around. The first man was created for the purpose of being loved by God. That is still our primary function. That may seem controversial, since we have been taught that we are made for the purpose of loving Him. However, the Bible is clear; we love Him because He *first* loved us. Whether or not we return that love, He will continue to love us.

He is fiercely, violently in love with His people, not just in a warm, fuzzy, paternal way, like Jesus in a centuries-old painting or stuffy Hollywood production, but as the intended groom desires His bride. I believe *Song of Solomon* is given to us as God's way of saying, "You think the desire of these lovers for each other is intense? My love for you is way beyond that."

We always think of the great love required for Jesus to allow Himself to endure the Crucifixion. Think also of the love for us that was the motivation for the Father in that event. He loves us so much that He would do that to His own son, for our benefit. He loves us so much that He would endure that outpouring of hell, both as Father and Son, to win us to Himself.

Nothing—not on earth, or in hell, or even sin itself—will be allowed to stand between God and those He loves. He will, and did, walk through hell to get to us. My God, what a love! Is it any wonder that it is described as "strong as death," and as "severe as the grave?" (8:6)

And don't forget an important point to the *SoS* story. This really did happen, and God has placed it here to show us that the type, as well as the anti-type, is blessed by God. Fierce love—romantic, even erotic—within the marriage relationship is pleasing to Him.

Here is what this song illustrates—"Yeah, God's love is like that, except more!" The love of these two lovers inspires us to love those whom we have on earth in a greater way, and then gives further inspiration to love Him Who first loved us.

24
Job and the Really Bad Day
Job

There is no compelling reason why *Job* was left until this late in this volume. Some experts say it may have been written before most of the rest of the books, so it could have gone in front. It contains much poetry, so it is usually placed with the books of wisdom in the Bible. We have it here, mainly because we haven't put it anywhere else. Here, it brings us back to the essence of faith in God.

Ever have a really bad day? Sometimes one or two bad things can "ruin" our day, but then there are days in which the bad things line up on the horizon and come swooping in, like planes at a busy airport.

Job had a season like that. His season of tragedy began with one day of hell, then it got worse. His story tells us many interesting things about God and His kingdom. However, there is at least one misconception we have to clear up at the start.

Occasionally, you may hear a discussion or study a book about *Job* that will state that the theme, or message of *Job* has to do with the question, "Why do the righteous suffer?" That's fine; all through this story, people are wrestling with that question. But if you come to the book thinking that reading it will give you a satisfying answer to the "why" question of suffering, you are likely to be let down. The "answer" isn't in there. You can gain insight into the nature of suffering, inspiration to help you deal with your own suffering, and illumination on the purpose of suffering, but the answer to the question "why" is not adequately covered in the text. I don't tell people that it is.

What it is about is faith. Not the kind of faith that just expects from God, but the deeper, darker, side of faith which trusts God, regardless of events or circumstances. Job could not reason why awful things were happening to him, but he trusted that God was always good and all-powerful, through whatever happened.

As I said, *Job* may be the oldest book in the Bible. Some scholars place it in the time of the patriarchs. According to this idea, during the era in which Abraham, Isaac, and Jacob were running around doing the things recorded in *Genesis* (or maybe even before that time), our hero was perhaps in another part of the world living through this story. This dating is based on the apparent absence of the Law, or of Tabernacle-style worship, or any mention of the people of Israel. However, it may also be possible that Job was just not a Jew, although he feared God. If the timing of the story were a matter of biblical importance to the Holy Spirit, we would have a clear date in the text. This book is about what, not when.

On to the story. There was, "in the merry old land of" Uz, a man named Job, who was both good and great. You must understand that he was a righteous man, not a sinner, a man who even offered sacrifices for his family, in case they had sinned. He was greatly blessed as a result of his pleasant relationship with God. Job was big rich, "the greatest man in the east." He had ten children, and life was sweet.

That lasts for five verses. In 1:6 there begins an intriguing passage which gives a little insight, and raises a few questions. It is easy to mis-understand what occurs, and to misinterpret this part of the story. We must not forget who God is. We must not place upon Him the limitations and motivations which characterize our own human existence.

There was a time when the "sons of God" (NASB) came into His presence, and spoke directly with the Almighty. In this context, "sons of God" seems to refer to angelic beings. It looks like there is a coming and going of the created (non-born) entities to give account for their actions. It is crucial to remember that this is not because God needs an accounting (*omniscience*, look it up) but because all created beings must give an account. We need this, God does not.

It was during this time that satan appeared before God. Apparently, getting kicked out of Heaven did not release him from accountability to God. Notice, it is God who directs the conversation. When you are allowed before God Himself, it is best not to speak until spoken to, unless you are a child of His, perhaps. One does not question the Sovereign Lord of Creation. Satan is not the opposite of God. There is no opposite of God. They were not old friends renewing acquaintances. Satan was being compelled before God, to recognize God's lordship and goodness.

Satan was asked what he had been up to. His response was that he had been going to and fro across the earth, walking about on it. This illustrates a bit of what it is like to be the devil. He must exist on the earth, no longer having a job in heaven. If he had a choice, he might be always in the presence of God, accusing people.

"Have you considered my servant Job? There is no one like him on the earth." It is a much deeper question than we usually appreciate. Remember again, God asks questions ONLY for the benefit of the "questionee." When God says, "Have you . . .?" that usually means, "You should . . ." That Job was willfully serving God proved that it could be done, and that humans on the earth would do it. Satan hates that, and God loves it.

Because it is the nature of satan to accuse, he cynically accused Job. Of course, Job serves God, the devil argues, only because Job's life is good. God has protected Job, and Job serves God out of self-interest alone. If it were not a sweet deal for Job, accuses satan, Job would just as easily curse God.

God knew better. He knew the substance of Job's faith. He knew what Job would do when that faith was tested. We all know, now. None of this story is about God finding out what Job is made of. God knows. He doesn't need to test us so that He can find out what we have. He tests us so that WE can find out. Or, in Job's case, to show the power of God's grace in us to everyone in Heaven and hell.

This was not a bet. God and satan were not equals placing a wager on what Job would do. Satan challenged God's ability to hold the love and faith of humans beyond His material blessing. God knew the end from the beginning, and only allowed the challenge because He knew the result would give more evidence (to us) of His power working in a man. Therefore, God would allow satan first to take away Job's stuff, but not yet to touch his person.

The man in question knew nothing of this. He was faithfully serving God to the best of his knowledge and ability, doing what he knew to do. He was trusting and obeying God, and seeing that trust and obedience open the path for God's blessing, as it still does.

In the midst of this, the bad news began. In came a messenger, with word for Job that his oxen and donkeys were all taken, and the servants attending them all slain, except the one who escaped to bring the report. This was a terrible disaster, but it was just the beginning.

Before the first servant concluded his tale, a second one appeared, with a disaster report from the sheep herds. Remember, he described the event as he saw it; he knew nothing of who was to blame for it. Therefore, he said that the "fire of God" came down and obliterated the herds and the shepherds. He was the only one who got away.

Immediately, at his side there was a third messenger. The camels were taken, the servants dead, and only the messenger got out with the story. By now Job must have been reeling, but it got worse. So much worse.

A fourth messenger filed in behind the other three, and by now, Job had probably stopped breathing. He may have anticipated the message, but there was no way he could be prepared for it. His children were all together in their eldest brother's home, when a wind blew the house down on them. All Job's sons and daughters were dead, and once again, one lonely servant escaped to bring word.

Finally, the messengers stopped coming, because Job had nothing else to lose. He could now respond, and he did, in keeping with the culture of his people and time. He tore his robe, he shaved his head, he fell to the ground, all acts which were to be expected. Then he did something very unexpected. *He worshipped.* All that he had owned, even his blessed family, were not the source of his faith. Their loss did not cast a shadow on his trust in God. Instead of breaking faith and turning from God, Job ran to refuge in God. "The Lord gives, and the Lord takes away. Blessed be the name of the Lord." Job knew that whatever had happened to his life, God was not to blame.

Back to the presence of God. Again, these beings were presenting themselves before God, and satan appeared as summoned. The interview began with the same questions, and God pointed out to the accuser that Job had responded admirably, in spite of the things God had allowed satan to do.

Satan responded with his usual cynicism, "Nothing a man has is as important to him as his life. Touch his body, and he will roll over on you." God still knew that this was not true. Job had not sinned yet in all his unhappiness, and he would not. God did not need proof, but satan did, and we do.

"Touch him, but don't kill him," God allowed. Satan ran back to earth and smacked Job with a horrible bunch of boils, all over his body. This made Job miserable, and loathsome to be around. He felt bad, and looked bad, and likely smelled bad. Job began the only remedy he knew, scraping off the rotten flesh and corruption with a piece of pottery. He was ruined and pitiful. His wife, who, to her credit, was still with him, was ready to give up. She marveled at Job's integrity, and suggested that he just curse God and die.

Job gave this not a moment's consideration. "You talk like a fool, woman! Shall we just accept good from God, and no bad things?" Job was trusting that whatever was causing his misery, God was good, and not to blame.

Right after the exchange with his wife, Job's friends enter the story. Eliphaz, Bildad, and Zophar came from separate locations, and met together to come to Job. They were good men. Everyone in this story is pretty good, except the devil. Sometimes you will hear preaching which bad-mouths Job's friends, but there was a lot of good in them. They had the intention of sympathizing with and comforting Job.

The friends came weeping, and tearing their clothes, and throwing dirt in the air, all signs of great distress and grief. Then they did an extraordinary thing. They sat down on the ground with Job and said not a word for seven days and seven nights, because his misery was so great. Whatever follows, their desire to identify with Job in his distress has to be remembered.

After the week of silence, it was Job who spoke first. He began with a poetic curse, not of God, but of the day upon which he was born. This opens the conversation, and what follows for nearly thirty chapters is the back-and-forth between Job and his three friends. Summarized, their positions are as follows: the visiting friends believe that God gives no distress to the righteous, so Job must have sin which requires repentance. Job retorts that he is a righteous man, and calls upon God to show up and vindicate him. Job challenges God to come explain what this is all about.

Along the way, Job gives what may be the earliest promise of the Resurrection. In 19:23-27, he speaks of his confidence that his Redeemer lives, and that there is coming a day beyond all this, in which Job will see God. In what is likely one of the earliest stories of the Bible, Job expressed his faith in a Redeemer. Had the story been passed down from

Adam's family, kept alive through Noah's descendants, of the coming rescue and redemption of mankind? Job knew about it from somewhere.

Job's friends ceased their reasoning with Job because he wouldn't budge. Job recognized no deliberate sin of which he should repent in order to be restored. This is the scene when another voice comes up. Elihu, who up to now has been silent, is angry and can hold his peace no more. He is angry at Job, because Job just keeps justifying himself, which isn't moving the conversation forward, nor is it helping the situation to improve.

Elihu is also angry at the other three friends of Job, because even though they had found no answer to Job's self-justification, they condemned him. Everyone else was much older, so Elihu had not spoken. However, when he saw that no one else was getting anywhere, he could be quiet no longer.

Elihu delivered a long speech, most of which was a rebuke of Job for not listening to God. Job had been hard-headedly replying, "Am not, am not!" instead of listening to what God was trying to say in his suffering. Elihu challenged Job to get his fingers out of his ears, and hear God.

As soon as Elihu finished, God finally spoke to Job. When He did, he ignored the questions that Job and his friends had been asking. God asked some good questions of His own.

"Who is this who talks without knowledge? And you were *where*, when I laid the foundations of the earth?" A whole series of rhetorical questions follow. (In one sense, perhaps all God's questions are rhetorical, since He does not need to be told anything.) God asked, "Who did . . .?" "Who can . . .?" and "Have you ever. . .?" The questions piled one upon another in a beautiful assertion of God's omnipotence. Job was left without a word in reply, and said so.

"Behold, I am insignificant; what can I reply to thee?
I lay my hand on my mouth." (40:4 NASB)

At the end of all of God's questions, Job did finally repent, not of any sin which caused his suffering, but for presumptuously justifying himself, and by doing so, insinuating that God was unjust. God then turned to Job's three contemporaries, and rebuked them, because they had misrepresented God, not speaking the words of trust that Job had. Sacrifices were ordered, and Job was healed as he prayed for his friends.

The restoration continued, and Job ended up with twice what he started out with in riches and livestock, as well as ten more children. If we remember that Job's first ten were still alive on the other side (not true of the cattle), we can understand how this fits in with a general "double for his trouble" blessing. There is no mention of concubines or other wives, although that is possible. If we assume that the additional children were borne by the original wife, bearing twenty children means that she would have been pregnant for fifteen years, total. Serves her right for telling her husband to curse God and die.

The next conversation between God and satan has not been recorded, but it must have been very interesting.

25
God's Fish Story
Jonah

I have threatened to write a book about our adventures in pastoring the "single digit" church. While the attendance did occasionally soar into the teens in those days, on most occasions, it did not reach that level. There are blessings in this kind of ministry, mostly hidden ones. For instance, I had a brief period in which I was also the teacher of the youth class.

One Sunday morning I sat in the classroom with two junior high-age girls. I do not remember the subject of the lesson, but at some point I made reference to Jonah and his experience. I could tell that one of the girls, who was not very much churched, was not registering any recognition. I gave another piece or two of the story, to jog her memory. No click. I paused to give her a brief synopsis of the events described in *Jonah,* and as I did, the look on her face made it startlingly clear to me that she had never heard this story before.

Okay, you go try this. Find someone of near adult age, who does not know this story, and tell them. With a straight face, inform them that a man heard God's voice, and disobeyed it. He ran away, and God made a big storm. The storm caused him to eventually tell his companions to throw him overboard, which they did. Not to worry, God created a special big fish to swallow the man. And the man lived. For three days and nights, inside the fish. And so he changed his mind, and told God "Okay, I'll go where You want me to." And SHAZAM —he was right there at the place, when the fish barfed him up on the shore. Yeah, just like Pinocchio.

It's a pretty wild story. It sounds like a fairy tale, or an old myth, and the fact that it is true does not make it sound less like a whopper. But just let me tell it to you from the beginning, and I hope you'll appreciate it more.

When the adventure started, Jonah was already a prophet. God's instructions were to go to the wicked city of Nineveh, and cry out against it. These awful people deserved God's judgment, and Jonah wanted them to receive it, so he was not keen on the idea of warning them. Jonah knew about God's mercy, and didn't want to see any of it wasted on Nineveh.

Therefore, Jonah took off as fast as he could in the other direction, to Tarshish. He chose the road to disobedience. Verse three of chapter one describes it well:

He went from the presence of the Lord —That's where you go when you disobey. It is the only direction available.

He went down—Yeah, I know it's really talking about a geographical direction, but I can't help thinking that there's a lesson for us there. When you flee God's presence in disobedience, it's all down from there.

He found a ship that was going—If you don't want to obey God, you will find a way not to. There will be an alternative. Our own fleshly nature will make sure of it.

He paid the fare—There is a cost for disobeying God, but you don't find out the price until you are too far from the shore to go back. Jonah thought he paid the full fare at the dock, but little did he know what the actual cost would be.

Then the story repeats; he went down into the ship, to flee the presence of the Lord. But wait—it's not that easy to get away from God, apparently. The Lord Himself hurled a big storm against the ship, and the boat was about to break up. The sailors did what people often do when faced with judgment.

First, *each man cried to his god*. When trouble comes, everyone looks to the thing they trust in. For some today it is money, relationships, accomplishments, or possessions. But sometimes, your stuff won't get you out of trouble. You're trusting in the wrong things. So, we take the next step.

They threw the cargo into the sea, to lighten the ship. Have you ever been there? "God, just get me through this, and I'll quit, I promise!" "Just let the test be negative, please God, and I'll . . ." We can each fill in the blank with the offer of our choice. And we may be sincere. It may even last, after the crisis. It may actually be good for us. Regardless, this is what we do. None of the things they threw overboard helped them, however, because the problem was the disobedient prophet who was asleep in the bottom of the boat.

Asleep? Yes, sound asleep. At least two conditions will help you sleep in the middle of a storm. One is a clear conscience which gives you faith in God. That was not Jonah's case. He had the other condition, the exhausted stupor that satan puts on you when you are out of position with God. The devil wants to kill you while you are out there, and he'll put you to sleep at the point of greatest danger.

The captain woke Jonah up, and ordered him to cry out to his god, like everyone else. But Jonah knew that before he could call on God, he would have to come clean with Him. The sailors did another thing that we do when we are in trouble; *they found someone to blame*. The lot fell on Jonah, and he told his sad story. Now the group could put together a plan to appease someone's god, at least.

Jonah recommended that he be thrown overboard. He didn't like the Ninevites, but he didn't want a ship full of innocent sailors to drown because of him, either. Best to just get out of there, and let the others go on. They tried to get control of the ship, but failed, so they were left with only Jonah's plan. The sailors pleaded with God not to hold the act against them, and they pitched Jonah over the railing. The storm stopped immediately, which impressed the crew greatly. Instead of fooling around with their own gods, they offered a sacrifice to the Lord.

Jonah noticed the way the water started to go calm as soon as he splashed down. At least he would have a little peace before the sea took him. As he looked toward the boat, he could see the sailors gathering on the deck to offer a sacrifice to the Lord. Hope they don't burn their boat down to the water now, he thought. That would be an ironic twist, wouldn't it? At least it wouldn't be his fault. Or, would it? And what would they be offering in the sacrifice? What was left on board? Tomorrow's lunch? The things you think, when you are floating in the sea, left adrift to die. He despaired of ever seeing land again, and began to wonder how this would end. How long would God make him wait to die?

And how would it come? Exhaustion, then drowning? A shark, maybe. Perhaps sunstroke. Then, before he could even be scared, he was thrust upward violently, then pulled down into darkness. Disoriented, he could not at first imagine what had happened. As his head stopped spinning, he took inventory of his situation. Very wet. Yet, he was still intact. Totally dark. A sense that he was moving, downward. The smell of fish overpowering. Everything he touched was slippery.

No, this doesn't happen. No, this isn't happening. Couldn't God just kill me, and be done? As he felt the undulating walls around him, resignation settled in. He was inside a fish. He had been totally swallowed in one gulp. What next? Job was unimaginably sorry—now— that he had disobeyed God.

The fish stopped moving. Jonah was pinned. The fish must be way under the water now, so if it opened its mouth again, Jonah thought, he would most likely drown. If he had any claustrophobic tendencies, this would set them off. He pushed in each direction. No way out. Well, he was still breathing air, so perhaps there was no need to panic yet. No need to panic? He was INSIDE A FISH, at the bottom of the ocean!

It was about then, that Jonah broke. It all came crashing down on his heart, this whole sorry business. Where he was. How he'd gotten there. Whose fault it was. If he died here, he would be dying in disobedience. Were the people of Nineveh so bad? He began to weep at the foolishness of it all. Because of his hatred for Nineveh, he had put himself in this sorry place.

Jonah cried out from his heart to God. Before he was finished, from starvation or drowning or fish digestion, he would call upon the Name of the Lord. If he were going to go out, he would do it calling on the Lord, not defying Him. It was the first good decision he had made in a while, and from somewhere, inexplicably, the beginnings of joy began to stir in his heart.

The fish began moving again.

I can't imagine what three days in a fish is like. Or three nights. Can't be much difference between the two, I would think. Jonah passed the time by praying. He cried for help, and he worshipped God. He renewed his vows, and he submitted to God's will, whatever that was going to be. Finally, the fish came to the beach at Nineveh, and hurled the prophet at his destination. Even being a "fish chunk" had to be a relief. Fresh air. Sunlight. Life.

As Jonah picked himself up from the sand, God spoke again. What a beautiful statement of God's mercy! *"Now the word of the Lord came to Jonah the second time."* The message was the same as the previous time, "Arise, go to Nineveh. . ." This time Jonah obeyed.

Nineveh was a great city. Apparently it took three days to walk through it. As he was walking in the first day, Jonah began his crying out. In forty days, the city would be destroyed. Jonah must have been carrying some serious prophetic power. The people of Nineveh believed him right away. Perhaps he told them things they knew were true, and they knew they deserved judgment. Maybe it was an especially convincing anointing that Jonah ministered under. Maybe word had gotten around that the prophet had ridden into town inside a fish. For whatever reason, they all believed.

The Ninevites repented and declared a fast, even putting sackcloth on the animals. The repentance went all the way up to the king, and they all cried out to God for His mercy. Wouldn't it be great if we would do the same? Everyone repenting of THEIR OWN wickedness? Lord, let it be.

As they repented and called out to God for mercy, God called off the scheduled destruction, for the time being. Nineveh would not be overthrown in forty days. Both people and animals would be spared. A happy ending for all, right?

No, not for all. Jonah was an angry prophet. He complained to the Lord that this was just what he thought would happen, that Nineveh would repent, God would have mercy, and they would get off the hook. He even tells God that this was why he fled to Tarshish in the first place! I find it remarkable that Jonah was now justifying his disobedience of God by citing God's own mercy. God, who did NOT kill Jonah in the storm, and did NOT kill Jonah with a fish, and did NOT allow Jonah to be murdered by a mob or a psychopath in Nineveh, now had to endure being dressed down by Jonah for showing mercy to the repentant city. God puts up with a lot.

Jonah requested to die, and God responded with a question. You know by now that when God asks a question, someone is going to learn something. His question to Jonah was, "Do you have good reason to be angry?" Jonah did not reply. He left town to sulk.

Jonah found a good place on the edge of town from which to observe, and made himself a little shelter, and waited. I'm not sure for what. Maybe he didn't know either. As he waited, God appointed a plant to grow over Jonah, to provide shade. This put the prophet in a much better mood. Next day at dawn, God sent a worm to gnaw the plant, and kill it. It withered fast, and when the sun came up, the day was a scorcher. A hot east wind blew, and the sun beat down, and Jonah was miserable. Again he begged to die.

Again God asked His question, "Do you have good reason to be angry about the plant?" Jonah was really crabby, "I have reason to be angry unto death!" Then God made His point with a second question.

"Jonah, you are feeling compassion for a plant, which you did not even work for, which came up overnight, and disappeared overnight. Shouldn't I have compassion on Nineveh, a great city, in which there are over 120,000 people who do not know their right hand from their left?"

Exactly what God meant by "right hand from their left" is not unanimously agreed upon. Many cultures clearly differentiate their right hand (the eating and greeting hand) from their left (the toilet hand). Perhaps God was referring to the deep and nasty ignorance of the Ninevites, or maybe He was counting the number of little children in the city. Whichever, it is the only book of the Bible that ends with a question. God leaves Jonah, and us, with the question hanging. Implied in the question is the conclusion that if God should have compassion on the lost multitude, shouldn't we? Roll the credits. End of story.

How did Jonah answer? It's not recorded.

How will you answer? Your life will tell.

26
Prophesying With the Big Boys
Isaiah
Ezekiel

"Major Prophets" are so titled only because of the size of the books attributed to them. Those books are longer, but of no more importance than those called "Minor Prophets." Any prophet of God who gives you the message you need at the time is pretty important, and all the biblical prophets shared that distinction during their times.

Prophets, then and now, have a three-fold ministry. First, they do "fore-telling." This is what most of us think of when we hear about prophets. However, it may not be the most useful ministry of a prophet at a particular time. Fore-telling is speaking what will be, through supernatural revelation.

Another common function of the prophets is "forth-telling." This often made them unpopular. Forth-telling is speaking out about what is. It may not always require supernatural revelation, but if you are going to do it, you better have heard from God.

The third thing we see prophets doing is acting as God's covenant representatives. God had a covenant with His people, and they were often unfaithful to it. He used the prophets to remind them, and to call the nation and its rulers back to Him. These second and third functions are why some people define prophetic ministry as "speaking truth to power." This is accurate, but not complete.

Liberal hermeneutics often takes the supernatural element out of the ministry of the prophets, leaving them with a role as mere defiant protesters, little more than the consciences of their people. This is why you will find interpreters who vary greatly in their placement of the dates of these writings.

If you have already decided that supernatural revelations are not going to be allowed, you can't very well place the date of a prophetic book hundreds of years before the events prophesied come to pass. You have to date it after the events have taken place, so that your writer is telling what he already knows has happened, but just writing it as if he were foretelling the future. Yeah, you're right, that would be dishonest, but some Bible interpreters seem to have no problem with calling the authors of Scripture liars. Don't worry, however. There are plenty of Bible scholars who still believe God's Word, and they can tell you why you should believe it, too.

As priests were the representatives of the people before God, prophets were often the representatives of God before the people. If you are going to step up into that role, you'd better be ready to "bring it." Rebuking people who can kill you is demanding work, and it makes public opinion much less relevant to your ministry. Prophets tended to be pretty hard-nosed, thick-skinned guys. Sometimes, they still are.

Those whom we usually call "Major Prophets" are Isaiah, Jeremiah, Ezekiel, and Daniel. One of these, Jeremiah, was the author of two books, as we have already learned. He and Daniel got their own chapters in this work, because this book is all about the stories, and those guys had some stories to tell.

Another distinction between biblical prophets is between literary and non-literary prophets. There were numerous Old Testament prophets to whom no writing has been attributed which has made it into our Bible today. Some of these guys could have been real heavyweights (Elijah and Elisha, for instance), but writing was not a known part of their ministry.

There are two major prophets left from whom we have not yet heard. They spoke of the days in which they were living, and of future days to come. Their messages are dramatic and important, to both the people of their time, and to us. These are their stories.

Isaiah

Isaiah is the "majorest" of the Major Prophets. Among the prophets, he is generally regarded as "the man." His book is the largest (sixty-six chapters), and his prophecies are greater in scope than all the rest. If you had just one book to read in order to get the message of the prophets, it would be *Isaiah*. Isaiah saw pretty much the same things as the other prophets, but where they each saw a specific thing or two, Isaiah saw nearly everything.

You will find Bible scholars who will explain to you that this book has numerous authors. You don't have to believe that. Even if there was more than one scribe, the book is the prophetic work of Isaiah. Take it as his prophecy. Most of us who just read the Bible and live by what we read bring this perspective.

The book starts out with some visions, then backs up to tell the story of Isaiah's calling and commissioning in chapter 6. This is something to savor, because we don't get this from all the prophets. Isaiah had a powerful, life-changing vision of God's glory.

Some people seem very casual with God. They talk about their conversations with the Almighty like He is their personal attendant. I think this is mostly psychological, but we should all have a great "comfort level" with God. He should not be distant, but we must remember that He is so much more than our "tagalong buddy." He wants to be that close to us, but it is good for us to experience a manifestation of His presence like Isaiah got from time to time.

Isaiah's prophetic ministry seems to have started about the time King Uzziah died. That year, Isaiah saw the Lord on His throne, exalted above all, with the train of His robe filling the temple. In His presence were glorious angels, seraphs, with multiple wings. These beings called to each other continuously, "Holy, holy, holy, is the Lord Almighty; the whole earth is full of His glory!" Their voices shook the house, and smoke filled the place.

What would have been your response? I must tell you, there is a lot of flippancy in worship in churches today. Sometimes I feel that I am getting entertainment while my heart is aching for intimacy. If you have ever been in the house of God (the corporate body, not the building) when "God came down," you will never again be satisfied with merely a "pep rally for God."

Isaiah's response was not casual. His book, you will notice, is not about "My Time at the Throne." One chapter of sixty-six is devoted to this experience. I have heard some pretty spectacular testimonies from people who had similar stories to Isaiah, but what I want to hear from them is "What is God saying to us? Do you have anything else to say?" Sometimes I think, "God called you into His presence, and *that's* all the message He gave you?"

I have had my own experiences with The Presence. There are times when God comes in heaviness. I have seen praise start with singing, then explode into dancing, and laughing, then continue until the glory of the Lord comes in such thickness that the dancers end up on their faces. Sometime, their cries become a great corporate moan, and sometimes, everyone just shuts up and prostrates themselves in silence before Him. Once the goosebumps are gone, however, we have to have a word we can live on.

Isaiah had one. He spoke to Judah and Jerusalem about their sin and the coming judgment. In the middle of the vision of judgment he spoke of salvation. A remnant would persevere and receive redemption for their repentance. The Branch of the Lord will be beautiful and glorious.

After King Uzziah followed his son, Ahaz. Judah came under attack. God sent Isaiah to speak to the king. He prophesied calm, assuring Ahaz that the attack would fail. "Ask for a sign," God commanded.

Ahaz would not; being religiously polite, I suppose. If God gets irritated, this seems to have done it. At least Isaiah seems a little chapped. He declares, "God will give you a sign, anyway!" And what a sign it was! A prophecy of Messiah, who would be born of a virgin, and be called Immanuel! While he was at it, Isaiah delivered the promise that those who were attacking would be laid waste.

This is how things went with this prophet. He spoke the words about deliverance right now, judgment in a little while, and ultimate salvation. In doing so, he may have gotten a better look at Christ than anyone in the Old Testament.

In chapter two, he tells us how the Lord will judge between the nations.

In chapter four, he speaks of the "Branch of the Lord."

In chapter seven, he prophesies that "a virgin will conceive" Immanuel.

In chapter nine, he speaks to "Galilee of the Gentiles," telling them that they have a wonderful future:

For to us a child is born, to us a son is given,
And the government will be on his shoulders,
And he will be called
Wonderful, Counselor, Mighty God, Everlasting Father
Prince of Peace.
Of the increase of his government and peace
There will be no end. (9:6,7a NIV)

In chapter eleven he says that a "Branch" from "the stump of Jesse" will arise, and that the Spirit of the Lord will rest upon him.

Chapter forty-two is another picture of "the Servant."

In chapter forty-nine we are promised that the Servant will be "a light for the Gentiles."

In chapters fifty-two and fifty-three, an especially important picture of the Servant is portrayed. He will be pierced for our transgressions. He will be crushed for our iniquities. The punishment that brings us peace will fall upon him, and by his wounds we will be healed.

In chapter sixty-one is the very text that Jesus would one day use to announce his ministry.

That's a partial list, but you get the idea. Isaiah saw what was going on in his time, but he saw through to the coming of Messiah, both the first time, and the ultimate Day of the Lord to come. He gave the word to all the nations in the neighborhood, Assyria, Babylon, Cush, Damascus, Egypt—right down the alphabet. There was no doubt left that God was over all.

In reading all this judgment, Isaiah never got far from his primary objective of bringing word to Judah. He covered all three bases of prophetic ministry. There were songs of praise among the "woes." There were a lot of pictures of the future time, when God would be able to make everything right, because His people were right. The faithful remnant is in for better days.

Isaiah has some narrative right in the middle. *Second Kings* describes the reigns of the kings from Uzziah to Hezekiah. This was Isaiah's time. During Hezekiah's reign, Sennacherib came up from Assyria and conquered many cities. He came to Jerusalem, and made great bullying boasts and blasphemies against Jerusalem and her God. We get this story from *2 Kings* 19, from *2 Chronicles* 32, and from *Isaiah* 37.

Hezekiah got a particularly nasty letter from Sennacherib, and he knew that it was not just idle boasting. The Assyrians had brutally destroyed every place they had encountered. The king took the letter into the temple, and laid it before the Lord. He acknowledged how great

God was, but also how terrible the Assyrians were. He put his trust in the God who was a real God, not just wood or stone. He believed that God would deliver His people, so that all the nations would know who alone was God.

God's answer came from Isaiah, who heard the word of the Lord, and passed it on to the king. God spoke of Jerusalem as the "Virgin Daughter of Zion." This feminine designation may have been particularly galling to Sennacherib, since the "girl" was "mocking" and "tossing her head" at him as he fled. God quite forcefully informed "Nachy" that this time, he had cluelessly insulted the Real God, the Holy One of Israel. Furthermore, God had been the One giving the Assyrians all the success they had enjoyed so far. Now, as the devil often does, they had overplayed their hand. God said, in effect, "I heard what you said about Me, so I'm going to send you right back out in the direction you came in."

As soon as the word had been delivered, an angel from the Lord went out overnight and killed 185,000 Assyrians. Sennacherib woke up with an army of corpses; time to slink out with your tail between your legs, quickly. He went lying and boasting and threatening all the way home, but after he got there, his sons whacked him. (If all this sounds familiar, it's because you have already read about it in chapter 17. Now we are getting it from Isaiah's point of view.)

This was kind of the high point in Hezekiah's career. After those days, he got sick, and Isaiah told him that this was his final chapter. The king was not ready for that, however, and rather pitifully pleaded for more time. God gave him fifteen more years, and even did a miracle with the sun as a sign. Hezekiah did not use the fifteen years well. (You can see that in chapter 17, too.)

You remember from earlier in our story (chapter 21), how Cyrus came along and was so helpful to the Jews as they returned to rebuild Jerusalem and the temple. Many years earlier, during the reign of Hezekiah, perhaps, Isaiah prophesied that this would happen, even calling Cyrus by name.

Isaiah reveals much of what God wants to say to all His people, at all times. If we are unfaithful, we can expect discipline. Discipline, however, will always be under His loving control, and repentance will bring restoration. It seems that God is so excited about His coming Redeemer that He can't help talking about Him whenever He gets a chance. He is proud of "the Servant," and His people haven't even seen Him yet.

Ezekiel

Ezekiel begins with a clear statement of the date, so there should be no question about when the first vision took place. Ezekiel was "with the exiles" when he saw visions of God— and what visions he saw! He saw amazing creatures above, and wheels below. He saw brightness and lightning, and he heard a voice. Above the creatures and the wheels was a throne, and upon the throne was a man. This man was full of fire and light, and radiance, and Ezekiel knew that this all was an appearance of the "likeness of God's glory." He fell on his face, a reasonable response.

The voice instructed Ezekiel to stand, and the Spirit came within him, so that he could, and he was given a call and commission. His calling was sort of a "good news/bad news" sort of thing. God said, "I am giving you a message, but the people won't listen to it." God literally placed His words in Ezekiel's mouth, and Zeke had to eat them.

God called him, "son of man," as a representative of the human race. He had been called before God to receive and deliver the message to the house of Israel, the people who were in exile by the Kebar River. Ezekiel returned from the presence of God to his people, and sat there, for seven days, completely gobsmacked. After seven days, God spoke to him again, and clarified his calling. Ezekiel was to be a watchman to the house of Israel, warning them of what God was saying. If they did not listen, their blood was upon their own hands, and head.

God was sending Ezekiel not only to a back-slidden and stubborn people, but apparently also a non-literate bunch. Ezekiel was always providing visual aids, under God's direction. This is also because, for a good part of the time, Ezekiel was made mute, unable to prophesy what God was saying. We call these illustrations "prophetic actions," and they can still be useful, from time to time.

They start for Ezekiel with his drawing a picture of Jerusalem on clay, then laying siege to it. (The picture, not the city.) He built little siege works, a ramp, and a battering ram, just like the real thing. It must have been really cute. Then he made a little iron wall out of an iron skillet, and placed it between him and the miniature Jerusalem. He was besieging a diorama.

God ordered that Ezekiel lie on his left side representing the sins of Israel for 390 days, as many days as there had been years in their apostasy. Then he was to turn over, and spend forty days on his right side, representing Judah's sin. That's a total of 430 days. Divided by thirty, it comes to over sixteen months. That's way over a year, people. This was his job for that period. If you came to town, looking for Ezekiel during that time, they might have told you something like this:

"Ezekiel? Oh, you mean that goofy prophet out on the plain. Yeah, head out in that direction, and you will come to his house. You may smell it before you see it, since he cooks his meals with cow patties. When you come to the house, you may have to go on in, because he's probably tied up in there, talking to his clay picture and his army toys."

Israel had been carried away to Assyria, and their land had been resettled. Judah had lasted longer, but was guilty of the same sins. They had been conquered by Nebuchadnezzar's Babylon, and a puppet regime had been placed on the throne in Jerusalem. It was against this poor remnant that Ezekiel was prophesying. You can see his prophecy fulfilled in *2 Kings* 25.

Really bad times were coming. God promises a time of punishment, with disaster, doom, and calamity, to use His words. God teleported Ezekiel to Jerusalem (either physically or spiritually) to show him the terrible idolatry that was taking place, even in the temple. God showed him that there would soon be judgment, even to the point of the glory of the Lord leaving the temple.

Just as the vision became overwhelming, God spoke a word of encouragement. A remnant would repent and return. God had scattered, and He would gather.

Ezekiel showed the people what they would look like when they headed into exile. At the command of the Lord, he packed up his stuff all day, then at dusk he dug a hole through the wall and went out of it. This is how the ruler of the city would leave it.

God declared an end to the false prophets and diviners who had been prophesying out of their own imaginations. They were making a meager living out of their falsehood, but the Sovereign Lord set His face against them. Some of the elders of Israel came and sat before the prophet. God had no word for them but to repent of their idolatrous ways.

Ezekiel delivered the message that even Noah, Daniel, and Job could not save these people, so great had their idolatry become. God was going to send such a whammy upon the land, that if these three men had been in it, they wouldn't even be able to save their families, only themselves. I find this choice of heroes interesting. Noah and Job were men of old, but Daniel was a contemporary, suffering the same exile as the rest of them. Yet there would be a remnant, to 1) testify of God's righteousness, and Judah's sin, and 2) be the recipients of God's faithful promise to restore.

God told a story. It was not a pretty story. Jerusalem was an abandoned baby when God found her, the daughter of Canaanites. He came by and saw her, naked and bare, kicking in the blood of her birth. He rescued her, cleaned her up, and watched her grow into a beautiful young woman. When she came of age, He entered into a marriage covenant with her, and she became a lovely queen, because of His blessing.

She trusted in her beauty and fame, and took on other lovers, said the Lord. The gifts that God had given, she gave to others in her gross prostitution. She became not just a "working girl" turning tricks for a living, but an obsessive slut, paying her lovers, instead of being paid. That not being evil enough, she offered up her children, the children of the Lord, to the detestable idols (this was literally true; they had taken up the practice of child sacrifice).

In her adulterous lust, she had slept around with every guy on the block, you might say; all the neighbors—Egypt, Assyria, Babylonia! The daughters of the neighbors, the Philistines, were shocked. Because she had been so adulterous with the neighbors, God said He would bring the neighbors in to be instruments of her humiliation. They would see, and participate in, her judgment. We know that they will not get off lightly either—their judgment is already foretold—but first, they will come watch as God punishes His own.

God knows what the king of Judah is planning, and he makes it clear that the Lord's plan is the only one that will succeed. All nations, and all souls, belong to Him. He will judge all men by their own righteousness, God tells Ezekiel.

Ezekiel continued to speak in word pictures, but also spoke plainly, delivering the message that judgment was coming, followed by restoration. The promise of restoration was partially fulfilled in the return from the exile, but will have its ultimate fulfillment in days yet to come. In our time, we have seen the gathering of the people back into the land of Israel, and we will see the eventual restoration of their full covenant relationship.

Meanwhile, the sword of judgment was coming, and its name was Babylon. Just as the other prophets had spoken, Ezekiel agrees that Babylon is a sword in the hand of the Sovereign Lord. And, when we read the indictment God instructs the prophet to release in what we know as *Ezekiel* chapter 22, we can surely see why. The princes, the priests, the prophets—all the officials of Israel—had become corrupt, and were being gathered into Jerusalem like ore, to be refined by the Lord's wrath.

God told another story. Read literally, it sounds like a porn novel (Not that I would know about those, but I can guess). Samaria and Jerusalem were described as sisters, a couple of "ho's" who learned their lust down in Egypt. Samaria lusted after the Assyrians, and God gave her over to them. They treated her brutally, and her end was sad.

Her sister saw the judgment Samaria received, but her lust was just further inflamed. She prostituted herself to the same Assyrians, and then to the Chaldeans (Babylon). After she had them, she was disgusted, and turned from them. (This speaks of Jerusalem submitting, then rebelling against, Babylon.) God got pretty explicit here, to make His point. Especially if you read the NIV.

God's correction is going to drive the lust and lewdness out of them. Adultery and sexual promiscuity were used here as symbols of the idolatry of Israel and Judah. They had a covenant with the One True God, but were worshipping the foreign gods of their neighbors with great dedication. This was despicable to God, but they had gotten used to it. He used the picture of something they still despised, adultery, to show them the real condition of their nations.

The illustrated sermons just continued, and in the midst of this, Ezekiel's wife died. The prophet was told by God that it would happen, and he was instructed not to mourn or grieve publicly, as was the custom. This was a sign to the exiles, that the beloved city of Jerusalem, which they had left behind was going to be destroyed. They would not be able to mourn, but would just have to get over it.

Ezekiel delivered words of judgment to all the nations round about. One of them, Tyre, is of special interest, because their prophecy looks beyond the earthly king of Tyre to Satan, who stands behind him. We get some insight into the very origins of the devil in this passage.

God taught Ezekiel (and us) about the ministry of the watchman. Watchmen are responsible only to be faithful; it is the responsibility of the people to hear their warning. Apparently, Jerusalem's people were comforted by having Ezekiel in their midst, but they would not heed his warnings. They were like people you may know, who enjoy gospel music and good, heartfelt, anointed preaching—but won't change their lives. This made the judgment of Jerusalem even more severe, and I fear that it still may have that effect.

God was disappointed in the way that those whom He had appointed shepherds over his sheep were performing. He declared that He Himself would become their shepherd. God will give them the best shepherd of all, not the earthly David, but the Eternal David, to watch over them. This is a beautiful prophetic promise (*Ezekiel* 34) that you should read on your bad days.

It was not for Israel's sake that God would do these things. It was for the sake of His own holy name. It was not because of who they were, but because of Who He was. God had a name to redeem. Israel had pretty well trashed His name, but by what He was doing, in judging His own, then restoring them, He was rebuilding His reputation before the nations.

There is a great old spiritual that we sing about *Ezekiel* 37. Some have misinterpreted this vision of the valley of dry bones as a prophecy of the resurrection. God says the vision is about the restoration of Israel. The nation would be coming back, and not only that, but the divided kingdom was coming back together into one.

Ezekiel seemed to leap forward to way "future days" for a while. He prophesied about a coming attack on Israel, one which does not seem to have happened even in our day. It is not the local neighbors who make this war, but folk from farther away, led by a nation called, "Gog."

It is also worth thinking about that Ezekiel prophesied that this attack would come against "a land that has recovered from war." "Now all of them live in safety," says Ezekiel. When has that ever been the case in modern Israel? Those who scoff at efforts to bring peace to the Middle East might want to think about this. Israel will be "a land of unwalled villages," "a peaceful and unsuspecting people—all of them living without walls and without gates and bars."

Some people get all excited and goose-bumpy when we talk about rebuilding the temple and turning up the ashes of the red heifer, because they believe that this is hastening the return of Christ. Why does nobody get excited about the idea of Israel being at peace with her neighbors? It may be because some believe that no one except the Antichrist will be able to accomplish this miracle. Hmmmn. Perhaps. If you are looking for a definitive interpretation of this prophecy that you can argue with, I suggest another book. All I am saying here is "Hmmmmn."

Oh, we should mention the results of this attack. God will simply turn loose the land itself against the attackers. Earthquake, confusion, plague. Rain, hail, and burning sulfur from the sky. While the nations of the world look on, Gog and its allies will be eliminated. *"Then they* (the nations) *will know that I am the Lord." (38:23)*

Now that God had showed Ezekiel the ultimate triumph of His name, He gave him a vision of the ultimate temple. Measurements and descriptions of the temple were given, and Ezekiel watched as the glory of the Lord returned to it. The temple would be restored; the priesthood would be cleansed. Trained for the priesthood himself, Ezekiel is a logical choice to be given these instructions.

As the temple is restored, life will come to the land. It will flow from the restored throne of God. The land was even reapportioned. Israel was getting a major do-over.

The judgment still had its course to run, but with repentance would come restoration. This was the message of Ezekiel and the other prophets of the exile. Once Israel was back in its land, and the temple was rebuilt, that pesky old idolatry habit would never again trouble them. Making an idol of the temple itself, however, was another matter.

27
No Prophet is Minor to His Mother

Hosea	Joel
Amos	Obadiah
Micah	Nahum
Habakkuk	Zephaniah
Haggai	Zechariah
Malachi	(Jonah)

Here is the last "story" in this volume. We will end our retelling of the Old Testament with the story of the "Minor Prophets." One, *Jonah*, you have already read about. His story was so compelling, and so basic to understanding The Big Story, that I dealt with him separately. However, much of what is generally true of the others is true of him also.

There are a few different ways of classifying the prophets, and as you study the Bible, you will come across them. I will give you some that are relevant to our purpose here. I have already told you that there are "Major" and "Minor," according to length, and that some were literary, and others not. Another way to get our minds around "who is who" is by dating the prophecies.

You remember that Israel had a great kingdom, then a split, resulting in the monarchies of Israel and Judah. Both of these backslid into idolatry, then were judged by God and taken into exile. This exile, and their eventual return, were prophesied long before the events happened. After some disciplinary years in foreign lands, God brought the exiles home, just as He had promised.

Some prophets are known as "Pre-exilic," because they warned of the coming judgment. Others are called "Post-exilic," because they prophesied after the hammer fell. This includes those who were themselves part of the Exile. When you are trying to understand the message of a biblical prophet, it is very helpful to know where he is located on this timeline. This is true of both "Majors" and "Minors." We have heard the stories of each of the "Major Prophets." All that is left to hear are the "short stories." I am going to tell you some of what I find interesting about each one.

Coming into Judgment

These are the prophets who spoke of God's coming judgment upon the lands and peoples:

Hosea

Hosea's story is noticeably bizarre. God instructed the prophet to marry an adulterous woman; perhaps already a prostitute. Not only was he to marry her, apparently he was to love her as well. She would not be faithful to this covenant, but the prophet would.

Her name was Gomer. I have never met anyone named Gomer; it has not been a popular name, since she got through with it. Three children came, and they were given prophetic names to indicate how God felt about Israel. Yet, even while God was speaking through this adulterous woman and her children, He was promising restoration. Just not yet.

Hosea was sent by God to get his wife out of her whoredom after she had returned to it. Yeah, you got the picture—the preacher's wife went back to turning tricks, and he had to go out on the street, and buy her back. How humiliating was that? God was showing Israel the depth and fierceness of His love for His people.

Much of Hosea's prophecies were to tell Israel what this object lesson meant. He had redeemed them from slavery, only to see them surrender to idolatry. This would cause judgment to fall upon them. Yet, He would redeem them still because of His everlasting love.

Perhaps we should study *Hosea* and *Song of Solomon* together. *Song of Solomon* shows us the sweet side of God's eternal love for us.

Hosea shows us that faithful love can have a very painful, nasty side. Jesus will later show us just how much pain and nastiness that love has had to endure.

Joel

We do not have to wait for judgment to come before we repent. Joel pleads with the inhabitants of Zion to start repenting now, before the great and terrible day of the Lord comes. He describes judgment in terms of a vast army of locusts, devouring everything that can be seen. There will be starvation—repent now, or repent later. However, as repentance comes, there will be restoration, and a coming day of salvation.

On the Day of Pentecost, Peter will point to Joel's prophecies of the "Day of the Lord" as being further fulfilled in the outpouring of the Holy Spirit upon the Jerusalem church. Luke will faithfully record his sermon and text, lifting *Joel* from obscure minor prophet status to one of the most-quoted of the minor prophets.

Amos

Amos was a farmer, a shepherd. God began to speak through him to give a warning of judgment to the neighbors of Israel and Judah. The book opens with a statement that the Lord's voice is roaring "from Zion." Damascus, Gaza, Tyre, Edom, Ammon, and Moab were indicted and convicted in the Lord's court, and sentences were read. Looks like scores were being settled all over the block.

Then, without a pause, Amos turned the prophetic guns homeward. *"For three sins of Judah, even for four I will not turn back my wrath."* Here we go. The neighbors were judged for their mistreatment of others, and Judah caught judgment for their mistreatment of God. Next, Amos settled in on the big target, Israel.

For several chapters, *Amos* calls judgment on Israel for their unfaithfulness. This got him a rebuke from Amaziah the priest in Bethel. You remember that Israel had left the worship of God in Jerusalem, and had put up those golden calves in convenient locations in Israel. Amaziah didn't want another out-of-towner prophet coming in and obnoxiously preaching judgment against their local idolatry, and he told Amos to go back home to Judah.

This got Amaziah a particularly nasty response from Amos on behalf of the Lord. After all, Amos was not a professional prophet, but a farmer who was just delivering mail for the Almighty. After telling the priest that his wife would end up peddling it on the street, his kids would die by the sword, and that Amaziah himself would die in exile, Amos went back to his business of warning Israel.

Plenty of destruction was prophesied. God asserts His Lordship over Israel, saying in effect, "I raised you up out of Egypt, and I'll wipe you out as quickly as I did them." Yet, not completely. God just can't seem to finish a good prophecy of judgment without a promise of restoration. This is because even His judgment is redemptive. *Amos* ends like many other of the minor prophets, with a promise of how great it will be when God's people come back from the woodshed.

Obadiah

This is the shortest book in the Old Testament, but a pungent one. It is directed primarily at Edom, the descendants of Esau, who have been unkind to their brothers, the children of Jacob/Israel, for a long time. Edom has lived in pride, but they are about to be humbled.

As Israel has been descending into captivity, Edom has gloried in their own security, wisdom, and shrewd alliances with neighboring kingdoms. All of this is about to go very bad. The Lord is Sovereign, and He will arrange the nations for His own purposes. Edom has rejoiced over the destruction of Judah, and God says, *"As you have done, so it will be done to you; your deeds will return upon your own heads"* (v. 15).

We cannot leave, however, without a promise of deliverance to the people of God. *"But on Mount Zion will be deliverance; it will be holy, and the house of Jacob will possess its inheritance."* (v. 17) God promises deliverance to Zion, but extermination to the nation of Edom. Both received their promised future.

Jonah

Since *Jonah* gets its own treatment in another chapter, we won't repeat it here. I will point out, however, that it is interesting that God sent Jonah, and later Nahum, to a people (Nineveh) who were not covenant partners. God is Lord of everybody, and He deals with them as He desires. When they are facing judgment and are in need of repentance, He does not hesitate to send His ambassador, even if the people claim to be worshippers of other gods. Notice that Jonah does not violate the human rights of the people of Nineveh, but neither does he flinch at telling them that they are in trouble with a God to whom they have had no commitment.

Micah

Micah prophesied during the reigns of Jotham, Ahaz, and Hezekiah in Judah. He got visions for both Israel and Judah. He talks a lot about Samaria and Jerusalem. Micah prophesied destruction because of the idolatry of both cities.

Because of the devastation to come, Micah seems to have acted a bit strange. He speaks of going "naked and barefoot," and of howling like a jackal and moaning like an owl. (Some commentators explain that he wasn't really walking about buck nekkid, but I don't know on what basis they make that claim. The man says he was naked; he should know.) Chapter one includes a clever series of puns involving the names of the afflicted cities; study the meanings of those town names to get the message.

Micah predicts bad outcomes for false prophets and unfaithful leaders, but like the other prophets, he prophesies restoration for God's people after the time of discipline. He looks forward to the Messiah, and even names Messiah's birthplace. The prophecies alternate between judgment and restoration, with a well-known passage in chapter six explaining just what God requires of His people—to act justly, and to love mercy, and to walk humbly with God.

Nahum

Nahum's vision was of the downfall of a bully. *Second Chronicles* 32 gives the story of Sennacherib and his threatening of Jerusalem. He was a nasty guy, and had done nasty things to just about everyone around. This was the nation of Assyria, who caused great grief to its neighbors, and Nineveh was its major city. Nahum came about a century and a half after Jonah, and by that time, Nineveh had gotten over their repentance.

Two attributes of God are stressed in this book. One is His anger. The other is His goodness. How can we talk about both, at the same time? It is His goodness that gives righteousness to His anger. If He were not totally good, He would have less right to be angry. However, because of His goodness, when He says, *"Many casualties, piles of dead, bodies without number, people stumbling over the corpses, . . . "* (3:3), you can be assured that these are people who had it coming.

Nahum knows,

The Lord is good, a refuge in times of trouble.
He cares for those who trust in him,
But with an overwhelming flood he will make an end of Nineveh;
He will pursue his foes into darkness (1:7).

Nineveh had their time to turn to the Lord and trust in Him. They repented of their repentance, and now their fortresses would fall like ripe figs (3:12) and their warriors would be "women." God had allowed Assyria to be His instrument of discipline to His backslidden and unfaithful people, but He was taking note of their iniquities, as well. Retribution was called for. To Nineveh, this is the anger of God's judgment, but to those whom Assyria had oppressed and abused, it is assurance that the

Righteous Judge would act righteously. Let all the surrounding people know that there is a good God in heaven, and He is keeping score.

Habakkuk

Habakkuk questioned God. He didn't question God's existence, or His righteousness, or His omnipotence. No, he asked questions of God directly. There were many things which Habakkuk did not understand. In that, he was much like us. However, many of us take our questions about God, and bail out of faith, altogether or in part. Habakkuk took his questions straight to God, and he waited for answers. The answers he got, as well as his questions, are still informing us today.

"How long, O Lord?" Habakkuk asked. How long would evil come out on top? How long would violence be tolerated? How long would justice be denied, and the wicked be in charge?

God responded, "Watch the nations and be amazed! I am doing something unbelievable. I will raise up the wicked Chaldeans (Babylon) to discipline My people." In other words, it is going to get worse before it gets better!

Habakkuk did not argue, but questioned further. "OK, but you are too pure to watch evil, so why do you allow these wicked ones to swallow up those more righteous than themselves?" Habakkuk thought this required a summit, of sorts, with God. He found a rampart, and stationed himself there to inquire of God until he received an answer. The answer came, and we are still putting it on our refrigerators, and screensavers, today:

Record the vision and inscribe it upon tablets
That the one who reads it may run.
For the vision is yet for the appointed time
It hastens toward the goal and it will not fail.
Though it tarries, wait for it, for it will certainly come,
It will not delay (2:2, 3 NASB.)

Have you ever received a promise from God? Have you had the assurance that God was working in your situation, only to see it remain
the same, or get worse? It doesn't always happen on our schedule, to our
understanding. Years ago I felt that God was promising me some spectacular things. I even told some people. I started a journal, to record the
miracles as they happened. More struggles have ensued, and I haven't
made an entry in that journal for a while. (That's my failing.)

Habakkuk tells me that I can ask God, "What's up with that?" He can
handle the questions, if I can handle the answers. A couple of years ago,
He directed me to *Habakkuk* 2:3, along with the 126th psalm. Those
things God has promised are much closer now, and I believe Him still.

God went on to assure Habakkuk that He would indeed set things
straight, just not on the "Habakkuk plan." After hearing God's reply to
his honest questions, the prophet prayed. He worshipped, and gave God
glory. If you want to work up a good shout, read Habakkuk 3 aloud. The
book concludes with Habakkuk's declaration that he would exult in the
Lord "no matter what!"

Zephaniah

Zephaniah was apparently the last of the prophets to declare God's
word before judgment came to Judah. He lived during the reign of Josiah, and it will be helpful to review what was happening then. Zephaniah was descended from Hezekiah, who had been a godly king. After
that good king came a wicked one, Manasseh, and God pronounced
judgment on Judah (2 Kings 21; 2 Chron. 33). Judah's sand was now
running through the hourglass.

It is interesting to note that Josiah and Zephaniah were relatives and
possibly of the same generation. There was a great time of revival under
Josiah. A careful reading of the account, however hints that it was largely a "top-down" revival. Josiah served the Lord and went on a "Purify
Judah" campaign, but it is unclear how committed the people were to

this. Josiah's revival would only delay the inevitable judgment. A Pharaoh would come up from Egypt, kill Josiah, and make Judah a colony of Egypt. Pharaoh Neco would then be displaced by Nebuchadnezzar, and the Babylonians would be in charge.

We are not sure where Zephaniah's prophecy occurred in relation to all this. It does not seem to matter much. Although they had a righteous king who was cleaning up the place, the hearts of the people were still far from God, and they were still marked for judgment. The oracle starts out, "I will completely remove all things from the face of the earth, declares the Lord." No warm-up. No easing into the heavy part. God is announcing judgment, and insinuating that not only Judah, but the whole creation is going to be judged. This is one of the striking features of *Zephaniah*; universal judgment.

God says that punishment will be distributed all around Jerusalem, and BTW, the rest of the earth, too. While He is at it, God declares destruction on a grocery list of Judah's enemies, then promises to give their place to His people. You see, God still can't pronounce bad things on His people for very long without a promise of restoration. First however, Judah's idolatry must be dealt with.

The nations will be gathered up and judged, but God also intends to give them "purified lips," so that they can call on His name. From "beyond the rivers of Ethiopia" will come His worshippers. And, in the midst of the idolatry and resultant judgment, there will be a remnant of Judah, who have been faithful. There is always a remnant.

We end the book with great praise, for God is not just our Judge, but our Savior! Again, God reminds His people that discipline will be severe, but restoration will be so worth it! So it was, and so it still is.

Coming Home

After the Exile, there came the times of restoration. Much of this is told about in *Ezra* and *Nehemiah*, so you might want to review those to get a good sense of context.

Haggai

The first verse of the book gives us the time and context. Darius is king of the Empire, Zerubbabel is governor of Judah, Haggai is a prophet, and Joshua is the high priest. The second verse gets right to the problem addressed by the book. God was "unhappy" because the people had said, "It is not yet time to build the Lord's house."

Not that God needed a house, you understand. God has made it ever so clear that He needs no house built by human hands. So, what's the problem? By de-prioritizing the rebuilding of the Temple, the people were ignoring the Covenant, and their relationship with God. They were building nice houses for themselves, while the Temple was in ruins.

God did not need a house, but the people needed to build one. They were hindering God's blessings to their nation by ignoring Him. Through Haggai, God brings their attention to the situation. God/Haggai sounds a little like Andy Rooney here; "D'ja ever notice that you are sowing a lot, but harvesting just a little? You eat but you're still hungry. You drink, but you still are thirsty. Your clothes don't even seem to be keeping you warm. You oughta think about this."

God explained that the crops were not producing because He had withheld His blessing. God wanted to bless His people, and He still does. Their disregard for Him had taken them out from under the place of blessing. It still will.

This first word from Haggai got Zerubbabel, Joshua, and the rest all stirred up for temple-building. The makeover was on. About a month later, God spoke again. "To those old men who remember what this temple looked like before, I say, 'It doesn't look like much now, does it?' But wait—its glory will be greater than before, because the 'desired of all nations' will come, and fill this house with glory and peace." Silver and gold belong to the Lord; He created them, and He is not impressed with their glory. The true glory of the Lord's House is His presence, and He promised that this temple they were rebuilding would see His presence.

Jesus Himself would one day come into the Temple and cleanse it. Shortly after, the Veil of the Temple would be ripped from top to bottom, as God's presence left its captivity in the Holiest of Holies and filled the whole Temple—and the hearts of His people. Great days were ahead for the Temple, and God can't help starting to talk about it ahead of time.

Another couple of months went by, and perhaps the commitment of the people was fizzling. God came to Haggai once more to warn the folk that whatever they did would be defiled if they did not pursue their service to God with a whole heart. However, what God really wanted to do was point out that right now, they did not have much, but that from that day on they would prosper under His blessing.

Haggai finishes up with a "p.s." prophecy for Zerubbabel. He would be as the Lord's "signet ring." I'm not sure exactly what all that means, but it has to be good. The ring was a symbol of authority, and if you saw that, you knew that the owner was backing it up, even if it was being worn by an old yellow dog, or the village idiot. It speaks of trust and of delegated authority for a purpose. God placed the entire weight of His Kingdom behind Zerubbabel to accomplish His purpose. The book ends with some of the greatest words you could ever hear said to you, "'I have chosen you,' declares the Lord Almighty."

Zechariah

The story continues. Zechariah's prophecy begins later in the same year as Haggai's. Same town. Same people. The story is similar, but Zechariah saw things, while Haggai just heard from God. Zechariah had visions; myrtle trees and horses and stuff.

Zechariah illustrates some of the principles for understanding prophecy. The prophet is sitting in a particular point in time, speaking to a historical situation, but unable to restrict his visions to that time. He saw his immediate context, but he saw also the time that Messiah would come to Jerusalem and be rejected by His people. But wait—he saw not only Messiah's rejection, but he also saw the ultimate victory even further ahead in time.

Zechariah saw Zerubbabel, the king, and he saw Joshua, the high priest, but superimposed over them were images of Jesus, the Messiah. At one point Zechariah instructs that a crown be made for the high priest. We know that high priests in Israel had neither crowns nor thrones, but the prophet was looking forward to the One Who would be both Priest and King. Zechariah's Joshua is a type of the Yeshua Who is to come. (The name is the same, but it has been "greeked" and "Europe-ized" until we know Him as Jesus.)

I didn't make that up; it says so plainly in Zechariah 3:8 and 9. The Branch will come, and he will take away the sin of the world in a single day. The ultimate blessing of Jerusalem was promised to Zechariah, and the book gives us numerous prophecies of what's coming, both in the earthly ministry of Messiah, and in the time of the end. The New Testament writers will quote *Zechariah* frequently, because Zechariah was looking at Jesus.

We cannot read *Zechariah* without thinking about Jesus. It is like a movie trailer of what is ahead. His message to God's people was "Return to the Lord—there's a great day coming!"

Malachi

God is good. He is not just benevolently "good," He is competently, excellently "good." He knows what He is doing. He is a perfect editor, and He ends the Old Testament part of His Story with just the right message. The exile is past, the people are back, the Temple is rebuilt, and life is swell. Except, the people are complaining. They are bored. They have gotten used to the blessings of God again, and it is poisoning them.

There is sloppiness in their lives, and God is sending His man, Malachi, to warn the people. Malachi has a list, and the book has a very easy-to-follow rhetorical style. One by one, the prophet names the things that are troubling God, and gives evidence of their prevalence. Let's follow the list.

God starts by plainly stating His love for Israel. He has heard their whining, and anticipates their challenge to His assertion. "You say, 'How have you loved us?'" God answers, "I loved Jacob, and hated Esau." God chose Jacob, the younger twin, because He chose to. Nothing in Jacob, prior to birth, indicated that he should be preferred. He just was, because God wanted to. Jacob *became* Israel because God chose to love him. Esau, as a person, is as much loved by God as anyone, but as a nation, he was despised. Someone has said, "When you don't get that good thing you think you deserved, remember how many times you didn't get that awful thing you know you had coming." Israel's problems started with forgetting that God's love for them was special and undeserved.

God goes on. His people have dishonored Him. How? By disrespecting the altar of worship. Their sacrifices were how they worshipped. Instead of giving the best, first, perfect, sacrifices from their flock and produce, they were giving the "leftovers." The animals that were going to die, anyway. The stuff they couldn't sell. This was not just rude, it was disobedient. God had been patient, but He was tired of it. "Try giving these lame sacrifices to your governor!" says the Lord. They knew that would not be acceptable, yet they were giving cheap worship to God.

We "tsk,tsk" at Israel for being so careless in their worship, yet we should be examining ourselves. God is great, but do I worship like it? Is he getting my priority time, attention, and effort, or is He getting what

I can spare? Does my calendar planning start with devotion to Him, or am I just fitting worship in when I have time? Does my day begin in His presence, or do I usually find myself apologizing to Him at the end of the day for a quick and cheap, "now I lay me down to sleep" prayer. He is worth so much more.

"And while we are on the subject," says God, "I want to talk to my priests." Implied in this is the idea that the sloppiness of the people's worship was the responsibility of the priests. They were supposed to "preserve knowledge." The people were to look to them to "seek instruction." Our "five-fold" ministries (*Eph.* 4:11, 12) are in the place of these priests in today's churches. This passage from *Malachi* is sobering.

I believe in being relevant, but I shudder to think that some churches may be substituting the latest in religious marketing for the truth of God's Word. With the Holy Spirit's help and the guidance of the Word, we will recognize that, while there are some things that must change with each generation, there are also some things that must not. If the people are offering "injured, crippled, and diseased" sacrifices in worship, it is the responsibility of their leaders to rebuke them, and refuse to accept less than their best.

As many good prophets do, Malachi delivers a message about faithfulness to the Covenant. As he ticks off the next item on his list, he warns Israel about a two-fold problem they have with faithfulness. First, they are ignoring their covenant agreement with God, and marrying foreign wives. God is not speaking just about ethnicity, that is not the issue. These wives serve foreign gods.

In addition, and sometimes in connection with this, they were violating the sacred covenant with their wives by divorcing them. God clearly says He hates this, and because of it, He is ignoring their offerings. Anytime this subject is raised, there is opportunity to misunderstand. God does not hate divorced people; He is grieved by the breaking of covenant that occurs in divorce. Every marriage is a covenant before God; therefore, every divorce involves the breaking of a covenant. Those who do it casually are enjoying what God hates.

Much tragedy ensues when one marriage partner views marriage as a lifelong covenant and commitment, while the other partner treats fidelity as a hopeful good intention. When it's not "fulfilling" anymore and "our needs" are not being met. It is easy to excuse ourselves from our promise to the covenant, and our partner. Those who have been the victims of this unfaithfulness do not need to have it explained to them why God says He hates divorce. It's not the painless removal of a wart or a mole. It is more like the soul—searing amputation of a limb or two.

Next on the list, God said, "You weary Me." How? Israel was saying that God had no sense of justice, that evil prospered at the expense of good, and God was doing nothing about it. Just you wait, God says. He is going to send His messenger, and who will be able to stand up to Him? He'll purge the earth good. Just like in the first book of the Old Testament, God is in the last book promising again to set this thing right.

God reminded Israel that He does not change; that is why He didn't nuke them all a long time ago. If they will return to Him, He will return to them. Pretending (?) to be thick-headed, they must think, "What do you mean, 'Return'?" "Well," God asks, "will a man rob God?" Sounds like a stupid thing to try. Yet, they were doing it. They were robbing God in their tithes and offerings.

Much hot air and ink has been expended about this subject of tithing. Most of it has been useless over-complication. If we believe the Bible it's very simple. Man has always worshipped God by giving Him a portion of our material substance off the top. We do this by putting it in the hands of His servants. You can see it start in *Genesis* 14, with Abram tithing to Melchisedek, and it continues right through the Bible to the point where Jesus says the Pharisees were doing right by tithing (*Luke* 11:42). Along the way, there are references to tithing such as this one in *Malachi*, where it is spoken of as part of the people's worship and an indicator of trust in God.

That's what it is all about. Worship and trust in God. If we believe Him, and trust Him with our possessions, we tithe. If we don't, any excuse we make does not change the simple fact: we don't trust God. That's the problem Israel was having in Malachi's time, and God was addressing it directly. He says, "Withhold the tithe and rob me, or trust me and receive the blessing." He doesn't need our money. We need to trust Him.

They were telling lies about God. They were saying, "There is no benefit to serving God. Even evildoers prosper." But God was listening, and taking notes. Those who spoke the truth about Him had their words recorded, and God promised to remember them, and to make a distinction between the righteous and the wicked.

Malachi ends with an exciting promise. A day is coming in which God is going to make things right. The very sun (not "son") of righteousness will arise, with healing in His wings. This will burn away wickedness and those who cling to it. Meanwhile, God says, remember the law I gave you; another "Elijah" is coming.

It is no accident that the last word in the Old Testament is "curse." As good as God had been, redemption was not accomplished. The curse of sin still marred humanity, and as they looked forward to the promised righteousness, they still struggled with the effects of sin's curse. But not forever.

And then . . . Silence

After Malachi, the Storybook closes for a little while. There will be centuries of silence. Have you enjoyed The Story so far? Out of all mankind, God has selected His people, through whom He plans to work out His Story of Redemption for all people. He has chosen them, and entered into a Covenant with them. That Covenant has been severely tested, and God has been proven faithful, although His people have not. Even so, they are no longer just a family or tribe. They are now a nation.

I remember the movie, *The Next Voice You Hear,* from my childhood. I'd like to see it again. In that film, God begins speaking on the radio, interrupting normal programming with His own messages. As He begins, the announcer says, "The next voice you hear will be God." At first, the world doesn't pay much attention, but circumstances bring them around to rapt listening as each night's message comes. Then, just as everyone seems to be finally listening . . . the messages stop. At least, that's the way I remember it. It's probably been forty years since I saw it.

In our Story, God has called out a people. He has endured their unfaithfulness, until His holiness required that He bring discipline to His own. After the judgment, God has allowed them to return home and start over. They have rebuilt their city and His temple, but what's next? They know that Messiah is coming, but what until then—and what then? They proceed as best they can, but they long to hear the voice of God again. They listen, they strain. They study what He has already said. They wonder what God will say next.

And the next voice they hear . . .

. . . is a baby's cry.

**Intermedia
Publishing Group**

Publishing That Works For You

Do you need a speaker?

Do you want Jim Dempsey to speak to your group or event? Then contact Larry Davis at: **(623) 337-8710** or email: **ldavis@intermediapr.com** or use the contact form at: **www.intermediapr.com**.

Whether you want to purchase bulk copies of *40 Stories Behind the Story* or buy another book for a friend, get it now at: **www.imprbooks.com**.

If you have a book that you would like to publish, contact Larry Davis, Publisher, at Intermedia Publishing Group, (623) 337-8710 or email: ldavis@intermediapr.com or use the contact form at: www.intermediapub.com.